Modern Critical Views

These and other titles in preparation

Modern Critical Views

WILLIAM BLAKE

Modern Critical Views

WILLIAM BLAKE

Edited with an introduction by

Harold Bloom

Sterling Professor of the Humanities
Yale University

1985
CHELSEA HOUSE PUBLISHERS
New York

THE COVER:
William Blake appears in the context of his double vision of Innocence and Experience, with the dominant emphasis falling upon the dialectic wrath of the Tyger of Experience.

—H.B.

PROJECT EDITORS: Emily Bestler, James Uebbing
EDITORIAL COORDINATOR: Karyn Gullen Browne
EDITORIAL STAFF: Linda Grossman, Julia Myer, Peter Childers
DESIGN: Susan Lusk

Cover illustration by Robin Peterson

Printed and bound in the United States of America

Library of Congress Cataloging in Publication Data

William Blake.
    (Modern critical views)
    Bibliography: p.
    Includes index.
    1. Blake, William, 1757–1827—Criticism and interpre-
tation—Addresses, essays, lectures. I. Bloom, Harold.
II. Series.
PR4146.W46   1985   821'.7   84-29254
ISBN 0-87754-610-X

Chelsea House Publishers
Harold Steinberg, Chairman and Publisher
Susan Lusk, Vice President
A Division of Chelsea House Educational Communications, Inc.
133 Christopher Street, New York, NY 10014

Contents

Editor's Note

This volume gathers together a representative selection of the best criticism devoted to William Blake from 1950 until the present. In some sense, all of the contributors are of the school of the late Foster Damon, whose *William Blake: His Philosophy and Symbols* (1924) may be said to have founded modern criticism of Blake. Damon's work was brought to an apotheosis by the finest single study of Blake, Northrop Frye's *Fearful Symmetry* (1947).

The editor's "Introduction" on "Blake and Revisionism" is intended to provoke all settled readings of Blake, because Blake was a master of dialectics who is too easily and, frequently, too weakly misread. But the first four essays, while provocative, do set forth approaches to Blake that are not altogether unsettled or problematic. David Erdman, the greatest of Blake's historical and textual scholars, propounds the broad context of Blake's relation to the politics and social economics of his own times. Robert Gleckner introduces the complexities of perspectivism that govern the singers and readers of Blake's songs. The essay by Northrop Frye, written nearly twenty years after the publication of his major book on Blake, is an intricate guide to the levels of meaning of Blake's systematic myths. Since Blake invented a new mode of counterpointing poem and illustration, W. J. T. Mitchell's initial guide to this composite art is of great value to those who wish to grasp Blake's highly individual intentions.

The essay on *Jerusalem*, by the editor, seeks to relate the troubling form of that poem to the form of its central precursor text, the Book of Ezekiel. Thomas Frosch's essay on the idea of art and Blake's Eden, in particular regard to the burden of sexual division, is part of his remarkable study of Blake's vision of the body. The late Thomas Weiskel's essay departs from overly system-bound views of Blake to examine the critique of transcendence which is another aspect of Blake's vitalism. In her account of the state of being called Beulah in Blake's brief epic, *Milton*, Susan Fox intimates something of a gathering movement in recent feminist critiques of Blake.

A final movement of essays is begun by Leslie Brisman's study of cosmological origins in Night VII of Blake's abandoned epic, *The Four Zoas*. The essay on "Los and Apocalypse" by Leopold Damrosch attempts a complex distinction between Christian notions of apocalypse and Blake's very original aesthetic visions of finality. David Wagenknecht, describing the way in which Blake's myths war against prior myths, achieves a useful insight into the much disputed question of Blake's allusiveness. The final essay, by Diana Hume George, is both a Freudian investigation of Blake's troubled attack upon what he called the Female Will, and also a spirited defense of Blake against some recent feminist critiques.

Introduction

What happens to a poem after it has succeeded in clearing a space for itself? As the poem itself begins to be misread, both by other poems and by criticism, is it distorted in the same way or differently than it has been distorted by itself, through its own activity in misreading others? Clearly its meanings do change drastically between the time that it first wrestles its way into strength, and the later time that follows its canonization. What kinds of misreading does canonization bring about? Or, to start further back, why call the canonization of texts a necessary misreading of texts?

What is canonization, in a purely secular context, and why ought criticism to talk about it? Criticism in fact hardly has talked about canon-formation, at least for quite a while now, and the process is a troublesome one, and so not easy to discuss. Canon-formation, in the West, began in the creation of Scripture, when the rabbis accepted certain texts and rejected others, so as to arrive at last at the library of thirty-nine books now commonly referred to as the Old Testament. The rabbis were no more unanimous than any other body of literary critics, and some of the disputes about canonization were not settled for several generations. The three main divisions of the Hebrew Bible—the Law, the Prophets, the Writings or Wisdom literature—represent three stages of canon-formation. It is likely that the Law was canonized by about 400 B.C., the Prophets by about 100 B.C., the Writings not until A.D. 90.

"Canon" as a word goes back to a Greek word for a measuring rule, which in Latin acquired the additional meaning of "model." In English we use it to mean a church code, a secular law, a standard or criterion, or a part of the Catholic Mass, or as a musical synonym for a kind of fugue, or in printing for a size of type. But we also use it for authoritative lists of works, sacred or secular, by one author or by many. The Greek word *kanon* was of Semitic origin, and it is difficult to distinguish between its original meanings of "reed" or "pipe," and "measuring rod." Canon-formation or canonization is a richly suggestive word for a process of classic-formation in poetic tradition, because it associates notions of music and of standards.

But before considering poetic canon-formation, I want to go back to the biblical process of canonization. Samuel Sandmel makes the useful observation that before a text was canonized, it could be copied with inattention, as you or I tend to copy. But, he adds: "Once a writing became canonical, it was copied with such relentless fidelity that even the inherited mistakes and the omissions and the telescoping were retained." The late Edmund Wilson, perhaps not understanding the indirect descent of academic textual scholars from these pious copyists, complained bitterly at its modern continuance, but we can attain a critical realization about how a copying-canonization fosters misreading, of a peculiarly uninteresting, weak, and unproductive kind. A canonical reading, like a canonical copying, attempts to stop the mind by making a text redundantly identical with itself, so as to produce a total presence, an unalterable meaning. So many texts, so many meanings—might be the motto of weak canonization. But there is also strong canonization, and it is more dangerous, whether carried on by the Academy of Ezra, the Church, the universities, or most of all by strong critics from Dr. Samuel Johnson to the present day. Though my own texts-for-reading in this [essay] will be two famous lyrics by Blake, London and The Tyger, I will try to illustrate the ways in which strong canonization misreads by a religious example, before I turn to Blake. But before I come to my religious example, I want to say something about the transition from religious to secular canon-formation.

Whether in religion or in poetry, or (as I suspect) everywhere else as well, memory is a crucial mode of thought, as Hannah Arendt remarks in the context of political philosophy. We can make a more drastic assertion; in poetry memory is always the most important mode of thought, despite Blake's passionate insistences upon the contrary view. The reason why most strong post-Enlightenment poems end with schemes of transumption or metaleptic reversals, with defensive patterns of projection and/or introjection, with imagery of earliness and/or belatedness, in short with the revisionary ratio I have called the apophrades or Return of the Dead, is that, particularly in poems, the past, like the future, is always a force, and indeed, in poems, the future's force is directed to driving the poem back into the past, no matter what the poet is trying to do.

Hannah Arendt tells us that political thought as a tradition goes from Plato to Marx, and ends there. I suppose we could say that moral psychology as a tradition goes from Plato to Freud and ends there. But poetry as a tradition has no Marx or Freud (though Wordsworth came closest to that end-stop position) because you cannot break the tradition without ceasing to write poetry, in the sense that the tradition from Homer to Goethe defines poetry, and Wordsworth's best poetry paradoxically breaks the tradition only to extend it, but at the high cost of narrowing and internalizing the tradition, so that all subsequent attempts to get beyond Wordsworth have failed. Blake was a much less original poet than Wordsworth, as I think we are only beginning to understand. Despite his surface innovations, Blake is closer to Spenser and to Milton than he is to Wordsworth, and far closer than Wordsworth is to Spenser and Milton. Wordsworth imposed himself upon the canon; Blake, though a major intellectual revisionist, was more imposed upon *by* the canon than modern Blake scholarship is willing to accept or admit.

I return to the process of canonic imposition. E. R. Curtius sums it up by saying: "Canon formation in literature must always proceed to a selection of classics." But Curtius, so far as I can tell, hardly distinguishes between religious and secular canon-formation. A secular tradition presumably is open to intruders of genius, rather more readily than a religious tradition, and surely this difference is the crucial one between revisionism and heresy. Revisionism alters *stance*; heresy alters *balance*. A secular canon stands differently, after it subsumes a great revisionist, as British poetry manifested a different relation between the poet and the poem, after Wordsworth. But a religious canon is thrown out of balance by a great heretic, and cannot subsume him unless it is willing to be a different religion, as Lutheranism and Calvinism were very different religions from Catholicism. Joachim of Flora or Eckhart could not become canonical texts, but in the secular canon Blake has been legitimatized. What this has done to Blake is now my concern, a concern I want to illuminate first by one large instance of the reading peculiarities brought about through religious canonization. The book *Koheleth* or Ecclesiastes is, rather astonishingly, a canonical work, part of Scripture. The book Ecclesiasticus, or *The Wisdom of Jesus the Son of Sirach* was not taken into the canon, and is part of the Old Testament Apocrypha.

As literary works, they both are magnificent; in the King James version, it would be difficult to choose between them for rhetorical power, but Ecclesiastes is far stronger in the original. Their peculiar fascination for my purposes is that they exist in a relation of precursor and ephebe, with Koheleth or Ecclesiastes, written about 250 B.C., being the clearly dominant influence upon Ben Sirach or Ecclesiasticus, written about 200 B.C. By a splendid irony, the canonical Koheleth is a highly problematic text in regard to normative Judaism, while the uncanonical Ben Sirach is explicitly and unquestionably orthodox, a monument to normative Judaism.

Koheleth derives from the Hebrew word *kahal*, meaning "the community" or "the congregation." The Greek "Ecclesiastes," meaning a member of the *ecclesia* or assembly of citizens, is not a very exact equivalent. Neither word, Hebrew or Greek, means "the Preacher," which is a famous mistranslation for Koheleth. Tradition identifies Koheleth with Solomon, a beautiful but false idea. Like his imitator Ben Sirach, Koheleth worked in the literary genre of Wisdom Literature, a vast genre in the ancient Near East. "Instruction" is a synonym for "Wisdom" in this sense, and may be a better modern translation for *Hokmah*, which really meant: "How to live, what to do," but was also used as a synonym for poetry and song, which were not distinguished from Instruction.

Robert Gordis, in the most widely accepted modern study of Koheleth, shows that Koheleth was a teacher in one of the Wisdom academies in third-century B.C. Jerusalem, teaching aristocratic youths, in a quasi-secular way. His ambiance was anything but prophetic, and his highly individual vision of life and religion was much closer to what we would call skeptical humanism than it was to the central traditions of Judaism. God, for Koheleth, is the Being who made us and rules over us, but Koheleth has nothing more to say about Him. God is there at our beginning and at our end; in between what matters is our happiness. How did *this* book become canonized?

Not without a struggle, is part of the answer. The two great interpretative schools of the rabbis Hillel and Shammai fought a long spiritual war over Koheleth, and the Hillelites did not win a final victory until A.D. 90 when the Council of Jamnia (Jabneh) closed out Scripture by affirming that Koheleth was part of the canon. The school of Shammai sensibly asserted that the book was self-contradictory, merely literary, not inspired by God, and was marked plainly by skepticism towards the Torah. The Hillelites insisted that the book was by Solomon (though surely even they knew this was a pious fiction), and pointed to certain passages in the book that were traditionally Torah-oriented. What was the motive of the Hillelites? Theologically, they were liberals, and presumably Koheleth helped them to achieve more daring and open interpretations of the Law. Yet the deeper motive, as with the great Rabbi Akiba's passion for the *Song of Songs*, seems to have been what we call literary or aesthetic esteem. Koheleth was, rhetorically and conceptually, too good a book to lose. Though both a belated and an audacious work, it was taken permanently into Scripture. I myself am a mere amateur at biblical scholarship, yet I want to go further in expressing the misreading of this canonization, for as I read it, Koheleth is a revisionist poem, a strong misprision of Torah, which suffered the happy irony of being absorbed by the precursor against whom it had rebelled, however ambivalently. Koheleth 3:14 echoes Deuteronomy 4:2 and 13:1 in a revisionist way, so as to change the emphasis from the Law's splendor to human powerlessness. It echoes passages in Kings, Samuel, and Leviticus, so as to undo the moral point from a categorical insistence upon righteousness as a divine commandment to the skeptical view that moral error is inevitable and even necessary, but that righteousness is always more humanly sensible if only you can achieve it. Robert Gordis insightfully remarks that Koheleth refers only to Torah and to Wisdom Scripture, and wholly ignores the canonical prophets, as nothing could be more antithetical to his own vision than Isaiah and Ezekiel.

Let us contrast to Koheleth his eloquent and more traditionally pious ephebe Ben Sirach, who about a half-century later seems to have followed much the same profession, teaching pragmatic Wisdom, of a literary kind, at an upper-class academy in Jerusalem. Ben Sirach can be described as the Lionel Trilling of his day, even as his precursor, Koheleth, seems a figure not wholly unlike Walter Pater or even Matthew Arnold, in Arnold's more skeptical moments, though I hasten to add that Arnold was hardly in Koheleth's class as poet or intellect. Ben Sirach, by a charming but not unexpected antithetical irony, echoes or alludes constantly to Koheleth, but always canonically misreading Koheleth into a Shammai-like high Pharisaic orthodoxy. Wherever Koheleth urges the necessity of pleasure, Ben Sirach invokes the principle of echoing Koheleth while urging restraint, but in the vocabulary of his precursor. Robert Gordis observes that wherever Koheleth is literal in his meaning, Ben Sirach interprets him as being figurative. Any close comparison of the texts of Ecclesiastes and Ecclesiasticus will confirm the analysis that Gordis makes.

Let me sum up this rather intricate excursus upon Koheleth and the book of Jesus Ben Sirach. The revisionist work, through canonization, is misread by being overfigurated by the canonically informed reader. The derivative, orthodox work, left uncanonized because of its belatedness, is misread by being overliteralized by those who come after it, ourselves included.

I turn to two texts of Blake, two famous *Songs of Experience: London* and *The Tyger*. How are we to read these two revisionist lyrics that Blake intended us to canonize, that indeed now are part of the canon of British poetry? What kinds of misreadings are these poems now certain to demand? *London* is a revisionist text with regard to the book of the prophet Ezekiel; *The Tyger* is a revisionist text with regard to the Book of Job, and also in relation to *Paradise Lost*.

Here is the precursor-text for Blake's *London*, chapter 9 of the Book of Ezekiel:

> He cried also in mine ears with a loud voice, saying, "Cause them that have charge over the city to draw near, even every man with his destroying weapon in his hand."

And, behold, six men came from the way of the higher gate, which lieth toward the north, and every man a slaughter weapon in his hand; and one man among them was clothed with linen, with a writer's inkhorn by his side: and they went in, and stood beside the brasen altar.

And the glory of the God of Israel was gone up from the cherub, whereupon he was, to the threshold of the house. And he called to the man clothed with linen, which had the writer's inkhorn by his side;

And the Lord said unto him, "Go through the midst of the city, through the midst of Jerusalem, and set a mark upon the foreheads of the men that sigh and that cry for all the abominations that be done in the midst thereof."

And to the others he said in mine hearing, "Go ye after him through the city, and smite: let not your eye spare, neither have ye pity:

Slay utterly old and young, both maids, and little children, and women: but come not near any man upon whom is the mark; and begin at my sanctuary." Then they began at the ancient men which were before the house.

And he said unto them, "Defile the house, and fill the courts with the slain: go ye forth." And they went forth, and slew in the city.

And it came to pass, while they were slaying them, and I was left, that I fell upon my face, and cried, and said, "Ah Lord God! wilt thou destroy all the residue of Israel in thy pouring out of thy fury upon Jerusalem?"

Then said he unto me, "The iniquity of the house of Israel and Judah is exceeding great, and the land is full of blood, and the city full of perverseness: for they say, 'The Lord hath forsaken the earth, and the Lord seeth not.'

"And as for me also, mine eye shall not spare, neither will I have pity, but I will recompense their way upon their head."

And, behold, the man clothed with linen, which had the inkhorn by his side, reported the matter, saying, "I have done as thou hast commanded me."

Chapter 8 of Ezekiel ends with God's warning that he will punish the people of Jerusalem for their sins. Chapter 9 is Ezekiel's prophetic vision of the punishment being carried out, despite the prophet's attempt at intercession on behalf of a saving remnant. The crucial verse for Blake's *London* is clearly the fourth one, which gives Blake not only the central image of his poem but even the rhyme of "cry" and "sigh":

. . . And he called to the man clothed with linen, which had the writer's inkhorn by his side;

And the Lord said unto him: "Go through the midst of the city, through the midst of Jerusalem, and set a mark upon the foreheads of the men that sigh and that cry for all the abominations that be done in the midst thereof."

This mark is given to the saving remnant of Jerusalem, who alone are to be spared destruction. The Hebrew word for "mark" used here is *taw*, which is the name also of the letter *t*, the last letter of the Hebrew alphabet, even as zed (*z*) is last in ours, or omega is last in the Greek alphabet. Traditional commentary on Ezekiel interpreted this to mean that the *taw* set upon the forehead of the righteous would be written in ink and signify *tichyeh*, "you shall live," but the *taw* upon the forehead of the wicked would be written in blood and would signify *tamuth*, "you shall die."

The intertextual relationship between Ezekiel and Blake here is quite unmistakable, even though it also has been quite unnoticed, except by myself, in my role as what Blake denounced as a "Satan's Watch-Fiend." How is Blake revising Ezekiel?

Not, so far as I can tell, by his initial equation of London = Jerusalem, which means that from the start all received readings of this poem, including my own, are wholly mistaken in seeing Blake's poem primarily as a protest against repression, whether societal or individual. That is, all received readings have said or intimated that in the poem *London* Blake presents himself as a prophet or prophetic figure, akin to Ezekiel, with the people of London only roughly akin to those of Ezekiel's Jerusalem, in that they are shown as suffering beneath the counter-revolutionary oppression of the regime of William Pitt. On this view the people, however culpable for weakness or lack of will, are the righteous, and only the State and State Church of Pitt are the wicked. From this, a number of other interpretations necessarily follow throughout the poem, down to the famous lines about the harlot and the new-born infant at the poem's close.

I shall demonstrate, with the aid of what I call "antithetical criticism," that all such interpretations are weak, unproductive, canonical misreadings, quite alien to the spirit of Blake's strong misreading or misprision of Ezekiel, and alien in any case to the letter of Blake's text, to the words, images, figurations of the strong poem *London*.

Blake begins: "I wander thro' each charter'd street," and so we begin also, with that wandering and that chartering, in order to define that "I." Is it an Ezekiel-like prophet, or someone whose role and function are altogether different? To "wander" is to have no destination and no purpose. A biblical prophet may wander when he is cast out into the desert, when his voice becomes a voice in the wilderness, but he does not wander when he goes through the midst of the city, through the midst of Jerusalem the City of God. There, his inspired voice always has purpose, and his inspired feet always have destination. Blake knew all this, and knew it with a knowing beyond our knowing. When he begins by saying

that he *wanders* in London, his Jerusalem, his City of God, then he begins
also by saying "I am not Ezekiel, I am not a prophet, I am too fearful to be
the prophet I ought to be, *I am hid.*"

"Charter'd" is as crucial as "wander." The word is even richer with
multiple significations and rhetorical ironies, in this context, than criticism so far has noticed. Here are the relevant shades-of-meaning: There is
certainly a reference to London having been created originally as a city by
a charter to that effect. As certainly, there is an ironic allusion to the
celebrated political slogan: "the chartered rights of Englishmen." More
subtly, as we will see, there is a reference to *writing*, because to be
chartered is to be written, since a charter is a written grant from authority, or a document outlining a process of incorporation. In addition, there
are the commercial notions of hiring, or leasing, indeed of binding or
covenanting, always crucial in a prophetic context. Most important, I
think, in this poem that turns upon a mark of salvation or destruction, is
the accepted meaning that to be chartered is to be awarded a special
privilege or a particular immunity, which is established by a written
document. Finally, there is a meaning opposed to "wandering," which is
charting or mapping, so as to preclude mere wandering. The streets of
London are chartered, Blake says, and so he adds is the Thames, and we
can surmise that for Blake, the adjective is primarily negative in its
ironies, since his manuscript drafts show that he substituted the word
"chartered" for the word "dirty" in both instances.

As is often the case with strong, antithetical poems that are highly
condensed in their language, Blake's key-words in *London* are remarkably
interrelated, as criticism again has failed to notice. Walter Pater, in his
great essay on *Style*, urges that the strong poet, or "literary artist" as he
puts it, "will be apt to restore not really obsolete or really worn-out words,
but the finer edge of words still in use." Pater meant the restoration of
etymological or original meaning, "the finer edge," and in this Pater was
again a prophet of modern or belated poetry. But here Blake, who deeply
influenced Pater, was already a pioneer. Let us return to "wander" which
goes back to the root *wendh*, from which come also "turn," "weave," and
"wind." I quote from Blake's *Auguries of Innocence*, notebook jottings
clearly related to his *London*:

> The Whore & Gambler by the State
> Licencd build that Nations Fate
> The Harlots cry from Street to Street
> Shall weave Old Englands winding Sheet
> The Winners Shout the Losers Curse

> Dance before dead Englands Hearse
> Every Night & every Morn
> Some to Misery are Born

Contrast this to the final stanza of *London*:

> But most thro' midnight streets I hear
> How the youthful Harlots curse
> Blasts the new-born Infants tear
> And blights with plagues the Marriage hearse.

The harlot's cry or curse, a loser's curse, weaves a winding sheet for England and every marriage in England by blasting the infant's tear and by blighting with plagues. To weave is to wind is to wander is to turn is to blight and blast. Blight and blast what and how? The surprising answer is: voice, which of course is the prophet's one gift. Blake *wendhs* as the harlot *wendhs*, and both to the same result: the loss of human voice. For what is an "infant"? "Infant," "ban," and "prophet" all come from the same root, the Indo-European *Bha*, which is a root meaning "to speak." And "infant" means one incapable of speech; all the infant can do is weep. The Latin *fari* and the Greek *phanai* both mean "to speak," and "prophet" derives from them. A ban is a stated or spoken interdiction, which means that a ban *is* a curse, while to curse is to put something or someone under a ban. Ban and voice, in Blake's *London*, are natural synonyms and indeed we can say that the poem offers the following equation: every voice = a ban = a curse = weeping or a blasted tear. But the verbal network is even more intricate. The harlot's curse is not, as various interpreters have said, venereal disease, but is indeed what "curse" came to mean in the vernacular after Blake and still means now: menstruation, the natural cycle in the human female. Let us note the complexity of two more key words in the text: "mark" and "forg'd" in "mind-forg'd manacles." A "mark" is a boundary (or, as Blake said, a "Devourer" as opposed to a "Prolific"); it is also a visible trace, a sign in lieu of writing, and a grade of merit or demerit. To "forge" means to "fabricate" in both senses of "fabricate": to make, as a smith or poet makes, but also to counterfeit. The Indo-European root is *dhabh*, meaning "to fit together" and is related to the Hebrew *dabhar* for "word." "Mind-forg'd manacles" is a phrase deliberately evoking the Western metaphysical problem of dualism, since "manacles" for "hand-cuffs" involves *manus* or hand, and hence bodily act, which is at once made and yet feigned or counterfeited by the opposing principle of mind.

I have involved us in all of this verbal interrelation in order to suggest that Blake's *London* centers itself upon an opposition between *voice* and *writing*, by which I don't mean that somehow Jacques Derrida wrote the poem. No—the poem is precisely anti-Nietzschean, anti-Derridaean, and offers us a terrifying nostalgia for a lost prophetic *voice*, the voice of Ezekiel and religious logocentrism, which has been replaced by a demonic *visible trace*, by a mark, by the writing of the apocalyptic letter *taw*. With this as background, I am at last prepared to offer my own, antithetical, strong misreading of Blake's *London*, of which I will assert only that it is more adequate to the text than the weak misreadings now available to us.

I will commence by offering a very plain summary or paraphrase of what I judge to be the difference in meanings when we juxtapose Blake's *London* with its precursor-text in Ezekiel, chapter 9. Then I will proceed to an antithetical account of Blake's *London*, through a charting of its revisionary ratios, tropes, psychic defenses, and images.

In chapter 8 of Ezekiel, the prophet sits in his house of exile in Babylon, surrounded by the elders of Judah. The Spirit of God raises him, and carries him "in the visions of God to Jerusalem," to the outraged Temple, where graven, idolatrous images of Asherah have been placed as substitutes for the Living God. A further and final vision of the *Merkabah*, God's triumphal chariot, is granted Ezekiel, after which four scenes of idolatry *within* the Temple are revealed to him. Chapter 8 concludes with a fierce warning from God:

> Therefore will I also deal in fury; Mine eye shall not spare, neither will I have pity; and though they cry in Mine ears with a loud voice, yet will I not hear them.

Chapter 9, which I have quoted already, mitigates this only for a small remnant. There are six angels of destruction, with only Gabriel (according to the Talmud) armed with the inkhorn that will spare the righteous. Unlike Gabriel, Blake does not necessarily set a mark, since his "mark in every face I meet," primarily is intransitive, meaning "remark" or "observe."

Blake begins *London* with a curious irony, more a scheme than a figure, or if a figure, then more a figure of thought than of speech. For he adopts the outcast role he called Rintrah, the John-the-Baptist or un-heeded forerunner, in place of the prophetic vocation, but in the context of Ezekiel's Jerusalem as well as his own London. In the opening dialectic of presence and absence, precisely what is absent is prophetic direction and prophetic purpose; what is present are chartering and marks. So voice is absent, and only demonic writing is present. Blake's defensive reaction-formation to the call he cannot answer is to be a wanderer, and to mark passively rather than mark actively with the *taws* of righteousness and wickedness, life and death. But righteousness and wickedness are alike absent; present only are weakness and woe, neither of which merits a *taw*, whether of ink or of blood. The synecdoche of the universal human face represents Blake's turning against his own self, for he also is weak and woeful, and not the Ezekiel-like prophet he should be.

The litany of "every" becomes a weird metonymic reification, a regression in moving all men back to a state of infancy, but also an isolation, as this is an "every" that separates out rather than unifies people:

> In every cry of every Man,
> In every Infants cry of fear
> In every voice: in every ban
> The mind-forg'd manacles I hear.

"Every Man" includes the Londoner William Blake, whose voice also must betray the clanking sound of "mind–forg'd manacles," where the mind belongs to every man, again including William Blake. An infant's cry of fear is all-too-natural, for the infant is voiceless but for his fear and hunger, which for him is a kind of fear. When the crucial word "voice" enters the poem, it is put into a metonymic, reductive series with "cry of fear" and "ban," with terror and curse, fear and the threat of fear.

When Blake answers this reduction with a Sublime repressive hyperbole, it is governed by the same "I hear," as spoken by a Jonah, a renegade prophet who never does speak in his own poem, but only hears:

> I hear
> How the Chimney-sweepers cry
> Every blackning Church appalls,
> And the hapless Soldiers sigh,
> Runs in blood down Palace walls.

The chimney-sweepers' cry, as in the two Blakean songs of the sweeps, is "Weep, weep," due to the cockney lisp of the children, as they attempt to advertise their labor with a voiced "sweep, sweep." The cry of weep helps blacken further the perpetually blackening Church, possibly draping it in a pall through the mark of *taw* in a black ink, giving it an edge over the royal palace, which receives the bloody *taw* of destruction. The soldier's hapless sigh prefigures the curse of the harlot, as both are losers, in the term from *Auguries of Innocence*. But what about Blake's synaesthesia? How, even in Sublime representation, can you *hear* a Church being draped in a pall, and how can you *hear* a sigh running in blood down palace walls. The answer, I think, is given by our map of misreading. What Blake is repressing into this hyperbolical hearing-seeing is the visionary power of the *nabi*, the Hebrew prophet, and the running of the repressed voice *down* the repressive walls represents not only the soldier's hapless sigh, but the more powerful hapless sigh of the prophet who has repressed the voice that is great within us.

We come then to the final stanza, the most weakly misread of all. Here is the characteristic Romantic ending that follows a limiting metaphor by a representing transumption:

> But most thro' midnight streets I hear
> How the youthful Harlots curse
> Blasts the new-born Infants tear
> And blights with plagues the Marriage hearse.

I want to reject altogether the customary interpretation that makes "curse" here a variety of venereal infection, and that makes the infant's condition a prenatal blindness. Instead, I want to reaffirm my own earlier interpretation of the Harlot here as Blake's perpetually youthful Harlot, Nature, *not* the human female, but the natural element in the human, male or female.

The inside/outside perspectivism here gives us Blake as pent-up voice wandering still at midnight *through* the streets, and through that labyrinth he achieves another synaesthetic hearing-seeing, *how* another curse or ban or natural fact (menstruation) blasts or scatters another natural fact, the tearlessness of the new-born infant. For Blake every natural fact equals every other natural fact. The metalepsis that introjects the future here is one that sees enormous plagues riding along in every marriage coach, blighting life into death, as though every marriage carries the *taw* of destruction. Remember again the doggerel of *Auguries of Innocence*:

> The Harlots cry from street to street
> Shall weave Old Englands winding sheet
> The Winners Shout the Losers Curse
> Dance before dead Englands Hearse

If Old England is dead, then all her marriages are funerals. A cry that weaves a shroud is like a mark of *taw* or a ban chartering weakness and woe. Blake's poem is not a protest, not a prophetic outcry, not a vision of judgment. It is a revisionist's self-condemnation, a Jonah's desperation at knowing he is not an Ezekiel. We misread Blake's poem when we regard it as prophecy, and see it as primarily sympathy with the wretched of London, because we have canonized the poem, and because we cannot bear to read a canonical poem as being truly so altogether negative and self-destructive a text.

Even as a revisionist strong poem, Blake's *London* is more a deliberate parody of misprision than it is a revisionist text. Blake's tonal complexities are uncanny, *unheimlich*, here and elsewhere, and like Nietzsche Blake is something of a parodist of world history. There is a grotesque element in *London*, and what we take as Sublime hyperbole is actually more the underthrow of litotes, the characteristic rhetorical figure in grotesque representation. This parody is a clearer strain in Blake's *The Tyger*, which I want to introduce more by way of Nietzsche than by way of its origins in Job and Milton.

Like Nietzsche, and like every other revisionist, Blake desired always to keep origin and aim, source and purpose, as far apart as possible. Neitzsche, if I understand him, believed only in comic or preposterous schemes of transumption, in which a future laughter is introjected and a past tragedy is projected. An aphorism in *Beyond Good and Evil* says that we are

> prepared as was no previous age for a Carnival in the grand style, for laughter and a high-spirited revelry, for transcendental flights of Sublime nonsense and an Aristophanes-like mockery of the universe. Perhaps this is where we shall yet discover the realm of our *invention*, that realm in which we also still can be original, say as parodists of world history and the clowns of God—perhaps, even if nothing else today has a future, our laughter may yet have a future.

We can observe here that a poem, in this view, must be a parody of a parody, just as a man is a parody of God. But Nietzschean repetition is even more bewildering, for any copy is both a parody of its original, yet also a self-parody. In terms of poetic misprision, this means that any poem is both a misreading of a precursor poem and, more crucially, a misreading of itself. Whether Nietzschean parody is universally applicable I do not know, but it illuminates poems of deliberately cyclic repetition like Blake's *The Tyger* or *The Mental Traveller* or *The Crystal Cabinet*.

Blake's Tyger has a pretty exact analogue in a Nietzschean tiger, a grand deconstructive tiger, in the curious text called *Truth and Falsehood in an Extra-Moral Sense*:

> What indeed *does* man know about himself? Oh! that he could but once see himself complete, placed as it were in an illuminated glass case! Does not nature keep secret from him most things, even about his body . . . ? Nature threw away the key; and woe to the fateful curiosity which might be able for a moment to look out and down through a crevice in the chamber of consciousness and discover that man, indifferent to his own

ignorance, is resting on the pitiless, the greedy, and insatiable, the murderous, and as it were, hanging in dreams on the back of a tiger. Whence, in the wide world, with this state of affairs, arises the impulse to truth?

Nietzsche's tiger is human mortality; our illusive day-to-day existence rests us, in dreams, as we ride the tiger who will be, who is our own death, a metaphorical embodiment of the unbearable truth that the pleasure-principle and the reality-principle are finally one.

Nietzsche's precursors were Goethe, Schopenhauer, Heine, and Wagner; Blake's were Milton and the Bible. Of all the thirty-nine books of the Old Testament, Job obsessed Blake most. The forerunners of Blake's Tyger are the Leviathan and Behemoth of Job, two horrible beasts who represent the God-ordained tyranny of nature over man, two beasts whose final name is human death, for to Blake nature *is* death.

God taunts Job by asking him if these great beasts will make a covenant with man? Rashi comments on Behemoth by saying: "prepared for the future," and the apocryphal apocalypses, Enoch and IV Ezra and Baruch, all say that Leviathan and Behemoth are parted only to come together one day, in the Judgment, when they will be the food of the Righteous. As God says of Leviathan, if none dare face him, then "Who is able to stand before Me?" Milton brings in the Leviathan (evidently a crocodile in Job) as a whale, but Melville's Moby-Dick is closer to the beasts of Job, and to Blake's Tyger.

At this advanced date, I assert an exemption from having to argue against the usual run of merely trivial misreadings of *The Tyger*. I will oppose my antithetical reading to the received misreading of the earlier Bloom, in books like *The Visionary Company* and *Blake's Apocalypse*, or in the notes to *Romantic Poetry and Prose* in the Oxford Anthology. The fundamental principle for reading *The Tyger* is to realize that this is a dramatic lyric in which William Blake is not, cannot be, the speaker. *The Tyger* is a Sublime or hyperbolical monologue, with little movement in its tropes or images. It is dominated by the single trope of repression, by an unconsciously purposeful forgetting, but this is not Blake's repression. The psychic area in which the whole poem centers is hysteria. What does it mean for a major lyric never to deviate from its own hysterical intensity?

The answer is that Blake, more even than Neitzsche, is a master of creative parody, and he is parodying a kind of greatness that he loves and admires, but vehemently does not wish to join. It is the greatness of William Cowper, and the other poets of the Burkean or Miltonic Sublime in the later eighteenth century. The two dominant images of the poem are both fearful—the burning or fire and the symmetry. Fire is the prime perspectivizing trope in all of Romanticism, as we will see again and again. It stands, most often, for discontinuity or for the possibility of, or desire towards discontinuity. Its opposite, the emblem of repetition or continuity, tends to be the inland sound of moving waters. These identifications may seem purely arbitrary now; I will vindicate them in later chapters.

What are we to make of "symmetry"? Symmetry is a one-to-one ratio, whether on opposite sides of a dividing line, or in relation to a center. A one-to-one ratio means that no revisionism has taken place; there has been no *clinamen*, no catastrophe-creation or breaking-of-the-vessels in the making of the Tyger. Like Leviathan and Behemoth, the Tyger is exactly what his creator meant him to be. But who is his creator? Does this poem set itself, for interpretation, in a relatively orthodox Genesis-Milton context, or in the context of some Gnosis? How fearful is the Tyger's maker? Or is it a canonical misreading that we allow this poem to set itself a genetic context for interpretation, at all?

By common consent of interpreters, *The Tyger* is made up of a series of increasingly rhetorical questions. The model for this series certainly is to be found in the Book of Job, where God confronts Job with crushingly rhetorical questions, all of them reducing to the cruelty of: Where were you, anyway, when I made everything? After all, Job's plea had been "Call Thou, and I will answer" (13:22), and God therefore relies upon a continuous irony as figure-of-thought. But the speaker of *The Tyger* is incapable of deliberate irony; every one of his tropes is, as I have noted already, an hyperbole. What is this profound repression defending against? What furnace is coming up, at last, against the will of this daemonizing speaker?

No speaker could be more determined to insist that origin and aim were the same impulse and the same event. We can surmise that the unconsciously purposeful forgetting of this poem's speaker is precisely that he himself, as an aim or purpose, has been separated irreparably from his point of origin. Confronting the Tyger, who represents his own *daemonic* intensity, the form that is his own force, what Blake would have called Vision or his own Imagination, the dramatic speaker is desperately determined to identify completely the Tyger's aim and purpose with the Tyger's supposedly divine origins.

Yet it is not the speaker's text, but Blake's, and the meaning of the text rises parodistically and even with a wild comedy out of the intertextual juxtapositions between the text itself and texts by Cowper, by Milton, and the text cited from Job.

First Cowper, from Book VI of *The Task*:

> The Lord of all, himself through all diffused,
> Sustains, and is the life of all that lives.
> Nature is but a name for an effect
> Whose cause is God. He feeds the secret fire
> By which the mighty process is maintained,
> Who sleeps not, is not weary; in whose sight
> Slow circling ages are as transient days,
> Whose work is without labour; whose designs
> No flaw deforms, no difficulty thwarts;

Here origin and purpose are one, without strain, anxiety, or repression, or so it seems. Next Milton, from Book VII of *Paradise Lost*, part of the most Sublime creation-scene in the language:

> The grassy Clods now Calv'd, now half appear'd
> The Tawny Lion, pawing to get free
> His hinder parts, then springs as broke from Bonds,
> And Rampant shakes his Brinded mane; the Ounce,
> The Libbard, and the Tiger, as the Mole
> Rising, the crumbl'd Earth above them threw
> In Hillocks . . .

Milton shows rather less creative anxiety than the poet of Job, even allowing himself a transumption of a Lucretian allusion as if to indicate his own corrective confidence that God's origins and Milton's purposes are one and the same. Blake's speaker is not Blake, nor is he Milton, not even Blake's own Milton. He *is* Cowper or Job, or rather Cowper assimilated to Job, and both assimilated not to the strong poet or revisionist in Blake, but to Blake's own Spectre of Urthona, that is, the time-bound work-a-day ego, and not what Blake liked to call "the Real Man the Imagination."

I approach an antithetical formula. Blake's revisionism in *London* was to measure the ratios by which he fell short of Ezekiel. Blake's revisionism in *The Tyger* is to measure the ratio by which he surpasses Cowper and Job. Cowper's fearful ratio does not frighten Blake, whose entire dialectic depends upon separating origins, natural or natural religion's, from imaginative aims or revisionist purposes. Yet, in *London*, Blake shows himself knowingly incapable of separating prophetic voice as aim or purpose from the cry, curse, ban of natural voice as origin. We have underestimated Blake's complexities, and his own capacity for self-recognition. He is in no danger of falling into the repetition of the Bard confronting the Jobean Tyger. Yet, in the societal context in which a prophet must vindicate himself, Blake falls silent, and falls into the repetition of the wanderer who flees the burden of prophecy. There can no more be a mute prophet than there can be a mute, inglorious Milton. The prophet or *nabi* is precisely a *public orator*, and not a private mutterer or marker. The *nabi* never moans, as Blake did, "I am hid." Blake, who might have been more, by his own account was human—all too human—and gave in to natural fear. His belatedness, in the spiritual more than in the poetic sense, was a shadow that overcame him.

The Blake of *London* has become a canonical writer, unlike the Ben Sirach of Ecclesiasticus, but like Ecclesiasticus Blake gives us in *London* a text he lacks the authority to sustain. The Blake of *The Tyger*, like the Koheleth of Ecclesiastes, gives us a canonical text that tradition necessarily has misread and goes on misreading. Revisionism or belated creations is a hard task, and exacts a very high price, a price that meaning itself must pay for, by being emptied out from a plenitude to a dearth.

I conclude with a final juxtaposition between the skeptical Koheleth and the passionately certain Blake. Both Ecclesiastes and *The Tyger* are texts of conscious belatedness, though *The Tyger* parodies and mocks its own condition of belatedness. For the Tyger itself, as a Sublime representation, is a self-imposed blocking agent, what Blake called a Spectre, and what Ezekiel and Blake called a Covering Cherub. The guilt suffered by the speaker of Blake's *Tyger* is also Cowper's guilt, and the guilt of a very un-Cowperian figure, Milton's Satan. This is the guilt that Nietzsche, in his *Genealogy of Morals*, called the "guilt of indebtedness." I think that Blake meant something like this when he said in *Jerusalem* that it was easier to forgive an enemy than it was to forgive a friend. The speaker of *The Tyger* confronts a burning, fearful symmetry that exists in a one-to-one ratio with its Creator. Like Job confronting Leviathan and Behemoth, the Cowper-like bard confronts an unacceptable surrogate for the divine Precursor, a surrogate who grants him no priority, and who has authority over him insofar as he is natural. Blake, in mocking a canonical kind of poem, nevertheless is subsumed by the canonical traditions of misreading, as any student of *The Tyger*'s interpretative history could testify.

Where Blake's dramatic speaker is trapped in repetition, Koheleth is a theorist of repetition, not far in spirit from the Stoic Marcus Aurelius. "All words toil to weariness," Koheleth says early on in his book, and so he thinks that fundamentally all the books have been written already. Though he praises wisdom, Koheleth is weary of it. He too might have said: "The flesh is sad alas, and I have read all the books." But he adds: "For wisdom is a defense, even as money is a defense," and the Hebrew translated here in the King James version as "defense" is a word literally meaning "shadow." I end on that identification of the defense against influence with the metonymic trope of shade for wisdom or money, and for the forests of the night that frame the menace of the fire that meant a discontinuity from origins.

DAVID V. ERDMAN

Blake: The Historical Approach

"**I** have imposed on myself . . . grossly," wrote a schemer who had tried to impose on Blake but had mistaken his man, "I have imposed on myself . . . grossly in believing you to be one altogether abstracted from this world, holding converse with the world of spirits!" The miracle is common, but it is not exactly gross.

Blake himself encouraged it. "My abstract folly hurries me often away while I am at work," he told Thomas Butts, the muster clerk who bought his paintings, "carrying me over Mountains & Valleys, which are not Real, in a Land of Abstraction where Spectres of the Dead wander." A more straightforward person, or Blake in a more forthright record, might have said: I find it difficult to keep busy at this miniature portrait of Mrs. Butts, because my mind wanders to the battlefield where men are dying, and then I see in my mind's eye the spirits of the contending powers.

We do not impose on ourselves if we believe that Blake held converse with the world of spirits, but we do if we think of either the poet or his spirits as "altogether abstracted from this world." As an observer of his own introspection, Blake understood the process of abstraction better than that; he knew that "it is impossible to think without images of somewhat [something] on this earth." At the age of twenty-six he saw Lunardi's first English demonstration of lighter-than-air craft (unless he was one of the few hapless Londoners who did not come out of their houses that day), and he knew that balloon navigators take some earth with them for ballast. When Blake soared, he did not expect to escape from the world of Bacon and Newton and Pitt, but to change its laws of gravity: "I . . . with my whole might chain my feet to the world of Duty & Reality," he explained; "but . . . the faster I bind, the better is the Ballast, for I, so far from being bound down, take the world with me in my flights."

We now understand this about Blake, in the sense that we recognize that he kept his sanity in spite of what he called "Nervous Fear" at the terrors of the times he lived in. "Fires inwrap the earthly globe," he wrote in 1793, "yet man is not consum'd." We may also understand it as a clue to his meaning, in the sense that Blake always kept his visions oriented in time and space, always knew where the sun was rising and what his horizons were. A person who wanted to escape the world altogether would not bother about horizons. But Blake never expected to get rid of his Urizen; he hoped only to teach him to be elastic and responsive as "the bound or outward circumference of Energy"—he hoped only to change Urizen from a workmaster to a schoolmaster who would recognize his own limitations and never bind fast the infant "joys & desires." Blake did not like the *status quo*, but he loved England's green and pleasant land. He did not like the "turrets & towers & domes Whose smoke destroy'd the pleasant gardens, & whose running kennels Chok'd the bright rivers"; but his program was reconstruction, not emigration; he welcomed the "golden Builders" who were expanding London's suburbs. He stood "in London's darkness" when he wrote "of the building of Golgonooza, & of the terrors of Entuthon."

> I heard in Lambeth's shades.
> In Felpham I heard and saw the Visions of Albion.
> I write in South Molton Street what I both see and hear
> In regions of Humanity, in London's opening streets.

To William Blake, Time and Space were "Real Beings," and history was a very real, if "emblematic," texture.

II

The aim of the historical approach is to approximate Blake's own perspective, to locate, as nearly as we can, the moment and place in which he stood, to discover what he saw and heard in London's streets—what loomed on the horizon and what sounds filled the air.

The value of doing this for Blake's lyric poems may be open to question. For example, the "London" of *Songs of Experience* is a successful general symbol. In the lines

> In every voice, in every ban,
> The mind-forg'd manacles I hear,

everyone will agree that the phrase "mind-forg'd manacles" is an improvement in many ways over the rejected earlier wording, "german forgèd links." And since we can do pretty well with the poem in contexts of our own manufacture or out of our own experience, some people will doubt the value of pursuing the clue of the rejected reading, "german forgèd," to discover that when Blake wrote the poem there was alarm among freeborn Englishmen that German George, the King of England, might be preparing to bring in "subsidized Hessians and Hanoverians" "to cut the throats of Englishmen," by way of following up the reiterated royal "ban" or Proclamation against Seditious Writings, the intent of which was to put manacles on such men as Paine and Blake. Nevertheless, the poem does gain poignancy when read as a cry of anguish from a city in the toils of antijacobinism. And our footnote does at least discourage the assumption that Blake meant to say that victims of tyranny are victims simply of manacles forged in their own minds. We see that he was writing about thought control as well as controlled thoughts.

Again, "The Tyger" is everyone's private possession and an inexhaustible general symbol. Yet it is possible for us to enlarge our view of its cosmic blacksmithery by considering those points at which the images of "The Tyger" touch the images of Blake's *French Revolution* and *The Four Zoas*. In a synoptic vision of the defeat of royal armies, as at Yorktown and at Valmy, Blake says "the stars threw down their spears." At the climax of "The Tyger" he uses the same words. We can at least observe, if we wisely hesitate to draw conclusions, that Blake speaks of the vindication of the American and French revolutions in the same terms that he uses to suggest the vindication of the creation of the tiger.

In short, the *Songs of Experience* are well-nigh perfect crystals in themselves, and yet as critics of their essential force and brilliance—and of course as literary historians—we gain by knowing that they were created in the Year One of Equality, in the time of the birth of the French Republic and the London Corresponding Society.

The value of applying historical research to the avowedly prophetic and manifestly historical writings, on the other hand, should be beyond question. Yet not merely the difficulty of the task, but the sophisticated tradition through which Blake has come to us and which still directs our attention largely another way, have thus far prevented its being attempted in any thorough fashion.

Consider how the neglect of historical particulars impedes the progress of Professors Sloss and Wallis, the almost indefatigable editors of *William Blake's Prophetic Writings*, in their pursuit of the wandering Zoas. On the assumption that history and Blake's kind of "prophecy" are unrelated, they omit his *French Revolution* from their canon and with it many a passage that could shed light on later symbols. And when, in Blake's "long resounding, strong heroic verse," they come upon remarks about "War on the Rhine & Danube," they note in passing that Blake may be referring to the Napoleonic Wars. But these editors treat the wars of Urizen and Luvah as altogether abstract, for they have snipped off the clue thread that the poet provided when he said "Luvah is France" and they have neglected the trail that leads back from Urizen to George the Third, via the canceled plates of *America*. For example, at one point in *The Four Zoas*, near the end of Night I, aggressive Urizen, after having brooded "Eternal death to Luvah" and threatened a long war, suddenly reverses his field:

> But Urizen, with darkness overspreading all the armies,
> Sent round his heralds, secretly commanding to depart
> Into the north. Sudden, with thunder's sound, his multitudes
> Retreat from the fierce conflict . . .
> Mustering together in thick clouds, leaving the rage of Luvah
> To pour its fury on himself & on the Eternal Man.

"Points like this which do not explain themselves," say the editors, "can receive no light from without." I am afraid we must apply to the editors themselves, as well as to Urizen's armies, the lines which immediately follow: "Sudden down fell they all together into an unknown Space, Deep, horrible, without End."

This can happen to any of us on our way through *The Four Zoas*, and I do not mean to sound lofty. But the historical approach tells us that Night I contains a survey of the diplomatic and military relations between Britain and France up through 1799 and that at this point we have come to Britain's ill-fated Netherlands campaign, during which 36,000 men marched out and 20,000 marched back very precipitately, after fierce conflict, leaving the rage of Luvah or Napoleon to vent its fury on himself and on humanity ("the Eternal Man"). Napoleon was in a mood to do so, because he had just come through his coup of 18th Brumaire, which is described by Blake as a transformation of form from human to reptilian.

I do not mean to imply that everything comes clear with the application of a little current history. In Blake's writings, as he has warned us, "there are many angles," and even the historical angle is never constant. The bard prefers to "walk up & down in 6,000 years," transposing furiously, translating the acts of Robespierre into those of Moses or abstracting the British heroes into their spiritual forms or telescoping together the Biblical and modern rebellions of slaves against Pharaohs in "dark Africa."

Sometimes we can understand a good deal of Blake's argument without paying much attention to his historical referents or even being aware of them. A great deal of Blake criticism, some of it very valuable in literary and philosophical insight, gets along famously in the swirling vortex of Blake's oratory without attending to what, in the narrowest literal sense, he is talking about, or, to put the matter another way, without asking just precisely which historical persons or events have appeared to Blake as manifestations of eternal archetypes. The increasing interest in Blake's social thought, however, and in his excitement about the industrial revolution which did—and the social revolution which did not—take place while he was writing, now makes imperative the clearest possible definition of his minute particulars, especially of the dates and contexts of those works in which he deals with the history of his own times.

We speak loosely of all Blake's difficult works as "prophetic," yet in so figurative a sense that it is not customary to look for any literal message for the times—even in those two poems he himself called prophecies: *America, a Prophecy, 1793,* and *Europe, a Prophecy, 1794.* Yet Blake defined the nature of prophecy quite literally as an honest man's warning that "if you go on So, the result is So." And the warning of *America* is plain enough: that if kings such as Albion's Prince repeat against the Republic of France, in 1793, the crusade that failed against the Republic of America, they will reach the end of their rule over the people, who are "the strong."

The warning of *Europe,* in 1794, is more veiled and less specific in its prediction. But in its own language it is directed to Pitt and Parliament. It traces the steps leading to Britain's declaration of war in February, 1793, and describes the effect of the "gagging acts" of the following year. And its warning is that the trumpet of British power has marked the end of all royal power, for the war now raging is Armageddon, and the bloody sun now rising in France is the light of Christ's Second Coming. The peaceful child of 1789 seemed easy to wrap in swaddling clothes, but the "terrible Orc" of the embattled Republic will brook no counterrevolutionary attempt to crucify him. "The bloodthirsty people across the water," as Blake put it crudely in his notebook, "Will not submit to gibbet & halter."

If this interpretation can be demonstrated (and I believe that my chapter which does so is pretty securely based), how is it possible that with only one exception that I know of (Jacob Bronowski) critics have mistaken the obviously historical part of *Europe, a Prophecy* for a summary of events leading up to the French Revolution of 1789, a matter scarcely prophetic in any immediate sense? The answer is partly that even Mr. Schorer, with all his interest in the social theme, has been so busy dispelling the fogs of mysticism around Blake that he has left it to those who follow to explore the cleared ground. A more implicit difficulty is the fog in Blake's style itself. Nowhere is his private nomenclature more puzzling than in *Europe*; nowhere is there more sly shifting from one level of discourse to another, more difficulty with ambiguities of punctuation and sudden changes of pace. Yet once we have separated the central narrative (lines 60–150 and 198–206) from the surrounding mythological framework (which reaches from the morning of Christ's Nativity to the day of his Second Coming) we are dealing with an orderly sequence of events which can be fitted into the calendar of secular history as soon as we can date some of the minute particulars.

An example will illustrate the sort of detective work that can be done and that flows logically from the recognition that Blake's prophecy really deals with current events—and from an awareness that Blake, in dealing with current politics, is not altogether apart from the main stream of eighteenth-century political satire. Miss Miles has discovered a major source of Blake's language in the language of social satire. In a recent note in *The Art Quarterly* (Spring, 1949) I have called attention to Blake's use of themes in the political caricatures of James Gillray. In the text of *Europe* Blake describes a groveling "Guardian of the secret codes" in flight from Westminster Hall or the Houses of Parliament. He does not draw a picture of the incident, but in Gillray's caricatures there are two, "The Fall of the Wolsey of the Woolsack" and "Sin, Death and the Devil," published in May and June, 1792, which is acceptable as the year "before the trumpet blew" if we take the trumpet as Pitt's declaration of war against France. Both prints commemorate Pitt's ousting from his cabinet of the Lord High Chancellor Thurlow , Keeper of the Seal and Guardian of the King's Conscience. In the second print, which is a parody of Fuseli and of Milton, Thurlow is the Devil, Pitt is Death, and the Queen (for Pitt was a Queen's man at the time) is Sin, carrying the key to the backstairs and all our woe.

Pitt, who had been trying to rid himself of the formidable Thurlow for some time, found his opportunity when the chancellor ridiculed Pitt's Sinking Fund Bill as the work of "a mere reptile of a minister" and told

Parliament that no bill should attempt to bind future governments. The grain of sedition in this remark must have seemed infinitesimal even in 1792. But Pitt, counting on his own indispensability at a time when he had filled the royal mind with constitutional alarm, asked the king to dismiss his Guardian, and the king obliged.

Blake treats the episode as a sign that the revolutionary world crisis has singed even the great Guardian of British law:

> Above the rest the howl was heard from Westminster louder & louder;
> The Guardian of the secret codes forsook his ancient mansion,
> Driven out by the flames of Orc; his furr'd robes & false locks
> Adhered and grew one with his flesh, and nerves & veins shot thro' them.
> With dismal torment sick, hanging upon the wind, he fled
> Groveling along Great George Street thro' the Park gate: all the soldiers
> Fled from his sight: he drag'd his torments to the wilderness.

The "howl . . . louder & louder" of the judge driven out by the flames of rebellion may echo the "Irregular Ode" in the *Rolliad*, in which Thurlow on an earlier occasion is depicted as warning "every rebel soul" to tremble, as he grows "profane" with a "louder yet, and yet a louder strain."

Blake's particulars are unambiguous. The street that led from Westminster Hall, the mansion of the law, to St. James's Park was Great George Street. Blake's description of the chancellor in his dismal torment is as informed as the account in Thurlow's standard biography, where we read of his drive through the park to St. James's Palace to surrender the Seal, his dejection as "a solitary outcast," and his "diminished consequence" when seen "without his robes, without his great wig." There is no mistaking Blake's allusion to this unique event. In the whole span of time his poem might conceivably allude to, the only ermined justice driven out of Westminster was Baron Thurlow. Sloss and Wallis, it is true, conjectured that "this passage may be a reference to the London riots of . . . 1780, when the mob . . . burned Lord Mansfield's house." But this was poor guesswork. A simple check discloses that Mansfield's house was nowhere near Westminster or Great George Street or any park and that none of the fires of 1780 was in Westminster. This guess, missing the date by twelve years, demonstrates both the haphazard nature of Blake research when it has been a matter of seeking him in the material world and the sort of misleading commentary that still hedges Blake's historical clues from sight.

Much more is at stake, of course, than the right reading of a few historical allusions. Only when the central historical theme of *Europe* is cleared of misconceptions can we bring into focus the symbolism of the

"Preludium" and of the mythological framework that encloses the central narrative, and only then can we see and properly appreciate the subtle use of Miltonic allusions there—and the architectural brilliance of the whole poem. But these are not matters for a hasty exposition.

In my book [*Blake: Prophet Against Empire* (Princeton, 1954)] I show that a similar bringing into focus is possible for Blake's three epics, *The Four Zoas*, *Milton*, and *Jerusalem*, although these are not dated prophecies of the same sort as *America* and *Europe*.

III

I have been dwelling on the importance of the historical approach, and thus far my examples have been largely in the category of "light from without." For the rest of my time I want to talk about a method of reading Blake's "Visionary or Imaginative" language for clues or "Ulro Visions" which he himself supplies—for visions, that is, of the ultimate material starting-points of his visions. This method may be described as the reduction of Blake's fourfold vision to single vision. This is what I do when I say Rintrah "is" William Pitt, or Albion "is" the people of England. It is what Blake does when he says, "Luvah is France." So long as we recognize that we are dealing with only one side of Blake's fourfold, it is legitimate to do this—especially since the other sides are incomplete without this one, which is the ballast that keeps his balloon navigable.

I am well aware that Blake, in his impatience with people who would see only with the eye and attend only to the ballast and not the flight, asserted "for My Self that I do not behold the outward Creation & that to me it is hindrance . . . it is as the dirt upon my feet." But to a detective or "Watch Fiend" like the historical scholar, the dirt upon Blake's feet is a good clue: it tells us where he has been walking. (Most of it upon Blake's feet is that gray clay known locally as "London stone.") You are familiar with the rest of the passage:

> "When the Sun rises, do you not see a round disk of fire somewhat like a Guinea?" O no, no, I see an Innumerable company of the heavenly host crying, "Holy, Holy, Holy is the Lord God Almighty!" I question not my Corporeal . . . Eye. . . . I look thro' it & not with it.

Read backward, as I am suggesting for purposes of orientation, Blake's vision of an innumerable company singing Holy Holy "is" a sunrise.

When Blake writes to Flaxman, "The kingdoms of this World are now become the Kingdoms of God & His Christ, & we shall reign with him for ever & ever. The reign of Literature & the Arts commences," he is responding to rumors of peace between the kingdoms of France and Britain *just as he responded to the sunrise* (I quote a letter of October, 1801, but he used almost the same language at similar news a year earlier). Toward the end of the same letter he states more simply the hope "that France & England will henceforth be as One Country and their Arts One" and that he can soon go to Paris "to see the Great Works of Art." This simple and profound hope underlies much of the yearning in Blake's prophecies for an end to "the war of swords" or "corporeal war" and a commencement of the time of "intellectual war" when "sweet Science reigns." We impose on ourselves—yes, grossly—if we neglect the connection here between vision and history.

My point about method is that we can often work back from vision to starting-point if we but grant that the vision has a starting-point, is a vision "of" something. To Dr. Trusler, who told Blake "Your Fancy . . . seems to be in the other world, or the World of Spirits," Blake retorted: "I see Every thing I paint In This World, but Everybody does not see alike." Sometimes Blake's way of seeing what he paints is curiously close to the ways of Erasmus Darwin.

Fuseli, introducing Blake's designs to an orthodox audience, called attention to a quality of "taste, simplicity, and elegance" in Blake's "wildness." Miss Miles tells us that the major materials of Blake's language are those of mid-eighteenth-century poetry. And she makes the salutary observation that many of Blake's language habits which may have seemed unique are properly defined as *extensions* of eighteenth-century practice. With regard to some of the obscurities of Blake's figurative language, I suggest that they will often yield up their literal meanings when we approach them as the product of an exuberant *extension* of eighteenth-century practice in ornamental periphrasis, or Poetic Diction.

Blake enjoyed referring, in a letter, to his wife's ocean bathing as "courting Neptune for an Embrace." In his poems he liked to refer to the ear as "the Gate of the Tongue." And he liked to take away the scaffolding of his conceit, too: he crossed out manuscript readings which made it clear that by the tongue's gate he meant the "auricular nerves." The gate of my tongue is your ear, your "auricular nerves," ultimately your reason; it is not simply what my nerves do that make my speech incoherent, but the effect of the closing up of your inlets of soul. Urizen is your reason, not mine. In *The Four Zoas* a kind of Della Cruscan periphrasis is used in descriptions of battle. An iron gun is a "black bow" which shoots "darts of hail" or "arrows black." A smoking gun is a "cloudy bow." A cavalry charge under cover of artillery fire comes out like this: "Spur, spur your clouds Of death! . . . Now give the charge! bravely obscur'd With darts of wintry hail! Again the black bow draw!" The one who fires the first shot is the one who doth "first the black bow draw." When a Zoa and his Emanation are separated by the mischance of war, they do not say, "Farewell for the duration," but "Return, O Wanderer, when the day of Clouds is o'er."

In Blake's day the newspapers still referred to British soldiers as "the sons of Albion," and so does Blake. Often the Sons and Daughters of Albion represent the various institutions and vocations of English men and women. When the Daughters are at their "Needlework" they represent the textile trades. They strip wool ("Jerusalem's curtains") from sheep ("mild demons of the hills"), and the cellars and garrets where they work are "the dungeons of Babylon." When Blake walks about London "among Albion's rocks & precipices" and looks into Albion's "caves of solitude & dark despair," he is walking through the narrow cobbled streets and looking into dark shops and tiny hovels—"the caves of despair & death" in "the interiors of Albion's Bosom." In the neoclassical tradition employed by Darwin, labor is done by gnomes and nymphs. In Blake it is done by demons and spectres. When young men and women enter apprentice slavery or the army, they are "taking the spectral form." Blake the journeyman engraver is the "spectre" of Blake the poet.

For a concentrated exercise in this materialistic method of reading Blake's "emblematic texture," let us study some of the passages in which Blake is looking at himself at work, engraving or etching on polished copper plates with engraving tools or with varnish and nitric acid (aqua fortis). Here the material referents are palpable, and the differences between matter and manner stand out plain.

Blake's best known reference to the etching process, which he employed in all his "Illuminated Printing," is found in *The Marriage of Heaven & Hell*.

> On the abyss of the five senses, where a flat sided steep frowns over the present world, I saw a mighty Devil folded in black clouds, hovering on the sides of the rock. With corroding fires he wrote the following sentence now perceived by the minds of men, & read by them on earth.

The abyss into which Blake is looking is the mirrorlike surface of his copper plate. When he focuses on the surface itself, he sees a flat sided rock. When he looks into the mirror world and orients toward *that* as real, then the "present world" is beneath it, and the flat surface is a steep cliff overhanging the present world. The mighty Devil folded in black clouds and hovering on the sides of the rock is the mirror image of Blake in his black suit pouring aqua fortis ("corroding fires") onto the copper to destroy the abyss except where he has written with impermeable ink or varnish. His sentence, appearing on the plate in reverse, is only perceived by the minds of men when it is printed and reversed back from the abysmal state. The relationship between the mirror image and the direct image symbolizes the relationship between the vision conveyed to "minds" and the physical sentence on the copper. Thus a full understanding of this passage depends on—or begins with—our visualizing the rudiments of the process: once we "see" that, we can proceed to explore the further connotations of "the abyss of the five senses."

For the process of line engraving we may turn to *The Four Zoas*, where we will find a Spectre who "drave his solid rocks before Upon the tide." The tide is the pond-like surface of the plate, upon which the engraving Spectre lodges the bits of copper gouged out by the graver as he pushes it forward with his hand—driving "his solid rocks before Upon the tide." Here again is the abyss which is not an abyss, the apparently solid surface which opens to infinite meaning—represented by an apparently non-solid tide or abyss which supports rocks or a rock.

The pushing of the graver (or etching needle) makes channels for the ink, and since these channels are technically called furrows, the most obvious metaphor is that of plowing. The complaint that the poet's children have been "plow'd and harrow'd" for another's profit is a complaint that Blake's drawings have been engraved (and etched) by Schiavonetti for his profit. All the plowing mentioned in the prophetic works is not engraving, of course. But sometimes even the direct description of agriculture contains an implied comparison to the poet's own manner of earning his bread.

> Wisdom is sold in the desolate market where none come to buy,
> And in the wither'd field where the farmer plows for bread in vain.

Blake had English famine years in mind when he wrote this. But he had also recently plowed for bread in vain, metaphorically, in the sense that he had engraved forty-three plates for an edition of Young's *Night Thoughts* which none had come to buy.

But let us turn to a passage where the focus is, both literally and metaphorically, on the plowing which is engraving. Here the "weeping" of "clods" in "the plowed furrow" suggests that Blake, like his fellow craftsmen, is resorting to "the engraver's best auxiliary, aquafortis," which makes the bits of copper dissolve. And the "many" who speak are, according to the context, the multiple eyes of God, that is, of Blake's imagination. "Many conversed on these things as they labour'd at the furrows," says Blake, meaning that many ideas occurred to him as his eyes and imagination attended to the lines he was engraving.

The passage I have begun to quote, *Jerusalem 55*, contains another reminder that these material aspects of Blake's meaning are but the dirt on his feet, or, as he puts it here, but

> as the moss upon the tree, or *dust upon the plow*,
> Or as the sweat upon the labouring shoulder, or as the chaff
> Of the wheat-floor or as the dregs of the sweet wine-press.
> Such are these Ulro Visions: for tho' we sit down

—"we" are the Eyes speaking about themselves, "the Human Organs" who can at will contract "into Worms or Expand . . . into Gods,"—

> for tho' we sit down within
> The plowed furrow, list'ning to the weeping clods till we
> Contract or Expand Space at will; or if we raise ourselves
> Upon the chariots of the morning, Contracting or Expanding Time,
> Every one knows, we are One Family, One Man blessed for ever.

Blake is speaking about the unity of life in the Imagination which denies the limitations and divisions accepted by the eyes that see only matter. But our concern at the moment is with the dust and the sweat. What the eyes say is this: We may focus on the furrow being engraved, until we look through that and see a world in a grain of copper; or we may look out the window and in imagination follow the sun ("raise ourselves Upon the chariots of the morning") until we see past, present, and future Time. In that way we see the unity of all space and all time.

Through the wrong end of the telescope we (I mean you and I, now) can see William Blake, sweating at "the meer drudgery" of engraving, and accomplishing "not one half of what I intend, because my Abstract folly hurries me often away while I am at work."

The difference between engraving and relief etching, we must understand, represented the difference between the hack work Blake had to do for a living and the prophetic work he did "to lay up treasures in heaven" and as a soldier of the imagination. His Spectre did most of the plowing and could boast that his labor was necessary to put a world "underneath the feet of Los" and bring a smile of hope to "his dolorous shadow" of a wife. Many a time, declared the surly Spectre, his engraving kept them all from "rotting upon the Rocks" and put "spungy marrow" into the prophet's "splinter'd bones." Yet Blake longed to rise above the "meer drudgery" of engraving, longed to escape this Spectre's power and cast him "into the Lake," perhaps into the very tide upon which he drave his solid rocks.

The writing and etching of his own poems, on the other hand, was done by Los, bard and prophet, "without Fatigue." With corrosive fires he burnt apparent surfaces away to reveal the "eternal lineaments" of truth. Or he would "pour aqua fortis on the Name of the Wicked & turn it into an Ornament & an Example." Or, in his favorite imagery, he would forge "under his heavy hand the hours, The days & years" of Tyranny, and thus bind the wicked "in chains of iron."

This shift of image from etcher to blacksmith, from worker with acid on copper to worker with iron and steel in fire, was essential for the connotations of cosmic bardic power. In "The Tyger" Blake could scarcely have written: What the hand dare seize the acid-bottle? An engraver's shop did have a small anvil for leveling, and a hand-bellows for drying, copper plates. But the blacksmith's mighty hammer, anvil, tongs, chain, and furnaces of intellectual war were far more effectual equipment for a bard in competition with the dark Satanic mills which were producing "ramm'd combustibles" and "molten metals cast in hollow globes, & bored Tubes in petrific steel" (Wilkinson's new process for making cannon barrels was to bore them from solid cast steel). There was also the emotional identification with the working artisan rather than with the more isolated intellectual worker, who might talk about books and pen and paper. Los, as blacksmith, could quite legitimately "wipe the sweat from his red brow." Ultimately Blake pictured him as assisted by a thousand laboring sons, because Blake knew that a multitude of furnaces and fellow laborers, a whole intellectual movement, would be needed to build the new Jerusalem, when free men, "Young Men of the New Age," inherited "the Ruin'd Furnaces of Urizen."

Another strong symbol of effective energy is the printing press, especially in its apocalyptic analogue, the human wine press "call'd War on Earth." The figure of the printer, however, does not compare in power to that of the blacksmith. In the preface to *Jerusalem* Blake prays in humble fashion that his own "types" shall not be "vain." But only once, in *Milton*, is the press of Los specifically called a "Printing-Press," and even there our attention is quickly shifted to a fiercer image. As the poet "lays his words in order above the mortal brain," his types are compared to the steel teeth of a cogwheel which "turn the cogs of the adverse wheel."

At one point in *Jerusalem* Blake does speak of the publication of paper books, when he refers to the pages of a pamphlet against war as "leaves of the Tree of Life." But here he is referring, not to his own fire-seared labors, which he expects to have read only by "future generations," but to the milder and more ephemeral publications of men "scarcely articulate."

In the passage I refer to (*Jerusalem* 45–46), a considerable speech or sermon by someone called "Bath" is spoken of as a sheaf of pages and handed to someone called "Oxford, immortal Bard" with a request that Oxford write an introduction to the public—or so I interpret the following: "Oxford, take thou these leaves of the Tree of Life; with eloquence That thy immortal tongue inspires, present them to Albion: Perhaps he may receive them, offer'd from thy loved hands." Here is a pretty concrete situation, and it ought certainly to yield up its literal meaning to an assiduous Watch Fiend. Both prongs of our historical method must be employed. On the one hand we must establish the historical context of *Jerusalem* by pinning down various kinds of internal evidence. This I have done fairly thoroughly and have found that *Jerusalem* deals with the latter phase of the Napoleonic wars and that the poem's central prophetic theme is a plea to Albion and his Sons not to pursue the war with France to mutual ruin or to make a vengeful peace that would destroy the freedom and national brotherhood of the two nations. On the eve of Waterloo the latter probability weighs on Blake's mind: "What can I do to hinder the Sons of Albion from taking vengeance? or how shall I them perswade?" In the earlier speech by Bath, he fears for Albion's own destruction.

We must on the other hand examine Blake's hyperbole to see what kind of literal statement the eloquence of Bath and Oxford can be reduced to. Translated into ordinary language, Bath's speech is an anti-war tract addressed to the people of England ("O Albion") alluding to the abolition of the slave trade, a Parliamentary measure enacted in 1807, and inveighing against imperial selfhood or British national pride: "however high Our palaces and cities and however fruitful are our fields, In Selfhood we are nothing." The remark that Bath speaks "in midst of Poetic Fervor" suggests that the author of the tract has been currently engaged in writing verse, and the statement that Bath is one who "first assimilated with Luvah in Albion's mountains" means, within the framework of date and theme established for *Jerusalem*, that he was one of the first British intellectuals to preach peace with France in the present period, that is, since the renewal of war in 1803.

Armed with these clues, my assistant, Martin Nurmi, soon found the preacher-poet of Bath by looking into a bibliography of works written in that city. In 1808, shortly after the passage of the Abolition Bill, the Reverend Richard Warner published *A Letter to the People of England: on Petitioning the Throne for the Restoration of Peace*. In the same year he published such evidence of "Poetic Fervor" as *Bath Characters* and *Rebellion in Bath, an Heroico-Odico-Tragico-Comico Poem*. As for Warner's being one who "first assimilated with Luvah," in 1804 he startled Bath and London with the publication of a fast-day sermon entitled *War Inconsistent with Christianity*, which advocated that Englishmen refuse to bear arms even in case of invasion by Napoleon. Reviewed widely and heatedly, Warner's sermon went into four editions within a few months and continued to be reissued throughout the war. In *Bath Characters* Warner caricatures himself thus:

> Dick preaches foul DEMOCRACY;
> And forces luckless loyal sinners,
> To hear his rant, and spoil their dinners

—or so his foes say. But "On the *broad basis*" he'll rely "of GENUINE CHRISTIANITY."

"Stripped of its Oriental dress," says Warner in his Fast Sermon, "the declaration of CHRIST may fairly be taken as a direct and unequivocal reprehension of hostile violence, both in individuals and states." "However brilliant the successes are with which their arms shall be crowned; whatever acquisitions of territory conquest may unite to their ancient empire . . . WAR is the GREATEST CURSE with which a nation can be afflicted, and . . . all its imaginary present advantages, or future contingent benefits, are but as 'dust in the balance,' and as 'chaff before the wind.' " Warner's sentiments are undoubtedly those of Blake's "voice of Bath."

In his 1808 *Letter to the People* Warner's alarm that the "national spirit . . . is graduating into a spirit of lawless ambition, and aggressive violence" parallels Bath's concern lest Albion should "slay Jerusalem in his fearful jealousy," and on the other hand his warning, "Be *expeditious* . . . lest the concluding scene of the war be performed upon your own shores; lest [Britain's] peaceful plains exhibit those horrors which the nations of the continent have so long and so largely experienced," suggests the tenor of Bath's urgency: "his [Albion's] death is coming apace . . . for alas, we none can know How soon his lot [the lot of Jesus or of Luvah-France] may be our own."

None of the Warner pamphlets I have seen discusses the slave trade, although in the *Letter* a passing reference to the "deliverers of Africa, the friends of the poor," may have been enough to prompt Bath's lines. Nor have I yet encountered—though I do not despair of doing so—any of Warner's "leaves" with an introduction by an Oxford poet saying, "In mild perswasion," something like this:

> Thou art in Error, Albion, [in] the Land of Ulro. . . .
> Reason not on both sides. Repose upon our bosoms.

ROBERT F. GLECKNER

Point of View and Context
in Blake's Songs

A flower was offerd to me;
Such a flower as May never bore.
But I said I've a Pretty Rose-tree,
And I passed the sweet flower o'er.

Then I went to my Pretty Rose-tree:
To tend her by day and by night.
But my Rose turned away with jealousy:
And her thorns were my only delight.

from "My Pretty Rose Tree"

J oseph Wicksteed, the only critic to devote an entire book to Blake's songs, said this about Blake's poem, "My Pretty Rose Tree": it "shows how virtue itself is rewarded only by suspicion and unkindness." And Thomas Wright, Blake's early biographer, commented on the poem as follows: " 'My Pretty Rose Tree,' Blake's nearest approach to humour, may be paraphrased thus: 'I was much taken with a charming flower (girl), but I said to myself, No, it won't do. Besides, I have an equally pretty wife at home. Then, too, what would the world say? On the whole it would be policy to behave myself.' But his wife takes umbrage all the same. The thorns of her jealousy, however, instead

From *Bulletin of the New York Public Library* 61, no. 11 (November 1957). Copyright © 1957 by *Bulletin of the New York Public Library*.

of wounding him give him pleasure, for they excuse his inclination for the flower. Moral: See what comes of being good!"

On the contrary, the moral is that such off-the-mark commentary is what comes of ignoring the context of Blake's songs (that is, whether the poem is a song of innocence or a song of experience) and the point of view from which a given poem is written. "My Pretty Rose Tree" is not about virtue perversely rewarded, nor does it have to do with "policy" or morality in the ordinary sense of those words. Virtue by itself meant nothing to Blake unless clarified and qualified by context: in the state of innocence it is *The Divine Image*; in experience it is perverted to *A Divine Image* and *The Human Abstract*. Real virtue Blake defined in *The Marriage of Heaven and Hell*: "No virtue can exist without breaking these ten commandments. Jesus was all virtue, and acted from impulse, not from rules." In "My Pretty Rose Tree" the speaker acts from rules when he refuses the offer of the sweet flower. For, as Blake wrote elsewhere,

> He who binds to himself a joy
> Does the winged life destroy;
> But he who kisses the joy as it flies
> Lives in eternity's sun rise.

The speaker in "My Pretty Rose Tree" not only has let the moment go, but also has bound to himself a joy. Furthermore, since this is a song of experience about the state of experience, the flower offered the speaker is the opportunity for a joy, a love, an ascent to a higher innocence. We recall that it was not just *any* flower, but a superb one, "such a flower as May never bore." Still, the offer is refused—because the speaker already has a rose-tree. Now, conventionally, this is admirable fidelity; for Blake, however, it is enslavement by what he called the marriage ring. The speaker thus passes up the chance of a spiritual joy (sweet flower) to return to the limited joy of an earthly relationship (pretty rose-tree). He is sorely tempted—but his desire has fallen subject to an extrasensual force symbolized by the existence of, and his relationship to, the rose-tree.

The result, of course, is the speaker's retreat from desire to the only substitute for desire in Urizen's world of experience, duty:

> Then I went to my Pretty Rose-tree:
> To tend her by day and by night.

The last two lines of the poem are the crushing commentary on the whole affair. Virtuous in terms of conventional morality, the speaker is rewarded with disdain and jealousy, ironically the same reaction which would have been forthcoming had the speaker taken the offered flower. It is Blake's trenchant way of showing the "rules" to be inane.

How easily, then, in reading Blake's *Songs of Innocence and of Experience* we can ignore Blake's own individual method. Basically that method is simple, its roots lying in his concept of states and their symbols. Like many other artists Blake employed a central group of related symbols to form a dominant symbolic pattern; his are the child, the father, and Christ, representing the states of innocence, experience, and a higher innocence. These *major* symbols provide the context for all the "minor," contributory symbols in the songs; and my purpose here is to suggest a method of approach that is applicable to all of them—and thus to all the songs.

Each of Blake's two song series (or states or major symbols) comprises a number of smaller units (or states or symbols), so that the relationship of each unit to the series as a whole might be stated as a kind of progression: from the states of innocence and experience to the *Songs of Innocence* and *Songs of Experience*, to each individual song within the series, to the symbols within each song, to the words that give the symbols their existence. Conceivably, ignorance of or indifference to one word prohibits the imaginative perception and understanding of the whole structure. As Blake wrote in the preface to *Jerusalem*, "Every word and every letter is studied and put into its fit place; the terrific numbers are reserved for the terrific parts, the mild and gentle for the mild and gentle parts, and the prosaic for inferior parts; all are necessary to each other."

For the serious reader of Blake's songs, then, a constant awareness of the context or state in which a poem appears is indispensable; and since each state is made up of many poems, the other poems in that state must be consulted to grasp the full significance of any one poem. Each song out of its context means a great deal less than Blake expected of his total invention, and occasionally it may be taken to mean something quite different from what he intended. Blake created a system of which innocence and experience are vital parts; to deny to the *Songs of Innocence*, then, the very background and basic symbology which it helps to make up is as wrong as reading *The Rape of the Lock* without reference to the epic tradition. Without the system, Blake is the simplest of lyric poets and every child may joy to hear the songs. Yet with very little study the child of innocence can be seen to be radically different from the child of experience, and the mother of innocence scarcely recognizable in experience. The states are separate, the two contrary states of the human soul, and the songs were written not merely for our enjoyment, or even for our edification, but for our salvation.

Closely related to the necessity of reading each song in terms of its state is the vital importance of point of view. Often it is unobtrusive, but many times [a faithful interpretation of the poem depends] upon a correct determination of speaker and perspective. Blake himself suggests this by his organization of the songs into series, *Innocence* introduced and sung by the piper, *Experience* by the Bard. Superficially there seems to be little to distinguish one from the other since the piper clearly exhibits imaginative vision and the Bard "Present, Past, & Future sees." Yet for each, the past, present, and future are different: for the piper the past can only be the primal unity, for the present is innocence and the immediate future is experience; for the Bard the past is innocence, the present experience, the future a higher innocence. It is natural, then, that the piper's point of view is prevailingly happy; he is conscious of the child's essential divinity and assured of his present protection. But into that joyous context the elements of experience constantly insinuate themselves so that the note of sorrow is never completely absent from the piper's pipe. In experience, on the other hand, the Bard's voice is solemn and more deeply resonant, for the high-pitched joy of innocence is now only a memory. Within this gloom, though, lies the ember which can leap into flame at any moment to light the way to the higher innocence. Yet despite this difference in direction of their vision, both singers are imaginative, are what Blake called the poetic or prophetic character. And though one singer uses "mild and gentle numbers" and the other more "terrific" tones, both see the imaginative (and symbolic) significance of all the activity in the songs. The inexplicit, Blake said, "rouzes the faculties to act." The reader of Blake, then, must rouse his faculties to consider this imaginative point of view always, no matter who is speaking or seeing or acting in a poem.

Both singers are, of course, William Blake. And since he, or they, sing all the songs, [an understanding of] whether they are identifiable or not with a character in a poem contributes most importantly to the total meaning of the poem. To take an extreme example, in "The Little Vagabond" of *Songs of Experience* there are four points of view: that of the mother, who is now out of her element and can no longer protect her child as she did in *Songs of Innocence*; that of the parson, who is a part of the major symbol of experience, father-priest-king; that of the vagabond himself, a child of experience, not the carefree, irresponsible, thoughtless child of innocence; and that of the Bard, through whose vision each of the other points of view can be studied and evaluated. Without an awareness of this complexity in "The Little Vagabond" the poem dissipates into sentimental drivel. Another good example is "Holy Thursday" of *Songs of Innocence*.

From a conventional point of view it is thoughtful and kind of the "wise guardians of the poor" to run charity schools and to take the children occasionally to St. Paul's to give thanks for all their so-called blessings. But from the piper's point of view (and Blake's of course) the children clearly are disciplined, regimented, marched in formation to church in the uniforms of their respective schools—mainly to advertise the charitable souls of their supposed guardians. The point here (seen only through the piper's vision) is that in the state of innocence there is, or ought to be, no discipline, no regimentation, no marching, no uniforms, and no guardians—merely free, uninhibited, irresponsible, thoughtless play on the echoing green. Accordingly the children in *Holy Thursday* assert and preserve their essential innocence, not by going to church, but by freely and spontaneously, "like a mighty wind," raising to "heaven the voice of song." This simple act raises them to a level far above their supposed benefactors, who are without vision, without innocence, without love: "Beneath them sit the aged men, wise guardians of the poor." The irony is severe, but lost upon us unless we are aware of context and point of view.

As a final example consider the "Introduction" to *Songs of Experience*. The main difficulty here seems to be Blake's chaotic punctuation and the ambiguity it causes. Stanzas 1, 3, and 4 seem to be an invitation to Earth to arise from the evil darkness and reassume the light of its prelapsarian state. Such an orthodox Christian reading, however, is possible only if we forget (1) that this is a *Song of Experience*, and (2) that the singer of these songs is the Bard, not God or a priest. In similar fashion, while ignoring the context or the point of view, one might quickly point out the obvious reference in stanza 1 to Genesis iii, and forget that the speaker in that chapter is the Old Testament God, Jehovah, the cruel lawgiver and vengeful tyrant who became in Blake's cosmos the father-priest-king image. And finally, the Holy Word in Genesis walked in the garden not in the "evening dew" but in the "cool of day," not to weep and forgive but to cast out and curse his children, to bind them to the soil, and to place woman in a position of virtual servitude to man. In view of this, if the second stanza is read as a clause modifying "Holy Word," it is either hopelessly contradictory or devastatingly ironic.

Blake himself hints at the correct reading immediately by means of the ambiguity of the first stanza. There are actually two voices in the poem, the Bard's ("Hear the voice of the Bard"), and the Holy Word's ("Calling the lapsed Soul"); and the second stanza, because of its apparently chaotic punctuation, must be read as modifying both voices. The last two stanzas are the words of both voices, perfectly in context when the dual purpose of the poem is recognized. Only in this way can the poem be seen for what it is, an introduction to the state and the songs of experience, in which the Holy Word of Jehovah is hypocritical, selfish, and jealous, thinking and acting in terms of the physical phenomena of day and night and the earthly morality of rewards and punishments. The Bard, mortal but prophetically imaginative, thinks and acts by eternal time and according to eternal values.

But how does one discover the all-important point of view in Blake's songs? One way is to observe the reactions of various characters to the same symbolic act, object, or character, for both the characters and the symbols ultimately resolve themselves into aspects of the major symbol governing that particular poem. Thus the mother of *Songs of Innocence* is symbolic in that her protection of the child contributes to the overall picture of the child as major symbol of the state of innocence. In addition, many of Blake's symbols are recurrent, so that once a symbol's basic significance is revealed in a kind of archetypal context, each successive context adds association to association within the song series. When the beadle's wand appears in the first stanza of "Holy Thursday" of *Innocence*, for example, its immediate connotation is authority. But since a *beadle* wields the symbol, it is also religious authority, the organized church, institutionalized religion. It also represents an act of restraint which forces the children to act according to rule rather than impulse. The wand is "white as snow" to suggest the frigidity of man-made moral purity as opposed to the warmth of young, energetic, exuberant innocence. And finally, it suggests the worldly, non-innocent concept of duty (and its corollary, harm), the duty of worship which clashes with all of Blake's ideas of freedom and spontaneity. But all of this, it will be said, strongly suggests the world of experience, and "Holy Thursday" is a *Song of Innocence*; the overall point of view is the piper's. The point to be made here is simply this. If we do not read the poem as a *Song of Innocence*, about the *state* of innocence and its major symbol, the joyous child, we can read it as a rather pleasant picture of nicely dressed charity children being led to church by a gentle beadle to sing hymns, or as a terrible view of unfortunate, exploited charity children under the thumbs of their elders. And we would not see that despite outward appearance the children *are* innocent, essentially free and happy, as they spontaneously sing their songs. Without an awareness of context the symbols do not work as Blake intended them to, and the song becomes a fairly inconsequential bit of sentimental social comment.

Considering, then, the care Blake took with point of view, recurring symbols, and symbolic action, we can see that gradually many of Blake's characters merge. The final products of these mergers are what I have called the major symbols. Kindred points of view tend to unite the holders of those points of view; characters who are associated continually with the same or similar symbols tend to melt into one another; and a similar pattern of action reveals a fundamental affinity among the actors. In these ways the significance and value of any one character in any one song are intensified and expanded beyond the immediate context. The physical identity may shift, but the symbolic value remains constant—or better, is constantly enriched. When the beadle's wand in "Holy Thursday" is recognized as part of the basic scepter motif, the beadle's identity, while being retained as representative of church law, merges with that of Tiriel, say, and the father—and ultimately with the "selfish father of men" in "Earth's Answer," the pebble in "The Clod and the Pebble," the "cold and usurous hand" of "Holy Thursday," God in "The Chimney Sweeper," the mother, parson, and "Dame Lurch" in "The Little Vagabond," "Cruelty," "Humility," and the "Human Brain" in "The Human Abstract," and Tirzah in "To Tirzah." Within the identity are inherent all the other identities which combine to make up the major symbol of the context. The priests of "The Garden of Love" may bind with briars love and desire, but they do so because they are selfish, fatherly, cold and usurous, worldly, cruel, humble, hypocritical, and so forth.

One serious question remains: how does one distinguish among all these characters, or are they all precisely alike and hence redundant? Professor Mark Schorer answers the question this way—I know of no better [answer]: "The point is," he says, "that the individuality of these creations lies not in their rich diversity but in the outline that separates them from their backgrounds." That is, each individual identity in its specific context is . . . [an identity as] a part of the whole context and [identical with] the whole of which it is a part. Both the priest of "The Garden of Love" and the flower in "My Pretty Rose Tree" are self-sufficient for some understanding of these two poems. Blake simply asked his reader to do more than merely understand: that, he said, is a "corporeal" function. He wanted them to imagine as he imagined, to see as he saw, even to recreate as he created. Only then does his method make sense, only then can one see the minor symbols as parts of a major symbol, only then can the individual song take its rightful place as a song of innocence or [a] song of experience.

NORTHROP FRYE

The Keys to the Gates

The criticism of Blake, especially of Blake's prophecies, has developed in direct proportion to the theory of criticism itself. The complaints that Blake was 'mad' are no longer of any importance, not because anybody has proved him sane, but because critical theory has realized that madness, like obscenity, is a word with no critical meaning. There are critical standards of coherence and incoherence, but if a poem is coherent in itself the sanity of its author is a matter of interest only to the more naïve type of biographer. Those who have assumed that the prophecies are incoherent because they have found them difficult often use the phrase 'private symbolism'. This is also now a matter of no importance, because in critical theory there is no such thing as private symbolism. There may be allegorical allusions to a poet's private life that can only be interpreted by biographical research, but no set of such allusions can ever form a poetic structure. They can only be isolated signposts, like the allusions to the prototypes of the beautiful youth, dark lady, and rival poet which historians and other speculative critics are persuaded that they see in the Shakespeare sonnets.

When I first embarked on an intensive study of Blake's prophecies, I assumed that my task was to follow the trail blazed by Foster Damon's great book, and take further steps to demonstrate the coherence of those poems. My primary interests, like Damon's, were literary, not occult or philosophical or religious. Many other writers had asserted that while the prophecies were doubtless coherent enough intellectually, they would turn out to depend for their coherence on some extra-poetic system of ideas. A

From *Some British Romantics: A Collection of Essays*, edited by James V. Logan, John E. Jordan, Northrop Frye. Copyright © 1966 by Ohio State University Press.

student interested in Blake's prophecies as poems would have to begin by rejecting this hypothesis, which contradicts all Blake's views about the primacy of art and the cultural disaster of substituting abstractions for art. But as I went on I was puzzled and annoyed by a schematic quality in these prophecies that refused to dissolve into what I then regarded as properly literary forms. There were even diagrams in Blake's own designs which suggested that he himself attached a good deal of value to schematism, and such statements as 'I must create a system'. Perhaps, then, these critics I had begun by rejecting were right after all: perhaps Blake was not opposed to abstraction but only to other people's abstractions, and was really interested merely in expounding some conceptual system or other in an oblique and allegorical way. In any event, the schematic, diagrammatic quality of Blake's thought was there, and would not go away or turn into anything else. Yeats had recognized it; Damon had recognized it; I had to recognize it. Like Shelly, Blake expressed an abhorrence of didactic poetry, but continued to write it.

This problem began to solve itself as soon as I realized that poetic thought is inherently and necessarily schematic. Blake soon led me, in my search for poetic analogues, to Dante and Milton, and it was clear that the schematic cosmologies of Dante and Milton, however they got into Dante and Milton, were, once they got there, poetic constructs, examples of the way poets think, and not foreign bodies of knowledge. If the prophecies are normal poems, or at least a normal expression of poetic genius, and if Blake nevertheless meant to teach some system by them, that system could only be something connected with the principles of poetic thought. Blake's 'message', then, is not simply *his* message, nor is it an extra-literary message. What he is trying to say is what he thinks poetry is trying to say: the imaginative content implied by the existence of an imaginative form of language. I finished my book in the full conviction that learning to read Blake was a step, and for me a necessary step, in learning to read poetry, and to write criticism. For if poetic thought is inherently schematic, criticism must be so too. I began to notice that as soon as a critic confined himself to talking seriously about literature his criticism tightened up and took on a systematic, even a schematic, form.

The nature of poetic 'truth' was discussed by Aristotle in connection with action. As compared with the historian, the poet makes no specific or particular statements: he gives the typical, recurring, or universal event, and is not to be judged by the standards of truth that we apply to specific statements. Poetry, then, does not state historical truth, but contains it: it sets forth what we may call the *myth* of history, the kind of thing that happens. History itself is designed to record events, or, as we may say, to provide a primary verbal imitation of events. But it also, unconsciously perhaps, illustrates and provides examples for the poetic vision. Hence we feel that *Lear* or *Macbeth* or *Oedipus Rex*, although they deal almost entirely with legend rather than actual history, contain infinite reserves of historical wisdom and insight. Thus poetry is 'something more philosophical' than history.

This last observation of Aristole's has been of little use to critics except as a means of annoying historians, and it is difficult to see in what sense Anacreon is more philosophical than Thucydides. The statement is best interpreted, as it was by Renaissance critics, schematically, following a diagram in which poetry is intermediate between history and philosophy, pure example and pure precept. It follows that poetry must have a relation to thought paralleling its relation to action. The poet does not think in the sense of producing concepts, ideas or propositions, which are specific predications to be judged by their truth or falsehood. As he produces the mythical structures of history, so he produces the mythical structures of thought, the conceptual frameworks that enter into and inform the philosophies contemporary with him. And just as we feel that the great tragedy, if not historical, yet contains an infinity of the kind of meaning that actual history illustrates, so we feel that great 'philosophical' poetry, if not actually philosophical, contains an infinity of the kind of meaning that discursive writing illustrates. This sense of the infinite treasures of thought latent in poetry is eloquently expressed by several Elizabethan critics, and there is perhaps no modern poet who suggests the same kind of intellectual richness so immediately as Blake does.

Blake, in fact, gives us so good an introduction to the nature and structure of poetic thought that, if one has any interest in the subject at all, one can hardly avoid exploiting him. There are at least three reasons why he is uniquely useful for this purpose. One is that his prophecies are works of philosophical poetry which give us practically nothing at all unless we are willing to grapple with the kind of poetic thought that they express. Another is that Blake also wrote such haunting and lucid lyrics, of which we can at first say little except that they seem to belong in the centre of our literary experience. We may not know why they are in the centre, and some readers would rather not know; but for the saving remnant who do want to know, there are the prophecies to help us understand. The third reason is Blake's quality as an illustrator of other poets. If a person of considerable literary experience is reading a poem he is familiar with, it is easy for him to fall—in fact, it is very difficult for him not to fall—into a passive habit of not really reading the poem, but merely of spotting the critical clichés he is accustomed to associate with it. Thus, if he is reading Gray's 'Ode on the Death of a Favourite Cat,' and sees the goldfish described as 'angel forms', 'genii of the stream' and with 'scaly armour', his stock response will start murmuring: 'Gray means fish, of course, but he is saying so in terms of eighteenth-century personification, Augustan artificiality, his own peculiar demure humour,' and the like. Such a reading entirely obliterates Gray's actual processes of poetic thought and substitutes something in its place that, whatever it is, is certainly not poetry or philosophy, any more than it is history. But if he is reading the poem in the context of Blake's illustrations, Blake will compel him to see the angel forms, the genii of the stream, and the warriors in scaly armour, as well as the fish, in such a way as to make the unvisualized clichés of professional reading impossible, and to bring the metaphorical structure of the poem clearly into view.

I am suggesting that no one can read Blake seriously and sympathetically without feeling that the keys to poetic thought are in him, and what follows attempts to explain how a documentation of such a feeling would proceed. I make no claim that I am saying anything here that I have not said before, though I may be saying it in less compass.

EASTERN GATE: TWOFOLD VISION

The structure of metaphors and imagery that informed poetry, through the Middle Ages and the Renaissance, arranged reality on four levels. On top was heaven, the place of the presence of God; below it was the proper level of human nature, represented by the stories of the Garden of Eden and the Golden Age; below that was the physical world, theologically fallen, which man is in but not of; and at the bottom was the world of sin, death, and corruption. This was a deeply conservative view of reality in which man, in fallen nature, was confronted with a moral dialectic that either lowered him into sin or raised him to his proper level. The raising media included education, virtue, and obedience to law. In the Middle Ages this construct was closely linked with similar constructs in theology and science. These links weakened after the sixteenth century and eventually disappeared, leaving the construct to survive only in poetry, and, even there, increasingly by inertia. It is still present in Pope's *Essay on Man*, but accompanied with a growing emphasis on the limitation of poetic objectives. This limitation means, among other things, that mythopoeic literature, which demands a clear and explicit framework of imagery, is in the age of Pope and Swift largely confined to parody.

As the eighteenth century proceeded, the imaginative climate began to change, and we can see poets trying to move toward a less conservative structure of imagery. This became a crucial problem when the French Revolution confronted the Romantic poets. No major poet in the past had been really challenged by a revolutionary situation except Milton, and even Milton had reverted to the traditional structure for *Paradise Lost*. Blake was not only older than Wordsworth and Coleridge, but more consistently revolutionary in his attitude: again, unlike most English writers of the period, he saw the American Revolution as an event of the same kind as its French successor. He was, therefore, the first English poet to work out the revolutionary structure of imagery that continues through Romantic poetry and thought to our own time.

At the centre of Blake's thought are the two conceptions of innocence and experience, 'the two contrary states of the human soul'. Innocence is characteristic of the child, experience of the adult. In innocence, there are two factors. One is an assumption that the world was made for the benefit of human beings, has a human shape and a human meaning, and is a world in which providence, protection, communication with other beings, including animals, and, in general, 'mercy, pity, peace and love', have a genuine function. The other is ignorance of the fact that the world is not like this. As the child grows up, his conscious mind accepts 'experience', or reality without any human shape or meaning, and his childhood innocent vision, having nowhere else to go, is driven underground into what we should call the subconscious, where it takes an essentially sexual form. The original innocent vision becomes a melancholy dream of how man once posssessed a happy garden, but lost it for ever, though he may regain it after he dies. The following diagram illustrates the process as well as the interconnection of *Songs of Innocence and Experience*, *The Marriage of Heaven and Hell*, and the early political prophecies *The French Revolution* and *America* in Blake's thought:

child's
innocence   >   adult
experience   = Urizen = 'heaven' of *status quo*

frustrated
desire   = Orc   = 'hell, of rebelliousness

In place of the old construct, therefore, in which man regains his happy garden home by doing his duty and obeying the law, we have an uneasy revolutionary conception of conscious values and standards of reality sitting on top of a volcano of thwarted and mainly sexual energy. This construct has two aspects, individual or psychological, and social or political. Politically, it represents an ascendant class threatened by the growing body of those excluded from social benefits, until the latter are strong enough to overturn society. Psychologically, it represents a conscious ego threatened by a sexually-rooted desire. Thus the mythical structure that informs both the psychology of Freud and the political doctrines of Marx is present in *The Marriage of Heaven and Hell*, which gives us both aspects of the Romantic movement: the reaction to political revolution and the manifesto of feeling and desire as opposed to the domination of reason.

In the associations that Blake makes with Urizen and Orc, Urizen is an old man and Orc a youth: Urizen has the counter-revolutionary colour white and Orc is a revolutionary red. Urizen is therefore associated with sterile winter, bleaching bones, and clouds; Orc with summer, blood, and the sun. The colours white and red suggest the bread and wine of a final harvest and vintage, prophesied in the fourteenth chapter of Revelation. Orc is 'underneath' Urizen, and underneath the white cliffs of Albion on the map are the 'vineyards of red France' in the throes of revolution. In a map of Palestine, the kingdom of Israel, whose other name, Jacob, means usurper, sits on top of Edom, the kingdom of the red and hairy Esau, the rightful heir. Isaiah's vision of a Messiah appearing in Edom, with his body soaked in blood from 'treading the winepress' of war, haunts nearly all Blake's prophecies. There are many other associations; perhaps we may derive the most important from the following passage in *America*:

> The terror answerd: I am Orc, wreath'd round the accursed tree:
> The times are ended: shadows pass the morning gins to break;
> The fiery joy, that Urizen perverted to ten commands,
> What night he led the starry hosts thro' the wide wilderness:
> That stony law I stamp to dust: and scatter religion abroad
> To the four winds as a torn book, & none shall gather the leaves:
> But they shall rot on desart sands, & consume in bottomless deeps:
> To make the desarts blossom, & the deeps shrink to their fountains,
> And to renew the fiery joy, and burst the stony roof.
> That pale religious letchery, seeking Virginity,
> May find it in a harlot, and in coarse-clad honesty
> The undefil'd thro' ravish'd in her cradle night and morn:
> For every thing that lives is holy, life delights in life:
> Because the soul of sweet delight can never be defil'd.
> Fires inwrap the earthly globe, yet man is not consumd:
> Amidst the lustful fires he walks: his feet become like brass,
> His knees and thighs like silver, & his breast and head like gold.

At various times in history there had been a political revolution symbolized by the birth or rebirth of Orc, the 'terrible boy': each one, however, has eventually subsided into the same Urizenic form as its predecessor. Orc is the human protest of energy and desire, the impulse to freedom and to sexual love. Urizen is the 'reality principle', the belief that knowledge of what is real comes from outside the human body. If we believe that reality is what we bring into existence through an act of creation, then we are free to build up our own civilization and abolish the anomalies and injustices that hamper its growth; but if we believe that reality is primarily what is 'out there', then we are condemned, in Marx's phrase, to study the world and never to change it. And the world that we study in this way we are compelled to see in the distorted perspective of the human body with its five cramped senses, not our powers of perception as they are developed and expanded by the arts. Man in his present state is so constructed that all he can see outside him is the world under the law. He may believe that gods or angels or devils or fairies or ghosts are also 'out there', but he cannot see these things: he can see only the human and the sub-human, moving in established and predictable patterns. The basis of this vision of reality is the world of the heavenly bodies, circling around automatically and out of reach.

One early Orc rebellion was the Exodus from Egypt, where Orc is represented by a pillar of fire (the 'fiery joy') and Urizen by a pillar of cloud, or what *Finnegans Wake* calls 'Delude of Isreal'. Orc was a human society of twelve (actually thirteen) tribes; Urizen, a legal mechanism symbolized by the twelvefold Zodiac with its captive sun, which is why Urizen is said to have 'led the starry hosts' through the wilderness. The eventual victory of Urizen was marked by the establishing of Aaron's priesthood (the twelve stones in his breastplate symbolized the Zodiac as well as the tribes, according to Josephus), and by the negative moral law of the Decalogue, the moral law being the human imitation of the automatism of natural law. The final triumph of Urizen was symbolized by the hanging of the brazen serpent (Orc) on the pole, a form of the 'accursed tree', and recalling the earlier association of tree and serpent with the exile of Adam into a wilderness, as well as anticipating the Crucifixion.

Jesus was another Orc figure, gathering twelve followers and starting a new civilization. Christian civilization, like its predecessors, assumed the Urizenic form that it presented so clearly in Blake's own time. This historical perversion of Christianity is studied in *Europe*, where Enitharmon, the Queen of Heaven, summons up twelve starry children, along with Orc as the captive sun, to reimpose the cult of external reality, or what Blake calls natural religion, on Christendom. With the Resurrection, traditionally symbolized by a red cross on a white ground, Jesus made a definitive step into reality: the revolutionary apocalypse Blake hopes for in his day is a second coming or mass resurrection, which is why resurrection imagery is prominently displayed in *America*. Now, at the end of European civilization, comes another rebellion of Orc in America, bearing on its various banners a tree, a serpent and thirteen red and white stripes. The spread of this rebellion to Europe itself is a sign that bigger things are on the way.

The Israelites ended their revolt in the desert of the moral law: now it is time to reverse the movement, to enter the Promised Land, the original Eden, which is to Israel what Atlantis is to Britain and America. The Promised Land is not a different place from the desert, but the desert itself transformed (Blake's imagery comes partly from Isaiah 35, a chapter he alludes to in *The Marriage of Heaven and Hell*). The 'deeps shrink to their fountains' because in the apocalypse there is no more sea: dead water is transformed to living water (as in Ezekiel's vision, Ezek. 47:8). The spiritual body of risen man is sexually free, an aspect symbolized by the 'lustful fires' in which he walks. Man under the law is sexually in a prison of heat without light, a volcano: in the resurrection he is unhurt by the flames, like the three Hebrews in Nebuchadnezzar's furnace who were seen walking with the son of God. According to *The Marriage of Heaven and Hell*, Jesus became Jehovah after his death, and Jehovah, not Satan, is the one who dwells in flaming fire. The risen man, then, is the genuine form of the metallic statue of Nebuchadnezzar's dream, without the feet of clay that made that statue an image of tyranny and the cycle of history.

The Resurrection rolled the stone away covering the tomb ('burst the stony roof'). The stone that covers the tomb of man under the law is the vast arch of the sky, which we see as a concave 'vault of paved heaven' (a phrase in the early 'Mad Song') because we are looking at it from under the 'stony roof' of the skull. The risen body would be like the shape of one of Blake's Last Judgement paintings, with an 'opened centre' or radiance of light on top, in the place which is the true location of heaven. Finally, the entire Bible or revelation of the divine in and to man can be read either as the charter of human freedom or as a code of restrictive and negative moral commands. Orc proposes to use Urizen's version of the holy book as fertilizer to help make the desert blossom: what he would do, in other words, is to internalize the law, transform it from arbitrary commands to the inner discipline of the free spirit.

NORTHERN GATE: SINGLE VISION

The optimistic revolutionary construct set up in Blake's early prophecies is found again in Shelley, whose Prometheus and Jupiter correspond to Orc and Urizen. But in later Romanticism it quickly turns pessimistic and once more conservative, notably in Schopenhauer, where the world as idea, the world of genuine humanity, sits on top of a dark, threatening, and immensely powerful world as well. A similar construct is in Darwin and Huxley, where the ethical creation of human society maintains itself precariously against the evolutionary force below it. In Freud, civilization is essentially an anxiety-structure, where the 'reality principle', Blake's Urizen, must maintain its ascendancy somehow over the nihilistic upthrusts of desire. It may permit a certain amount of expression to the 'pleasure principle', but not to the extent of being taken over by it. And in Blake, if every revolt of Orc in history has been 'perverted to ten commands', the inference seems to be that history exhibits only a gloomy series of cycles, beginning in hope and inevitably ending in renewed tyranny. In Blake's later prophecies, we do find this Spenglerian view of history, with a good many of Spengler's symbols attached to it.

The cyclical movement of history is summarized by Blake in four stages. The first stage is the revolutionary birth of Orc; the second, the transfer of power from Orc to Urizen at the height of Orc's powers, accompanied by the binding or imprisoning of Orc; the third, the consolidating of 'natural religion' or the sense of reality as out there, symbolized by Urizen exploring his dens; the fourth, a collapse and chaos symbolized by the crucifixion of Orc, the hanging of the serpent on the dead tree. This fourth stage is the one that Blake sees his own age entering, after the triumph of natural religion or 'Deism' in the decades following Newton and Locke. It is an age characterized by mass wars (Isaiah's treading of the winepress), by technology and complex machinery, by tyranny and 'empire' (imperialism being the demonic enemy of culture), and by unimaginative art, especially in architecture. The central symbol of this final phase is the labyrinthine desert in which the Mosaic exodus ended. Jesus spent forty days in the desert, according to Mark, 'with the wild beasts': the passage from empire to ruin, from the phase of the tyrant to the phase of the wild beast, is symbolized in the story of Nebuchadnezzar, whose metamorphosis is illustrated at the end of *The Marriage of Heaven and Hell.* The figure of Ijim in *Tiriel* has a parallel significance.

As Blake's symbolism becomes more concentrated, he tends to generalize the whole cycle in the conception of 'Druidism'. The Druids, according to Blake's authorities, worshipped the tree and the serpent, the Druid temple of Avebury, illustrated on the last plate of *Jerusalem*, being serpent-shaped; and they went in for orgies of human sacrifice which illustrate, even more clearly than warfare, the fact that the suppression or perversion of the sexual impulse ends in a death wish (I am not reading modern conceptions into Blake here, but following Blake's own symbolism). This 'Druid' imagery is illustrated in the following passage from *Europe*, describing the reaction of the tyrannical 'King' or guardian angel of the reactionary Albion and his councillors to the American revolution and kindred portents of apocalyptic disaffection:

> In thoughts perturb'd they rose from the bright ruins silent following
> The fiery King, who sought his ancient temple serpent-form'd
> That stretches out its shady length along the Island white.
> Round him roll'd his clouds of war; silent the Angel went,
> Along the infinite shores of Thames to golden Verulam.
> There stand the venerable porches that high-towering rear
> Their oak-surrounded pillars, form'd of massy stones, uncut
> With tool: stones precious: such eternal in the heavens,
> Of colours twelve, few known on earth, give light in the opake,
> Plac'd in the order of the stars, when the five senses whelm'd
> In deluge o'er the earth-born man: then turn'd the fluxile eyes
> Into two stationary orbs, concentrating all things.
> The ever-varying spiral ascents to the heavens of heavens
> Were bended downward, and the nostrils golden gates shut,
> Turn'd outward barr'd and petrify'd against the infinite . . .
>
> Now arriv'd the ancient Guardian at the southern porch.
> That planted thick with trees of blackest leaf, & in a vale
> Obscure, inclos'd the Stone of Night; oblique it stood, o'erhung
> With purple flowers and berries red: image of that sweet south
> Once open to the heavens and elevated on the human neck,
> Now overgrown with hair and cover'd with a stony roof:
> Downward 'tis sunk beneath th' attractive north, that round the feet
> A raging whirlpool draws the dizzy enquirer to his grave.

It is an intricate passage, but it all makes sense. The serpent temple of Avebury is identified with the white-cliffed Albion in its final Druid phase. It is centred at Verulam, which, as the site of a Roman camp, a 'Gothic' cathedral, and the baronial title of Bacon, takes in the whole cycle of British civilization. As we approach the temple, it appears to be a Stonehenge-like circle of twelve precious stones, 'plac'd in the order of the stars', or symbolizing the Zodiac. The imagery recalls the similar decadence of Israel in the desert: the twelve Zodiacal gems of Aaron's breastplate have been mentioned, and the Israelites also built megalithic monuments on which they were forbidden to use iron (Jos. 8:31), hence 'uncut with tool', iron being in Blake the symbol of Los the blacksmith, the builder of the true city of gems (Isa. 54:16).

The central form of Druid architecture is the trilithic cromlech or dolmen, the arch of three stones. According to Blake, the two uprights of this arch symbolize the two aspects of creative power, strength and beauty, or sublimity and pathos, as he calls them in the *Descriptive Catalogue*, the horizontal stone being the dominant Urizenic reason. Human society presents this arch in the form of an 'Elect' class tyrannizing over the 'Reprobate', the unfashionable artists and prophets who embody human sublimity, and the 'Redeemed', the gentler souls who are in the company of the beautiful and pathetic. This trilithic structure appears in such later militaristic monuments as the Arch of Titus: in its 'Druid' form, it is illustrated with great power in *Milton*, Plate 6, and *Jerusalem*, Plate 70. In the former, the balancing rock in front may represent the 'Stone of Night' in the above passage. To pass under this arch is to be subjugated, in a fairly literal sense, to what is, according to the *Descriptive Catalogue*, both the human reason and the 'incapability of intellect', as intellect in Blake is always associated with the creative and imaginative. Another form of tyrannical architecture characteristic of a degenerate civilization is the pyramid, representing the volcano or imprisoning mountain under which Orc lies. Blake connects the pyramids with the servitude of the Israelites among the brick-kilns and the epithet 'furnace of iron' (I Kings 8:51) applied to Egypt in the Bible. The association of pyramids and fire is as old as Plato's pun on the word πύρ.

The temple of Verulam is a monument to the fall of man, in Blake the same event as the deluge and the creation of the world in its present 'out there' form. This form is that of the law, the basis of which is revolution in its mechanical sense of revolving wheels, the symbol of which is the *ouroboros*, the serpent with its tail in its mouth (indicated in a passage omitted above). We see the world from individual 'opake' centres, instead of being identified with a universal Man who is also God, who created what we see as alien to us, and who would consequently see his world from the circumference instead of the centre, the perspective reinstated in man by the arts. Such a God-Man would be 'full of eyes', like the creatures of Ezekiel's vision, and by an unexpected but quite logical extension of the symbolism, Blake makes him full of noses too. Burning meat to gods on altars, after all, does assume that gods have circumferential noses.

The 'Stone of Night', the opposite of the 'lively stones' (I Pet. 2:5) of the genuine temple, is an image of the human head, the phrase 'stony roof' being repeated from the passage in *America* quoted above. It is in the south because the south is the zenith, the place of the sun in full strength in Blake's symbolism. Now it is covered with purple flowers and red berries, probably of the nightshade: the colours are those of the dying god, which is what Orc (usually Luvah in this context) comes to be in Blake's later poems. The Stone of Night has fallen like a meteor through the bottom or nadir of existence, represented by the north, and now has the same relation to its original that a gravestone has to a living body. We may compare the 'grave-plot' that Thel reached when she passed under the 'northern bar', and the black coffin which is the body of the chimney sweep (and the enslaved Negro, who also belongs in the 'southern clime'). Blake's imagery of the north combines the magnetic needle and the legend of the northern maelstrom, the latter supplying a demonic parody of the ascending spiral image on the altar.

From the perspective of single vision, then, our original diagram of buried innocence trying to push its way into experience has to be completed by the death in which all life, individual or historical, ends. Death in Blake's symbolism is Satan, the 'limit of Opacity', reduction to inorganic matter, who operates in the living man as a death wish or 'accuser' of sin. His source in the outer world is the sky, Satan being the starry dragon of Revelation 12:4. Blake identifies this dragon with the Covering Cherub of Ezekiel 28, and the Covering Cherub again with the angel trying to keep us out of the Garden of Eden. Thus the sky is, first, the outward illusion of reality that keeps us out of our proper home; second, the macrocosmic Stone of Night, the rock on top of man's tomb designed to prevent his resurrection; and third, the circumference of what Blake calls the 'Mundane Shell', the world as it appears to the embryonic and unborn imagination. Thus:

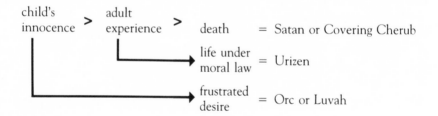

Ordinary human life, symbolized in Blake first by 'Adam' and later by 'Reuben', oscillates between the two submerged states.

The conception of Druidism in Blake, then, is a conception of human energy and desire continuously martyred by the tyranny of human reason, or superstition. The phrase 'dying god' that we have used for Luvah suggests Frazer, and Blake's Druid symbolism has some remarkable anticipations of Frazer's *Golden Bough* complex, including the mistletoe and the oak. The anticipations even extend to Frazer's own unconscious symbolism: the colours of the three states above are, reading up, red, white, and black; and Frazer's book ends with the remark that the web of human thought has been woven of these three colours, though the status of the white or scientific one in Blake is very different. The following passage from *Jerusalem* 66 illustrates Blake's handling of sacrificial symbolism:

> The Daughters of Albion clothed in garments of needle work
> Strip them off from their shoulders and bosoms, they lay aside
> Their garments, they sit naked upon the Stone of trial.
> The knife of flint passes over the howling Victim: his blood
> Gushes & stains the fair side of the fair Daughters of Albion.
> They put aside his curls: they divide his seven locks upon
> His forehead: they bind his forehead with thorns of iron,
> They put into his hand a reed, they mock, Saying: Behold
> The King of Canaan, whose are seven hundred chariots of iron!
> They take off his vesture whole with their Knives of flint:
> But they cut asunder his inner garments: searching with
> Their cruel fingers for his heart, & there they enter in pomp,
> In many tears: & there they erect a temple & an altar:
> They pour cold water on his brain in front, to cause
> Lids to grow over his eyes in veils of tears: and caverns
> To freeze over his nostrils, while they feed his tongue from cups
> And dishes of painted clay.

The imagery combines the mockery and passion of Jesus with features from Aztec sacrifices, as Blake realizes that the two widely separated rituals mean essentially the same thing. In the Mexican rites, the 'vesture whole' is the skin, not the garment, and the heart is extracted from the body, not merely pierced by a spear as in the Passion. As the passage goes on, the victim expands from an individual body into a country: that is, he is beginning to embody not merely the dying god, but the original universal Man, Albion, whose present dead body is England. The veils and caverns are religious images derived from analogies between the human body and the landscape. Serpent worship is for Blake a perennial feature of this kind of superstition, and the victim is fed from dishes of clay partly because, as Blake says in *The Everlasting Gospel*, 'dust & Clay is the Serpent's meat.' An early Biblical dying-god figure is that of Sisera, the King of Canaan, whose murder at the hands of Jael suggests the nailing down of Jesus and Prometheus; and the reference to 'needle work' in the first line also comes from Deborah's war song. The role given to the Daughters of Albion shows how clearly Blake associates the ritual of sacrifice, many features of which are repeated in judicial executions, with a perversion of the erotic instinct; and, in fact, Blake is clearer than Frazer about the role of the 'white goddess' in the dying god cult, the Cybele who decrees the death of Attis.

SOUTHERN GATE: THREEFOLD VISION

The conception of a cycle common to individual and to historical life is the basis of the symbolism of several modern poets, including Yeats, Joyce in *Finnegans Wake*, and Graves in *The White Goddess*. In its modern forms, it usually revolves around a female figure. *The Marriage of Heaven and Hell* prophesies that eventually the bound Orc will be set free and will destroy the present world in a 'consummation', which means both burning up and the climax of a marriage. When the marriage is accomplished 'by an improvement of sensual enjoyment', the world of form and reason will be their 'outward bound or circumference' instead of a separate and therefore tyrannizing principle. One would think then that a female figure would be more appropriate for the symbolism of the world of form than the aged and male Urizen.

In traditional Christian symbolism, God the Creator is symbolically male, and all human souls, whether of men or of women, are creatures, and therefore symbolically female. In Blake, the real man is creating man; hence all human beings, men or women, are symbolically male. The symbolic female in Blake is what we call nature, and has four relations to humanity, depending on the quality of the vision. In the world of death, or Satan, which Blake calls Ulro, the human body is completely absorbed in the body of nature—a 'dark Hermaphrodite', as Blake says in *The Gates of Paradise*. In the ordinary world of experience, which Blake calls Generation, the relation of humanity to nature is that of subject to object. In the usually frustrated and suppressed world of sexual desire, which Blake calls Beulah, the relation is that of lover to beloved, and in the purely imaginative or creative state, called Eden, the relation is that of creator to creature. In the first two worlds, nature is a remote and tantalizing 'female will'; in the last two she is an 'emanation'. Human women are associated with this female nature only when in their behaviour they dramatize its characteristics. The relations between man and nature in the individual and historical cycles are different, and are summarized in *The Mental Traveller*, a poem as closely related to the cyclical symbolism of twentieth-century poetry as Keats's *La Belle Dame Sans Merci* is to pre-Raphaelite poetry.

The Mental Traveller traces the life of a 'Boy' from infancy through manhood to death and rebirth. This Boy represents humanity, and consequently the cycle he goes through can be read either individually and psychologically, or socially and historically. The latter reading is easier, and closer to the centre of gravity of what Blake is talking about. The poem traces a cycle, but the cycle differs from that of the single vision in that the emphasis is thrown on rebirth and return instead of on death. A female principle, nature, cycles in contrary motion against the Boy, growing young as he grows old and vice versa, and producing four phases that we may call son and mother, husband and wife, father and daughter, ghost (Blake's 'spectre'), and ghostly bride (Blake's 'emanation'). Having set them down, we next observe that not one of these relations is genuine: the mother is not really a mother, nor the daughter really a daughter, and similarly with the other states. The 'Woman Old', the nurse who takes charge of the Boy, is Mother Nature, whom Blake calls Tirzah, and who ensures that everyone enters this world in the mutilated and imprisoned form of the physical body. The sacrifice of the dying god repeats this symbolism, which is why the birth of the Boy also contains the symbols of the Passion (we should compare this part of *The Mental Traveller* with the end of *Jerusalem* 67).

As the Boy grows up, he subdues a part of nature to his will, which thereupon becomes his mistress: a stage represented elsewhere in the Preludium to *America*. As the cycle completes what Yeats would call its first gyre, we reach the opposite pole of a 'Female Babe' whom, like the newborn Boy, no one dares touch. This female represents the 'emanation' or accumulated form of what the Boy has created in his life. If she were a real daughter and not a changeling, she would be the Boy's own permanent creation, as Jerusalem is the daughter of Albion, 'a City, yet a Woman'; and with the appearance of such a permanent creation, the cycle of nature would come to an end. But in this world all creative achievements are inherited by someone else and are lost to their creator. This failure to take possession of one's own deepest experience is the theme of *The Crystal Cabinet* (by comparing the imagery of this latter poem with *Jerusalem* 70 we discover that the Female Babe's name, in this context, is Rahab). The Boy, now an old man at the point of death, acquires, like the aged King David, another 'maiden' to keep his body warm on his death-bed. He is now in the desert or wilderness, which symbolizes the end of a cycle, and his maiden is Lilith, the bride of the desert, whom Blake elsewhere calls the Shadowy Female. The Boy as an old man is in an 'alastor' relation to her: he ought to be still making the kind of creative effort that produced the Female Babe, but instead he keeps seeking his 'emanation' or created form outside himself, until eventually the desert is partially renewed by his efforts, he comes again into the place of seed, and the cycle starts once more.

A greatly abbreviated account of the same cycle, in a more purely historical context, is in the 'Argument' of *The Marriage of Heaven and Hell*. Here we start with Rintrah, the prophet in the desert, the Moses or

Elijah or John the Baptist who announces a new era of history; then we follow the historical cycle as it makes the desert blossom and produces the honey of the Promised Land. We notice how, as in the time of Moses, water springs up in the desert and how Orc's 'red clay' puts life on the white bones of Urizen. Eventually the new society becomes decadent and tyrannical, forcing the prophet out into the desert once more to begin another cycle.

The poem called *The Gates of Paradise*, based on a series of illustrations reproduced in the standard editions of Blake, describes the same cycle in slightly different and more individualized terms. Here conception in the womb, the mutilation of birth which produces the 'mother's grief', is symbolized by the caterpillar and by the mandrake. The mandrake is traditionally an aphrodisiac, a plant with male and female forms, an opiate, the seed of hanged men, a 'man-dragon' that shrieks when uprooted (i.e. born), and recalls the frustrated sunflower of the *Songs of Experience*. The association of the mandrake with the mother in Genesis 30:14 is the main reason why Blake uses 'Reuben' instead of 'Adam' as the symbol of ordinary man in *Jerusalem*. The embryo then takes on the substance of the four elements and the four humours that traditionally correspond to them, of which 'Earth's Melancholy' is the dominant one. Then the infant is born and grows into an aggressive adolescent, like the Boy in *The Mental Traveller*, binding nature down for his delight. This attitude divides nature into a part that is possessed and a part that eludes, and the separation indicates that the boy in this poem also is bound to the cyclical movement. The youth then collides with Urizen, the spear in the revolutionary left hand being opposed to the sword of established order in the right. The caption of this emblem, 'My Son! My Son!' refers to Absalom's revolt against David. Orc is not the son of Urizen, but Absalom, hung on a tree (traditionally by his golden hair, like the mistletoe: cf. *The Book of Ahania*, II,9), is another dying god or Druid victim.

The other plates are not difficult to interpret: they represent the frustration of desire, the reaction into despair, and the growing of the youthful rebellious Orc into a wing-clipping Urizen again. Finally the hero, like the early Tiriel and like the Boy of *The Mental Traveller* in his old age, becomes a wandering pilgrim making his way, like the old man in the *Pardoner's Tale*, toward his own death. He enters 'Death's Door', the lower half of a design from Blair's *Grave* omitting the resurrection theme in the upper half, and is once more identified with Mother Nature, with a caption quoted from Job 17:14. The Prologue asks us why we worship this dreary womb-to-tomb treadmill as God—that is, why we think of God as a sky-god of automatic order, when this sky-god is really Satan, the corpse of God. The Epilogue returns to the same attack, and concludes by calling Satan 'The lost traveller's Dream under the Hill'. Apart from the general theme of the dreaming traveller which is common to this poem and to *The Mental Traveller* (where the 'mental' travelling is done by the poet and reader, not the hero), there is a more specific allusion to the passage in *The Pilgrim's Progress* where Christian, after falling asleep under Hill Difficulty and losing his roll, is forced to retrace his steps like the Israelites in the desert, to whom Bunyan explicitly refers.

The passage from death to rebirth is represented in Blake's symbolism by Tharmas, the power of renewing life. The ability of the individual to renew his life is resurrection, and the resurrection is a break with the cycle, but in ordinary life such a renewal takes place only in the group or species, and within the cycle. Tharmas is symbolized by the sea, the end and the beginning of life. As the original fall of man was also the deluge, we are in this world symbolically under water, our true home being Atlantis, or the Red Sea, which the Israelites found to be dry land. Tharmas and Orc are the strength and beauty, the sublime and the pathetic, the uprights of the Druid trilithon already mentioned, with Urizen, the anti-intellectual 'reason', connecting them. Thus:

childhood and youth	>	maturity and old age	>	death and return to place of seed	= Tharmas =	fallen power
				life under law	= Urizen =	fallen wisdom
				frustrated desire	= Orc =	fallen love

WESTERN GATE: FOURFOLD VISION

In *The Marriage of Heaven and Hell*, Blake presents the revolutionary vision of man as a self-centred anxious ego sitting on top of a rebellious desire, and he associates the emancipating of desire with the end of the world as we know it. The Proverbs of Hell say: 'He who desires but acts not, breeds pestilence.' Putting desire into action does not lead to anarchy, for the fires of Orc are 'thought-creating': what it does lead to is an apocalypse in which 'the whole creation will be consumed and appear infinite and holy, whereas it now appears finite & corrupt'. But when we read other works of Blake, we begin to wonder if this 'Voice of the Devil' tells the whole story. Blake certainly means what he says in *The Marriage of Heaven and Hell*, but that work is a satire, deriving its norms from other conceptions. As we read further in Blake, it becomes clear that the emancipating of desire, for him, is not the cause but the effect of the purging of reality. There was some political disillusionment as Blake proceeded—the perversion of the French Revolution into Napoleonic imperialism, the strength of the reactionary power in Britain, the contin- ued ascendancy of the slave-owners in America, and a growing feeling that Voltaire and Rousseau were reactionaries and not revolutionaries, were the main elements in it—but although this leads to some changes in emphasis in later poems, there is no evidence that he was ever really confused about the difference between the apocalyptic and the historical versions of reality.

Blake dislikes any terminology which implies that there are two perceivers in man, such as a soul and a body, which perceive different worlds. There is only one world, but there are two kinds of things to be done with it. There is, first, what Blake calls the natural vision, which assumes that the objective world is essentially independent of man. This vision becomes increasingly hypnotized by the automatic order and tanta- lizing remoteness of nature, creates gods in the image of its mindless mechanism, and rationalizes all evils and injustices of existence under some such formula as 'Whatever is, is right'. In extreme forms, this alienating vision becomes the reflection of the death wish in the soul, and develops annihilation wars like those of Blake's own time. Then there is the human vision, which takes the objective world to be the 'starry floor', the bottom of reality, its permanence being important only as a stable basis for human creation. The goal of the human vision is 'Religion, or Civilized Life such as it is in the Christian Church'. This is a life of pure creation, such as is ascribed in Christianity to God, and which for Blake would participate in the infinite and eternal perspective of God. We note that Blake, like Kierkegaard, leads us toward an 'either/or' dilemma, but that his terms are the reverse of Kierkegaard's. It is the aesthetic element for Blake which moves in the sphere of existential freedom; it is the ethical element which is the spectator, under the bondage of the law and the knowledge of good and evil.

We begin, then, with the view of an orthodox or moral 'good', founded on an acceptance of the world out there, contrasted with the submerged 'evil' desires of man to live in a world that makes more human sense. This vision of life turns out to be, when examined, a cyclical vision, completed by the more elaborate cycles just examined. But in addition to the cyclical vision there is also a dialectic, a separating-out of the two opposing human and natural visions. The categories of these visions are not moral good and evil, but life and death, one producing the real heaven of creation and the other the real hell of torture and tyranny. We have met one pole of this dialectic already in the conception of Satan, or death, as the only possible goal of all human effort from one point of view. The other pole is the impulse to transform the world into a human and imaginative form, the impulse that creates all art, all genuine religion, all culture and civilization. This impulse is personified by Blake as Los, the spirit of prophecy and creativity, and it is Los, not Orc, who is the hero of Blake's prophecies. Los derives, not from the suppressed desires of the individual child, but from a deeper creative impulse alluded to in Biblical myths about the unfallen state. These myths tell us that man's original state was not primitive, or derived from nature at all, but civilized, in the environment of a garden and a city. This unfallen state is, so to speak, the previous tree of which contemporary man is the seed, and the form he is attempting to recreate. Thus:

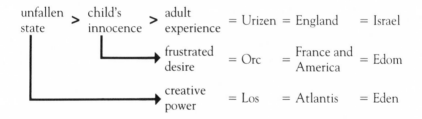

It seems curious that, especially in the earlier prophecies, Los appears to play a more reactionary and sinister role than Urizen himself. We discover that it is Los, not Urizen, who is the father of Orc; Los, not Urizen, who actively restrains Orc, tying him down under Mount Atlas with the 'Chain of Jealousy'; and Los who is the object of Orc's bitter Oedipal resentments. In the Preludium to *America*, he is referred to by his alternative name of Urthona, and there it is he and not Urizen who rivets Orc's 'tenfold chains'. These chains evidently include an incest taboo, for Orc is copulating with his sister in this Preludium. Evidently, as Blake conceives it, there is a deeply conservative element in the creative spirit that seems to help perpetuate the reign of Urizen. In fact, certain functions given to Urizen in earlier prophecies are transferred to Los in later ones. According to William Morris, the joy that the medieval craftsman took in his work was so complete that he was able to accept the tyranny of medieval society: similarly, Blake is able to live in the age of Pitt and Nelson and yet be absorbed in building his palace of art on the 'Great Atlantic Mountains', which will be here after the 'Sea of Time and Space' above it is no more.

This principle that effective social action is to be found in the creation of art and not in revolution is, of course, common to many Romantics in Blake's period. It should not, however—certainly not in Blake—be regarded as a mere neurotic or wish-fulfilment substitute for the failure of revolution. Apart from the fact that the creation of art is a highly social act, Blake's conception of art is very different from the dictionary's. It is based on what we call the arts, because of his doctrine that human reality is created and not observed. But it includes much that we do not think of as art, and excludes much that we do, such as the paintings of Reynolds.

We notice that in *The Gates of Paradise* cycle there is one point at which there is a break from the cycle, the plate captioned 'Fear & Hope are—Vision', and described in the commentary as a glimpse of 'The Immortal Man that cannot Die'. The corresponding point in *The Mental Traveller* comes in describing the form ('emanation') of the life that the Boy has been constructing, just before it takes shape as the elusive 'Female Babe':

> And these are the gems of the Human Soul,
> The rubies & pearls of a lovesick eye,
> The countless gold of the akeing heart,
> The martyr's groan & the lover's sigh.

The curiously wooden allegory is not characteristic of Blake, but it recurs in *Jerusalem* 12, where the same theme is under discussion. Evidently, Blake means by 'art' a creative life rooted in the arts, but including what more traditional language calls charity. Every act man performs is either creative or destructive. Both kinds seem to disappear in time, but in fact it is only the destructive act, the act of war or slavery or parasitism or hatred, that is really lost.

Los is not simply creative power, but the spirit of time: more accurately, he is the power that constructs in time the palace of art (Golgonooza), which is timeless. As Blake says in a grammatically violent aphorism, the ruins of time build mansions in eternity. The products of self-sacrifice and martyrdom and endurance of injustice still exist, in an invisible but permanent world created out of time by the imagination. This world is the genuine Atlantis or Eden that we actually live in. As soon as we realize that we do live in it, we enter into what Blake means by the Last Judgement. Most people do not make this act of realization, and those who do make it have the responsibility of being evangelists for it. According to Blake, most of what the enlightened can do for the unenlightened is negative: their task is to sharpen the dialectic of the human and natural visions by showing that there are only the alternatives of apocalypse and annihilation.

Blake obviously hopes for a very considerable social response to vision in or soon after his lifetime. But even if everybody responded completely and at once, the City of God would not become immediately visible: if it did, it would simply be one more objective environment. The real 'heaven' is not a glittering city, but the power of bringing such cities into existence. In the poem 'My Spectre around me', Blake depicts a figure like the Boy of *The Mental Traveller* in old age, searching vainly for his 'emanation', the total body of what he can love and create, outside himself instead of inside. The natural tendency of desire (Orc) in itself is to find its object. Hence the effect of the creative impulse on desire is bound to be restrictive until the release of desire becomes the inevitable by-product of creation.

The real world, being the source of a human vision, is human and not natural (which means indefinite) in shape. It does not stretch away for ever into the stars, but has the form of a single giant man's body, the parts of which are arranged thus:

<pre>
Urizen   = head = city
Tharmas = body = garden
Orc   = loins = soil or bed of love
Urthona = legs = underworld of dream and repose
(Los)
</pre>

Except that it is unfallen, the four levels of this world correspond very closely to the four traditional levels that we find in medieval and Renaissance poetry. The present physical world, by the 'improvement of sensual enjoyment', would become an integral part of nature, and so Comus's attempt to seduce the Lady by an appeal to 'nature' would no longer be a seduction or a specious argument. But the really important distinction is that for earlier poets the two upper levels, the city and the garden, were divine and not human in origin, whereas for Blake they are both divine and human, and their recovery depends on the creative power in man as well as in God.

The difference between the traditional and the Blakean versions of reality corresponds to the difference between the first and the last plates of the Job illustrations. In the first plate, Job and his family are in the state of innocence (Beulah), in a peaceful pastoral repose like that of the twenty-third Psalm. They preserve this state in the traditional way, by obeying a divine Providence that has arranged it, and hence are imaginatively children. There is nothing in the picture that suggests anything inadequate except that, in a recall of a very different Psalm (137), there are musical instruments hung on the tree above. In the last plate, things are much as they were before, but Job's family have taken the instruments down from the tree and are playing them. In Blake, we recover our original state, not by returning to it, but by re-creating it. The act of creation, in its turn, is not producing something out of nothing, but the act of setting free what we already possess.

W. J. T. MITCHELL

Blake's Composite Art

The illuminated poetry of William
Blake presents a unique problem in the interpretation of the arts, for
although there have been many artists who have worked in several
different media, rarely do we find one equally renowned in more than one
field, and even more rarely do we encounter an artist who can successfully
combine several art forms. Michelangelo's sonnets would not be read if he
had not carved in marble, and Wagner's libretti survive, not for their
inherent value, but because of their musical settings. Blake's "sister arts"
of poetry and painting, on the other hand, have survived at least a
century of misunderstanding without the mutual support of one another.
In the twentieth century his paintings and etchings have risen in
market value to equal and surpass those of his formerly better known
contemporaries, and the bare words of his poetry have appeared in edition
after edition. Until recently, Blake's two arts have gone their separate
ways in criticism as well, with only occasional bursts of cross fire
between the art historians and the literary critics. Today, however, the
question is no longer *whether* Blake's poetry and painting have anything
to do with one another, but *how* their relationship may best be
understood.

Since the two sides of Blake's genius have made their ways in the
world without the help of one another, it is proper to ask what is gained
by yoking them together. Suzanne Langer's observation that there are no
marriages of the arts, only successful rapes, must serve as a warning to
anyone who would deflower either of Blake's arts for the sake of elucidat-

From *Blake's Visionary Forms Dramatic*, edited by David V. Erdman and John E. Grant.
Copyright © 1971 by Princeton University Press.

ing the other. It is one thing to say that one form helps to explain or amplify the other; quite another to claim (as this essay does) that the illuminated poems constitute a composite art, a single, unified aesthetic phenomenon in which neither form dominates the other and yet in which each is incomplete without the other.

There may be a kind of ironic virtue, then, in the long period of division that Blake's composite art has undergone. If, as seems apparent from the tendencies of the present volume, the next major step in Blake studies is to be a critical reunification of text and design, it will be important to remind ourselves of how well the two art forms have done on their own, and to account for this fact even as we bring them together. The word "illustration," for instance, will have to be redefined when applied to Blake. It will simply not do to say that his designs illustrate the text if we mean only that they throw light upon, explicate, or provide a visual rendition of matters which have been sufficiently expounded in the test. If this were an adequate definition, it would be very difficult to explain the fact that Anthony Blunt has been able to write a very fine study of the paintings on the assumption that they are completely superior to the poems (especially the later prophecies), and that the text is in reality only a kind of pre-text for the real art in the designs. The poetry, thanks to the endless vocabularies of literary critics, will take care of itself; but the art is in danger of being infected by the concept of illustration. As a kind of verbal prophylactic, therefore, it might be appropriate at the outset to remind ourselves that when Blake "illustrates" a text, he expands and transforms it, and often provides a vision which can operate in complete separation from it.

Blake's reluctance to permit this separation has often been re-marked. In referring to a friend's request for separate plates from *The Marriage of Heaven and Hell, The Book of Urizen,* and several other minor prophecies, he objected strongly: "Those I Printed . . . are a selection from the different Books of such as could be Printed without the Writing, tho' to the Loss of some of the best things. For they, when Printed perfect, accompany Poetical Personifications & Acts, without which Poems they never could have been Executed." It is interesting to note, however, that a substantial number of the designs he sent to his friend do *not* illustrate specifically any of the "Poetical Personifications & Acts" in the poems to which they were attached. It is no accident that amid all the meticulous Blake scholarship that has appeared in recent years, there is still no authoritative index or commentary identifying the subjects of his illustrations. In *The Songs of Innocence and of Experience,* of course, the problem of specification of content is greatly simplified by the direct juxtaposition of the design with a limited text, but even in the case of these poems (especially *Experience*) there are problems. In the longer prophetic works, however, the relationship becomes very attenuated: illustrations often seem purposely placed as far as possible from their textual reference—when there is a reference to be found at all. As Blake increased his mastery of both poetic and pictorial techniques, it seems that he tended to minimize the literal, denotative correspondences between the two forms.

There is no difficulty in locating a context for composite art forms in Blake's intellectual milieu. The eighteenth century was, after all, the age which discovered that art could be spelled with a capital A, and Abbé Batteaux could title his 1746 treatise *Les Beaux Arts reduits à un même principe*. Book illustration was expanding into a minor industry, and individual poems such as Thomson's *Seasons* were illustrated so often that it has been possible for one modern critic to construct a history of late-eighteenth-century criticism largely on the basis of the illustrations of this one poem. Since the Renaissance an elaborate apologetics had developed around the illustrated book, especially the emblem book, taking the Horatian maxim *ut pictura poesis* for its central principle. The critical dogmas which calcified around Horace's innocent phrase had already provoked an adverse reaction from Lessing, however, and we should be surprised to find an independent mind like Blake's receiving them passively.

The two basic premises of the doctrine of *ut pictura poesis* were, first, that all art is to be understood as a species of imitation, and second, that the reality which is to be imitated is essentially dualistic. The personification of poetry and painting as the "sister arts" was no accident; it expressed concisely the eighteenth century's conviction that the two arts were daughters of the Nature which they imitated, and that they provided complementary representations of a dualistic world of space and time, body and soul, *dulce et utile*, sense and intellect. The emblem book enjoyed a particularly privileged position because it not only fulfilled the classical ideal of uniting the arts, but also could be seen as a means of providing the most comprehensive possible imitation of a bifurcated reality. "The emblem," as Jean Hagstrum points out, "seemed to be the completest and most satisfying form of expression imaginable, since body (the picture) and soul (the verse) were vitally connected." Painting was supposed to appeal to the senses, poetry to the intellect, and the union of the two arts, it was presumed, would counteract that "dissociated sensibility" which T. S. Eliot had not yet invented. Cesare Ripa, perhaps the most important of the emblematists, plagiarized Marino to affirm that the union of the arts "causes us almost to understand with the senses, . . . to feel with the intellect." An even more extravagant claim was made by the anonymous essayist of *The Plain Dealer* in 1724: "*Two Sister Arts*, uniting their different Powers, the one transmitting *Souls*, the other *Bodies* (or the outward Form of Bodies) their combining Influence would be of Force to frustrate *Death itself*: And all the ages of the World would seem to be Cotemporaries."

Blake's critique of the implications of *ut pictura poesis* can be understood most clearly in terms of his reception of the idea of Nature assumed by this doctrine. For Blake, the dualistic world of mind and body, time and space, is an illusion which must not be imitated, but which must be dispelled by the processes of his art: "But first the notion that a man has a body distinct from his soul, is to be explunged; this I shall do by printing in the infernal method, by corrosives, melting apparent surfaces away, and displaying the infinite which was hid" (*MHH* 14). The methods of relief etching here become a metaphor for the destruction of the appearance of dualism. Blake would agree with the attempt of the emblematists to unite the two arts, not, however, as a means of representing the full range of reality, but as a means of exposing as a fiction the bifurcated organization of that reality. The separation of body and soul, space and time, Blake sees as various manifestations of the fall of man, "His fall into Division" (*FZ* I 4:4). The function of his composite art is therefore twofold: it must "melt apparent surfaces away" by exposing the errors and contradictions of dualism; and it must display "the infinite which was hid," and overcome the "fall into division" with a "Resurrection to Unity" (*FZ* I 4:4).

Blake never refers to his painting and poetry as "the sister arts," a curious omission for a man who lived at the end of the age which had systematized this relationship so carefully. The reason lies in his conception of the nature of the dualities that his art was designed to overcome. Blake's most pervasive metaphor for the "fall into Division" is the separation of the sexes. In particular, the apparent division of the world into space and time is described as a sexual antinomy: "Time & Space are Real Beings, a Male & a Female. Time is a Man, Space is a Woman" (*VLJ*:E553/K614). In Blake's myth, the sexes do not exist as part of the ultimate reality, but are the product of pride and egotism: "When the Individual appropriates Universality / He divides into Male & Female" (*J* 90:51–52). The danger is, according to Blake, that this sexual polarity will be mistaken for the final nature of things: "when the Male & Female / Appropriate Individuality, they become an Eternal Death" (*J* 90:52–53). That is, in terms of space and time, when space becomes an individual, an end in itself, it becomes a prison-house, the "Mundane Shell" of matter which is mistakenly supposed to be independent of consciousness. In like manner, time becomes a nonhuman phenomenon, an endless Heraclitean flux or the "dull round" of a fatal, mechanistic determinism. Blake's poetry and painting must begin by invalidating these incontingent views of time and space, and end by replacing them with visions of eternity and infinity. His primary disagreement with eighteenth-century conceptions of composite art, then, is that they presuppose an incontingent Nature which is to be copied and represented in a complementary, additive manner. For Blake, the coupling of poetry and painting is desirable not because it will produce a fuller range of imitation, but because it can dramatize the interaction of the apparent dualities in experience, and because it can embody the strivings of those dualities for unification.

If we conceive of text and design as Blake did, as organized expressions of the polarized phenomena of space and time, their relationship becomes intelligible in terms of his theory of contrariety. If a purpose of his art is to dramatize the struggle of the antinomies of our experience into a unified vision, the vehicles of spatial and temporal form must embody this dialectic as well. Regarded in this way, the separation of text and design can be seen as having two functions. First, it has a hermeneutic function, in that the disparity between poem and illustration entices the mind of the reader to supply the missing connections. In this light, the illuminated book serves as an "Allegory address'd to the Intellectual Powers" which is "fittest for Instruction because it rouzes the faculties to act." Second, the separation has a mimetic function, in that the contrariety of poem and picture reflects the world of the reader as a place of apparent separation of temporal and spatial, mental and physical phenomena.

It is important to remember the adjective "apparent" when talking about the discrepancies between Blake's designs and text, however, for if we are correct, the most disparate pictorial and verbal structures must conceal a subtle identity of significance. The title page of *The Marriage of Heaven and Hell* {3} exemplifies the way in which the apparent unrelatedness of content in design and text belies the close affinities of formal arrangement. A pair of nudes embrace in a subterranean scene at the bottom of the page, the one on the left emerging from flames, the one on the right from clouds. The top of the page is framed by a pair of trees, between which are two sets of human figures. No scene in the poem corresponds to this picture, and yet it is a perfect representation of the poem's theme, the marriage of contraries:

> Without Contraries is no progression. Attraction and Repulsion, Reason and Energy, Love and Hate, are necessary to Human Existence.

> From these contraries spring what the religious call Good & Evil.
> Good is the passive that obeys Reason. Evil is the active springing from
> Energy.
>
> Good is Heaven. Evil is Hell.

(MHH 3)

Every aspect of the composition is deployed to present this vision of
contraries: flames versus clouds, red versus blue, the aggressive inward
thrust of the female flying up from the left versus the receptive outward
pose of the figure on the right. At the top, the trees on the left reach their
branches across to the right, while the trees on the right recoil into
themselves. The couple beneath the trees on the left walk hand in hand
toward the right. The couple on the right face away, and are separated,
one kneeling, the other lying on the ground. This last detail suggests that
the composition is not simply a visual blending of contraries, but also a
statement about their relative value. The active side presents a harmoni-
ous vision of the sexes; the passive, an inharmonious division, in which
the male seems to be trying to woo the female from her indifference by
playing on a musical instrument. This tipping of the balance in favor of
the "Devil's Party" is accentuated by the direction of movement that
pervades the whole design. If we were simply to have a balanced presentation of contraries such as the text suggests, we would expect a simple
symmetrical arrangement, with a vertical axis down the center (see fig.
1a). But, in fact, the whole kinesis of the composition, accentuated by
the flying nudes in the center, produces an axis which goes from the lower
left corner to the upper right. If one were to draw vectors indicating the
probable course of the figures in the center of the design, the result would
be the diagonal axis of figure 1b.

This tilting of the symmetry of the contraries, is, of course, exactly
what happens to the theme of the *Marriage* as Blake treats it. Although

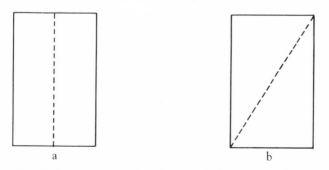

FIG. 1. Thrust of implied movement in the title page of *The Marriage of Heaven and Hell*

the contraries are theoretically equal, Blake has all his fun by identifying himself with the side of the devils. The poem is not simply a self-contained dialectic; it is a dialogue with Blake's own time, and he felt that the "Angels" already had plenty of spokesmen, such as Swedenborg and the apologists for traditional religion and morality. At his particular historical moment, Blake felt that the axis needed to be tilted in favor of energy. Hence, all the good lines in the work and the advantageous pictorial treatments are reserved for the representatives of Hell. But the style of lettering in the title page returns us to the theoretical equality which Blake sees between the contraries. Both "Heaven" and "Hell" are printed in rather stark block letters; the flamboyant, energetic style of free-flowing lines and swirls is reserved for the key term in the poem, "Marriage."

Blake's departure from the literalist implications of *ut pictura poesis* was not, however, simply confined to the avoidance, in his own work, of mere illustration. The doctrine also had implications for the nature of poetry and painting in general, apart from their employment in a composite form like the illustrated book. The concept of the ideal unity of the arts was used to encourage, on the one hand, "painterly," descriptive poetry like Thomson's, and on the other, "poetical," literary painting like Hogarth's. Poetry was to become pictorial by evoking a flood of images which could be reconstituted in the reader's mind into a detailed scene. Painting was to become poetical by imitating a significant action, with beginning, middle, and end, not just a fleeting moment, and by representing not only the surfaces of things but also the interior passions and characters of men. Each art was expected to transcend its temporal or spatial limitation by moving toward the condition of its sister.

This conception of the unification of the arts can only be applied very meagerly to Blake's practice. His poetry, like Milton's, avoids "painterly" descriptions in favor of visual paradoxes like "darkness visible" and "the hapless Soldiers sigh" which "Runs in blood down Palace walls." When he does have an opportunity for "iconic" passages describing a fixed object, such as the building of the art-city of Golgonooza in *Jerusalem*, the result is anything but a set of visualizable images:

> The great City of Golgonooza: fourfold toward the north
> And toward the south fourfold & fourfold toward the east & west
> Each within other toward the four points: that toward
> Eden, and that toward the World of Generation,
> And that toward Beulah, and that toward Ulro:
> Ulro is the space of the terrible starry wheels of Albions sons:
> But that toward Eden is walled up, till time of renovation:
> Yet it is perfect in its building, ornaments & perfection.
>
> (J 12:46–53)

It is no accident that Blake, for all his ability to visualize the unseen, never illustrated this passage. In fact his prophetic illustrations generally do not provide visual equivalents for specific passages, but often expand upon some point of only minor importance in the text, or even convey an opposed or ironic vision.

Blake's refusal to illustrate an "iconic" passage such as the description of Golgonooza is a clue, moreover, to the extent of his departure from the tradition of "literary" painting. Architectural backgrounds, the standard setting of the history painting, naturally generated a more or less "objective" and mathematically constructed spatial container for the human form. But Blake, who considered himself a history painter (see the subtitle of his *Descriptive Catalogue*) could hardly be more perfunctory in his treatment of this kind of subject matter. He is interested not in the mechanically determined form of the material city but in its spiritual (i.e., human) form, as in *Jerusalem* 57, where he specifies the cities of York, London, and Jerusalem with tiny geographical emblems (fig. 18), but defines them pictorially as gigantic women. Jerusalem, particularly, while both a city and a woman in the text, is primarily a woman in the illustrations.

Blake's rejection of the architectural background is only one symptom of his general refusal to employ very extensively the techniques of three-dimensional illusionism which had been increasingly perfected since the Renaissance. This kind of illusionism was particularly popular with "literary" painters, since it provided an easy metaphor for the temporal structure of the scene being depicted. The earliest event in the narrative could be placed in the foreground, and the later events could be placed in increasingly distant perspective planes. Blake avoids this kind of illusionism in his designs for his own works. As a rule, he concentrates on a few foreground images, often arranged symmetrically, to encourage an instantaneous grasp of the whole design rather than an impression of dramatic sequence. Sometimes, to be sure, he does present metamorphic sequences across the foreground plane, usually in his marginal designs, where (for obvious reasons) radial and bilateral symmetry must give way to some kind of linear presentation. These mural-like tableaux, however, embody the passage of time not as a progression from the near to the distant, or the clear to the obscure, but as a movement from the near to the near. All moments in the sequence are immediate and "immanent"; just as in the poetry, the prophet-narrator "present, past, & future *sees*" as an eternal *now*.

The other desideratum of "poetical" painting, the representation of the interior life of its human subjects, not just their outward features, likewise seems inapplicable to Blake's practice. His human figures have a kind of allegorical anonymity, and are clearly designed as types, not as subtly differentiated portraits. We see very little subjectivity in the faces of Blake's figures for the same reason we do not find "motivation" or novelistic personalities in his poetical personifications. Urizen cannot have his own interior life like the character of a novel; he is only an aspect of the interior life of the single human mind which constitutes the world of his poem. Blake certainly expresses the passions in his painting: but he does not present them as residing *within* particular human figures; he presents them *as* human figures. His portraits are not of men with minds, but of the mind itself.

The methods of pictorialist poetry and literary painting, then, shed only a negative light on the specific manner in which Blake approaches the problem of unifying the arts. He rejects the practice of mutual transference of techniques in favor of a methodology which seems rather to emphasize the peculiar strengths and limitations of each medium: the shadowy, allusive metamorphoses of language, and the glowing fixity of almost abstract pictorial forms.

In Blake's view, the attempt to make poetry visual and to make pictures "speak" and tell a story was bound to fail because it presumed the independent reality of space and time and treated them as the irreducible foundations of existence. As we have seen, Blake considers space and time, like the sexes, to be contraries whose reconciliation occurs not when one becomes like the other, but when they approach a condition in which these categories cease to function. In the simplest possible terms, his poetry exists to invalidate the idea of objective time, his painting to invalidate the idea of objective space. To state this positively, his poetry affirms the power of the human imagination to create and organize time in its own image, and his painting affirms the centrality of the human body as the structural principle of space. The essential unity of his arts, then, is to be seen in the parallel engagements of imagination and body with their respective media, and in their convergence in the more comprehensive idea of the "Human Form Divine." For Blake, in the final analysis the body and the imagination are separable principles only in a fallen world of limited perception; the business of art is to dramatize their unification: "The Eternal Body of Man is The Imagination. . . . It manifests itself in his Works of Art" (*Laocoön*: E271).

Blake's specific techniques for constructing his art forms as critiques of their own media are quite clear. In the poetry he creates a world of process and metamorphosis in which the only stable, fixed term is the imagining and perceiving mind. Cause and effect, linear temporality, and other "objective" temporal structures for narrative are replaced by an imaginative conflation of all time in the pregnant moment. The prophetic narrator-actor perceives "Present, Past & Future" simultaneously, and is able to see in any given moment the structure of all history: "Every Time less than a pulsation of the artery / Is equal in its period & value to Six Thousand Years" (M 28:62–63). Consequently, the narrative order of the poem need not refer to any incontingent, nonhuman temporal continuum. Most narrative structures employ what Blake would call "twofold vision": that is, the imaginative arrangement of episodes is always done with reference to an "objective" time scheme. The narrative selects its moments and their order in terms of some imaginative order: *in medias res, ab ovum,* or *recherche du temps perdu.* All of these selective principles assume, however, that there is an order of nonhuman, "objective," or "real" time which flows onward independent of any human, "subjective," or "imaginary" reorganization of its sequence. For Blake, this objective temporal understructure is an illusion which is to be dispelled by the form of his poetry. The beginning, middle, and end of any action are all contained in the present; so the order of presentation is completely subject to the imagination of the narrator. Hostile critics have always recognized this quality in Blake's major prophecies when they indicted them for being "impossible to follow." That is precisely the point. Blake's prophecies go nowhere in time because time, as a linear, homogeneous phenomenon, has no place in their structure. *Jerusalem* is essentially a nonconsecutive series of poetic "happenings," not a linear ordering of events. The one continuous and stable element in the course of the narrative is the idea of consciousness as a transformer of itself and its world. That is why Los, the vehicle of the imagination, is also cast as the personification of time. In this way, Blake could depict the poet's management of time and the prophet's quarrel with history as the struggle of the individual with himself.

An analogous technique can be observed in the whole range of Blake's paintings. Historical parallels have tended to confuse attempts at defining Blake's style because the historical concept always carries with it a freight of alien associations which have no relevance to the work at hand. His art has recognizable affinities with Michelangelo, Raphael, and the Mannerists in his treatment of the human figure, with Gothic painting in his primitivism and anti-illusionism, and with contemporaries such as Flaxman in his stress on outline, Fuseli in his use of the terrific and exotic. It is also clear, however, that these elements are transmuted into something unified and unique in Blake's hands. His art is a curious compound of the representational and the abstract, the picture that imitates natural forms and the design that delights in form for its own sake. The "flame-flowers" which are so ubiquitous in his margins, and which later provided inspiration for art nouveau, serve as a prime example of the interplay between representation and abstraction that informs all his work. The abstract vorticular composition may assume specific representational form as a whirlpool, a dance of lovers, or a spiral ascent to the heavens. The circle may serve as the structural skeleton of the mathematical enclosures of Urizen, or of the glowing sun created by the hammer of Los. Plate 39 [44] of *Jerusalem* makes this technique explicit by showing a serpent metamorphosing into a flame, then a leaf, and finally the tendrils of a vine. The effect of this pictorial strategy is to undercut the representational appearance of particular forms and to endow them with an abstract, stylized existence independent of the natural images that they evoke. Pictorial form is freed from the labor of accurately representing any idea of nature, and instead serves to show that the appearances of natural objects are arbitrary and subject to transformation by the imagination. All art, of course, even that which claims only to provide a mirror image of external reality, transforms its subject matter in some way. But the subject of Blake's art is precisely this power to transform, this ability of the artist to reshape and control his visual images, and, by implication, the ability of man to create his vision in general. That is why at the center of Blake's visual world of process and metamorphosis the form of the human body tends to retain its uniqueness and stability. The backgrounds of Blake's designs, his landscapes and prospects, all serve as a kind of evanescent setting for the human form. There are no mathematically determined perspectives, and very few landscapes which would make any sense without the human figures they contain. Pictorial space does not exist independently as a uniform, objective container of forms; it exists to provide contrast and reinforcement to the human figures it contains. The image of evil in Blake's designs, consequently, is not an arbitrary emblem, or simply a devil with horns, but the sight of the human body surrendering its unique form and dissolving into a nonhuman landscape, as in many designs in the Lambeth books and the later prophecies where bodies take root in the ground or sprout bestial appendages.

The essential unity of Blake's composite art, then, lies in the convergence of each art form upon the single goal of affirming the centrality of the human form (as both imagination and body) in the structure of reality. Blake's art imitates neither an external world of objective "Nature" nor a purely internal world of subjective, arbitrary abstractions. Neither representationalism nor allegory satisfactorily defines the nature of his art. This latter point perhaps needs to be stressed most forcefully, since no one is about to mistake Blake for a Dutch painter, and since the allegorists generally have more to say about Blake than anyone else. Interpretation would indeed be easier if certain colors and certain abstract linear patterns had fixed, iconic meanings, but Blake would certainly be less interesting. The whole vitality of his art arises from his refusal to settle for the fixed, the emblematic, and the abstract, and from his decision to concentrate instead upon dramatizing the activity of the imagination in its encounter with reality. "Men think they can Copy Nature as I copy Imagination This they will find Impossible" (PA:E563). Blake's use of the word "imagination" as an object here has misled many critics into supposing that he has in mind the archetypal forms of some Platonic system as the objects of his copying. But imagination is not simply a product for Blake, a fixed body of well-defined forms; it is the *process* by which any symbolic form comes into being. When Blake says he "copies imagination," then, he means that he renders faithfully the activity of the mind as it alters the objects of perception: both the finished product and the process by which it comes into being are "imagination."

The consequences of this definition of Blake's art are perhaps more apparent in his poetry than in his art. Since Northrop Frye's *Fearful Symmetry* the nonallegorical nature of Blake's poetry has regularly been acknowledged, if not fully grasped. Nevertheless, the question of form in the major prophecies is still open. *Jerusalem* is still treated primarily as a quarry for Blakean "philosophy," not as a poetic structure with its own nondiscursive logic. When attempts are made to understand its form, they usually concentrate on one of the structural topoi to which Blake often alludes—the prophecy, the epic journey, the dream vision—rather than on Blake's own peculiar ideas about the principles of narrative form. When these traditional ideas of form are recast in terms of Blake's own understanding of poetry as a critique of temporality and as a means of transcending it, we will see, I suspect, that *Milton* and *Jerusalem* have as much in common with *Tristram Shandy* as with *Paradise Lost*.

The basic groundwork for understanding Blake's pictorial symbolism remains to be done. Critics still tend either to content themselves with identification of subject matter (which assumes that the designs are mere illustrations) or to search for a fixed set of pictorial conventions. The attempts to formulate a color glossary, a left-right convention, or a set of denotative linear forms persist in spite of their continued failure to account for more than a very few pictures. Blake makes clear, however, that no system of abstractions is to be found beyond or behind his art, and gives us instead a fairly straightforward set of general principles for understanding the generation of symbols by the dialectics in his compositions.

His emphasis on the superiority of form and outline to light and color is well known yet misleading:

> The great and golden rule of art, as well as of life, is this: That the more distinct, sharp, and wiry the bounding line, the more perfect the work of art: and the less keen and sharp, the greater is the evidence of weak imitation.   (DC:E540)

> The Beauty proper for sublime art is lineaments, or forms and features that are capable of being the receptacles of intellect;   (DC:E535)

Blake's preference for linearity was probably in large measure a product of his early apprenticeship to James Basire, a master of the old-fashioned school of austerity in line engraving. The change in taste in late-eighteenth-century reproductive engraving to the softer lines and tonal emphasis of Woollett, Strange, and Bartolozzi left Blake in possession of an increasingly unfashionable style, and probably accounts for some of his bitterness at the "painterly" schools. He was not isolated, however, in his preference for linearity. The neoclassical primitivism which Winckelmann had introduced was having its effect both in England and on the Continent. Diderot's hope for a reincarnation of Poussin was being fulfilled by David's meticulous historicism and sculpturely purity; Flaxman and Cumberland, to name two of Blake's friends, were insisting on an even more radical purity and simplicity of outline. The seeds of this preference for linearity had always been present in idealist conceptions of art, and the theorists of the seventeenth and eighteenth centuries had consequently felt it necessary to defend the equal importance of color and light in painting long after it had been established in practice. Du Fresnoy, for instance, calls outline and color sisters, and defends the latter against the charge of prostituting outline: "And as this part, which we may call the utmost perfection of Painting, is a deceiving Beauty, but withall soothing and pleasing: So she has been accus'd of procuring Lovers for her Sister, and artfully engaging us to admire her. But so little have this Prostitution, these false Colours, and this Deceit, dishonour'd Painting, that on the contrary, they have only serv'd to set forth her praise." The writers on *ut pictura poesis* likewise justified the use of color by comparing it to the expressive qualities of poetry: the relationship of color to outline is regularly equated with the relationship of verse to fable. Color is seen by the Platonists as "art," a kind of cosmetic allurement to the "real meaning" which is contained in outline. To the Aristotelians, color permits a faithful imitation of nature's variety, and provides a verisimilitudinous setting for the general forms revealed by outline.

It is easy to say that Blake rejects these justifications of color, just as he rejects the Venetian "painterly" schools, and virtually makes a demonic trinity out of Rembrandt, Rubens, and Titian (see DC:E537–538). But it is not so clear what we should make of his actual use of color. We cannot say of Blake's designs, as we can of Flaxman's illustrations to Hesiod, Homer, and Dante, that they would gain nothing by the inclusion of color. Blake rarely produced an illustration to his own work without color, and black-and-white reproductions of his work are notoriously unsatisfying. Furthermore, to take at face value his claim that coloring is subservient to and determined by outline simply falsifies a good deal of his practice. In spite of his theoretical preference for clear outline and form, Blake often obscures his outlines with opaque pigments and heavy drapery.

The resolution of this apparent contradiction between theory and practice lies in a fuller understanding of the theory. The subservience of light to form is, for Blake, a visual equivalent of an ideal condition:

> In Great Eternity, every particular Form gives forth or Emanates
> Its own peculiar Light, & the Form is the Divine Vision
> And the Light is his Garment.
>
> (J 54:1–3)

The relation of form to light is defined as that of the Individual and his Emanation, or of consciousness and the external world which it projects. With the fall, however, consciousness becomes egotism (male will) and the external world becomes an independent Nature (female will). Form and light become, in this world, sexual principles working in opposition. The resolution of this opposition is attained by a procedure rather similar to the one we observed in the relation of text and design, a dialectic of contraries. When female nature, for instance, assumes an independent existence, it becomes "An outside shadowy surface superadded to the real Surface; / Which is unchangeable" (J 83:47–48); that is, color freed from outline and obscuring it is the visual equivalent of nature's obfuscating the imagination. The veil or garment is often used as a metaphor for this idea of color, and the disposition of drapery in Blake's pictures can be seen to follow the same principles as his treatment of color. Even though "Art & Science cannot exist but by Naked Beauty displayed" (J 32:49), Blake clothes many of his figures to exhibit their immersion into the fallen world of space and time. The frontispiece of *Jerusalem*, for instance, presents the clothed figure of Los-Blake entering the fallen world, the "Void outside of Existence, which if entered into Englobes itself & becomes a Womb." The return of Los (J 97 {102}) from this world of Ulro or "Eternal Death" into the world of imagination (or true existence) displays his naked beauty. In the "Death's Door" illustration to Blair's *Grave* Blake similarly contrasts the entry into death (i.e., the fallen world) with the "awaking to Eternal life" by setting the clothed figure who enters the grave against the naked figure atop the grave. "The Drapery is formed alone by the Shape of the Naked" (Annotations to Reynolds: E639/K462) in theory, but in practice Blake often covers his figures (especially Urizen) with heavy, oppressive garments which obscure rather than reveal their lineaments.

It would be a mistake, however, to conclude that Blake's art is constructed simply on the principle that outline is "good" and the color or drapery which obscures it is "bad." The two compositional elements, like the two aspects of his composite art, engage in a dialectic that ranges from antagonism (when color becomes "An outside shadowy Surface" obscuring outline) to unity (when light serves as an aureole or halo around form), and all the stages of this dialectic are integral to the total vision. Blake provides us with a vocabulary for describing the range of his possible uses of form and light in the terms which he probably drew from his own experience as a painter. When man falls from his state of visionary perfection in Blake's myth, a universe or space must be created to set a limit to his fall: "The Divine Hand found two Limits: first of Opacity, then of Contraction" (M 13:20). These two limits are personified as Satan and Adam, and represent the lower boundaries of man's fall into spiritual darkness and the shrinking of his soul into an egotistic, self-enclosed organism. "But there is no Limit of Expansion! there is no Limit of Translucence" (J 42:35), except in the limitations of the painter's ability to create glowing images of bodily freedom. The applicability of these two terms to Blake's art is strongly suggested by his making them the basic structural principles of his art-city, Golgonooza, like Yeats's Byzantium, a regular metaphor for the total form of his artifices of eternity. (See *FZ* VIIa 87:E354.)

Two of Blake's most famous designs, the frontispiece to *Europe* and *Albion rose*, exemplify the contrast between contraction / opacity and expansion / translucence. The figure captioned "Albion rose from where he labourd at the Mill with Slaves . . ." {91} expands in a veritable sunburst of radiance. Blake wisely avoids trying to convey this radiance by direct means, such as mere whiteness, and instead depicts Albion as the light-source of all the colors of the spectrum; he serves as both the hub and spokes of a color-wheel. Just below Albion's knees the outer boundary of his radiance seems to expand into and dispel the darkness around his feet. The ground, which corresponds to the spiritual darkness and deformity from which he has risen, is presented as a riot of disorganized, opaque pigments, such as Blake used in depicting the seat of "that most outrageous demon," Newton. Anthony Blunt has shown that this figure may have been derived from a diagram of the perfect human proportions in Scamozzi's *Idea dell'architettura universale*, in which the limbs of the figure are measured against a wheel with the center located at the navel. Blake has moved the center of his figure down to the loins to enforce his idea that "The improvement of Sensual Enjoyment" (which corresponds, among other things, to the use of the erotic image, "Naked Beauty Display'd") is the proper means for reawakening the infinite in man. More important, Blake has freed his figure from the enclosing wheel, except perhaps for the token reminder of enclosure just below Albion's knees. If the design is indeed to be taken as employing a quotation from Scamozzi's treatise, it is certainly an ironic allusion, expressing Blake's conviction that his art is to be seen as a triumph over the tyranny of "mathematic form."

The contrasts with the frontispiece to *Europe* {8} need hardly be elaborated. Urizen is shown with his body bent and contracted into itself, enclosed in a circle. His one outward gesture is a thrust downward into the darkness to inscribe another circle on the abyss. Unlike Albion, who is the center of all the dynamism in his design, Urizen is the subject of the elements, as is revealed by the wind blowing his hair and the clouds closing in to obscure his radiance. If Albion is to be seen as bursting the circle of mathematical restriction, Urizen is the creator of that circle, and Blake's treatment of him must remind us of one of his most audacious epigrams:

> To God
> If you have formed a Circle to go into
> Go into it yourself & see how you would do
> (E508/K557)

The concepts of expansion and translucence, contraction and opacity are not to be placed in a simple equation with "good" and "evil," any more than outline and color can convey value in themselves. Blake always had a "contrary vision" in mind, in which any given symbolic organization could reverse its meaning. The act of creation, for instance, is a demonic act in that it encloses man in the "Mundane Shell," but it is, from another point of view, an act of mercy in that it prevents man from falling endlessly into the "Indefinite." In like manner, there is a sense in which contraction is a good, as in the state of Innocence when the mother creates a womblike space to protect the child. In *The Songs of Innocence* this aspect of contraction is given visual expression by "embracing" compositions. The space of the design is generally encircled in vines, or framed by an overarching arbor. Opacity also has its beneficial aspect, as can be seen in both text and design of *The Little Black Boy*, where it serves as a temporary protection from the overpowering translucence of God:

> And we are put on earth a little space,
> That we may learn to bear the beams of love,
> And these black bodies and this sun-burnt face
> Is but a cloud, and like a shady grove.

The protective functions of opacity and contraction in Innocence are transformed, of course, in *The Songs of Experience*. The tranquil, angel-guarded darkness of *Night* gives way to the threatening opacity of the "forests of the night" in Experience. The protective contraction of the arbor becomes the stark frame of a dead tree, the encircling vines become choking briars.

On the other hand, expansion and translucence are not unequivocally good. Blake often presents the figures of warfare or revolution as bright, expansive nudes. The figure of Orc, for instance, the personification of energy and rebellion against the circumscribed order of Urizen, is often depicted as a bright, youthful nude in an expansive pose. A good example of this kind of composition is plate 10 of *America* {38}, which shows Orc surrounded by flames, his arms extended in a kind of parody of the exultant expansion of *Albion rose*. Just two plates before this appears the well-known "Urizen on the Stone of Night," a design which has a completely different affective value from plate 10. But a close comparison of the two figures and the positions of their limbs reveals a point-for-point similarity. (See {36} and {38}.) The two pictures have, of course, completely opposite effects. Orc seems to rise and burst outward, the downward movement of his hands only providing thrust to his expansive movement, which is accentuated by his flaming hair and the exploding surroundings. The old man in his white robes, on the other hand, anatomically identical to Orc, produces the effect of contraction. His arms seem to merge into the stony background, pressed down by a great weight and weariness. The horizontal curves of the rocks reinforce the gravity which seems to push against and bend down the space of the picture. The juxtaposition of these two designs provides us with a visual equivalent of what Northrop Frye calls "the Orc cycle," the cyclical repetition of tyrannic repression and rebellious reaction. This essential identity of the rebel and his oppressor becomes the basis of Blake's critique of his own historical time, and in the later prophetic books a structural metaphor for time in the fallen world.

This identity of Orc and Urizen is also a further example of the interplay between abstraction and representation which is the basic mode of Blake's symbolism. The linear skeleton which permits us to identify these two figures has no particular meaning in itself: it does not "equal" Urizen or Orc, or the sum of their qualities. On the other hand, the particular representation of each of these mythical figures does not achieve its full symbolic status until we recognize that each is potentially the other, each is a metaphor for the other. Orc *is* Urizen, because the spirit of violent rebellion always degenerates into oppression when it has gained power. Urizen *is* Orc, because the tyrant inevitably begets the revolutionary reaction against his rule. Neither abstraction nor representation, however, is permitted to become in itself the locus of this meaning. Significance is located in the dialectic between the permanence of outline and the mutability and momentary reality of color, just as in the poetry the continuity of consciousness is affirmed and realized in its ability persistently to give form to the changing manifestations of itself and the world it perceives.

The total design of the illuminated page affirms the identity of poem and picture by actualizing the continuity and interrelatedness of the most abstract linear patterns with the most representational forms. At the one extreme, visual form is constructed in accord with what is, from the point of view of the visual arts, a completely abstract, nonvisual system (language); at the other extreme, the picture exists to imitate the peculiarly visual aspects of experience. The word "Marriage" on the title page of *The Marriage of Heaven and Hell* affirms, appropriately enough, the actual marriage of these two concepts of form by serving as a bridge between the abstraction of typography and the mimesis of naturalistic representation. This may sound like an unnecessarily involved way of pointing out that Blake decorates his letters with foliage, as the medieval illuminators did. But the keystone of a complicated structure is always in the obvious, the inevitable place. The continuity which Blake manages to establish between the world of ideality and reality, subject and object in the dynamics of his two art forms is an integral part of the process of uniting these two forms into a single entity. And it is also the means by which the strange and wonderfully consistent world of his imagination manages to retain its own uncompromising otherness while establishing a continuity with and relevance to our own worlds.

HAROLD BLOOM

"Jerusalem":
The Bard of Sensibility
and the Form of Prophecy

also out of the midst thereof came the
likeness of four living creatures. And this
was their appearance; they had the likeness of a man.

from Ezekiel 1:5

"T he midst thereof" refers to "a fire
infolding itself," in the Hebrew literally "a fire taking hold of itself," a
trope for a series of fire-bursts, one wave of flame after another. Blake's
Jerusalem has the form of such a series, appropriate to a poem whose
structure takes Ezekiel's book as its model. *The Four Zoas*, like Young's
Night Thoughts, is in the formal shadow of *Paradise Lost*, and *Milton* less
darkly in the shadow of Job and *Paradise Regained*. In *Jerusalem*, his
definitive poem, Blake goes at last for prophetic form to a prophet, to the
priestly orator, Ezekiel, whose situation and sorrow most closely resemble
his own.

Ezekiel is uniquely the prophet-in-exile, whose call and labor are
altogether outside the Holy Land. Held captive in Babylon, he dies still in
Babylon, under the tyrant Nebuchadnezzar, and so never sees his prophecy fulfilled:

From *The Ringers in the Tower*. Copyright © 1971 by The University of Chicago Press.

> Thus saith the Lord God; In the day that I shall have cleansed you from
> all your iniquities I will also cause you to dwell in the cities, and the
> wastes shall be builded.
>
> And the desolate land shall be tilled, whereas it lay desolate in
> the sight of all that passed by.
>
> And they shall say, This land that was desolate is become like the
> garden of Eden; and the waste and desolate and ruined cities are become
> fenced, and are inhabited.

Everything in Ezekiel except this ultimate vision is difficult, more
difficult than it at first appears. Blake's *Jerusalem* is less difficult than it
first seems, even to the informed reader, but still is difficult. Both books
share also a harsh plain style, suitable for works addressed to peoples in
captivity. Ezekiel, like *Jerusalem*, is replete with the prophet's symbolic
actions, actions at the edge of social sanity, violence poised to startle the
auditor into fresh awareness of his own precarious safety, and the spiritual
cost of it. As early as *The Marriage of Heaven And Hell*, Blake invokes
Ezekiel as one who heightens the contradictions of merely given existence:

> I then asked Ezekiel. why he eat dung, and lay so long on his right and
> left side? he answered the desire of raising other men into a perception of
> the infinite

The central image of Blake, from whenever he first formulated his
mythology, is Ezekiel's; the *Merkabah*, Divine Chariot or form of God in
motion. The Living Creatures or Four Zoas are Ezekiel's and not initially
Blake's, a priority of invention that Blake's critics, in their search for more
esoteric sources, sometimes evade. Ezekiel, in regard to Blake's *Jerusalem*,
is like Homer in regard to the *Aeneid:* the inventor, the precursor, the
shaper of the later work's continuities. From Ezekiel in particular Blake
learned the true meaning of prophet, visionary orator, honest man who
speaks into the heart of a situation to warn: if you go on so, the result is
so; or as Blake said, a seer and not an arbitrary dictator.

I have indicated elsewhere the similarities in arrangement of the
two books, and the parallel emphases upon individual responsibility and
self-purgation. Here I want to bring the poets closer, into the painful area
of the anxiety of influence, the terrible melancholy for the later prophet
of sustained comparison with the precursor, who died still in the realm of
loss, but in absolute assurance of his prophetic call, an assurance Blake
suffered to approximate, in an isolation that even Ezekiel might not have
borne. For Ezekiel is sent to the house of Israel, stiffened in heart and
rebellious against their God, yet still a house accustomed to prophecy.
God made Ezekiel as hard as adamant, the *shamir* or diamond-point of the

engraver, and that was scarcely hard enough; Blake knew he had to be even harder, as he wielded his engraver's tool.

Jerusalem begins with the Divine Voice waking Blake at sunrise and "dictating" to him a "mild song," which Blake addresses in turn to Albion, the English Israel, at once Everyman and an exile, a sleeper in Beulah, illusive land of shades. When the Divine Voice orders Ezekiel to begin his ministry, the prophet has already had a vision of the four cherubim and their wheels, a manifestation of glory that sustains him in the trials ensuing. But Blake has never seen the Living Creatures of the *Merkabah*, his Four Zoas as one in the unity of a restored Albion. The fourth, final book of *Jerusalem* begins with a demonic parody of the *Merkabah*, with the Wheel of Natural Religion flaming "west to east against the current of/Creation." A "Watcher & a Holy-One," perhaps Ezekiel himself, "a watchman unto the house of Israel," identifies this antagonist image for Blake, who is afflicted throughout by demonic epiphanies, as Ezekiel was not. The form of Ezekiel's prophecy depends upon the initial vision, for the glory is thus revealed to him before his task is assigned, though the emphasis is on the *departure* of the *Merkabah*, interpreted by the great commentator David Kimchi as a presage of the Lord's withdrawal from the Jerusalem Temple, thus abandoned to its destruction.

In the England of *Jerusalem*, everything that could be seen as an image of salvation has been abandoned to destruction. No poem could open and proceed in a profounder or more sustained despair, for the next level down is silence. The temptation of silence, as in the self-hatred of Browning's ruined quester, Childe Roland, type of the poet who has given up, is to turn, "quiet as despair," into the path of destruction. Blake's antagonist, in *Jerusalem*, is what destroys Browning's quester: selfhood. What menaces continued life for the imaginative man is the quality of his own despair:

> But my griefs advance also, for ever & ever without end
> O that I could cease to be! Despair! I am Despair
> Created to be the great example of horror & agony: also my
> Prayer is vain I called for compassion: compassion mocked,
> Mercy & pity threw the grave stone over me & with lead
> And iron, bound it over me for ever: Life lives on my
> Consuming: & the Almighty hath made me his Contrary
> To be all evil, all reversed & for ever dead: knowing
> And seeing life, yet living not; how can I then behold
> And not tremble; how can I be beheld & not abhorrd

The imaginative man's despair is the Spectre of Urthona, who speaks these lines, and who may be thought of as holding the same relation to

Blake the poet as the Solitary of *The Excursion* has to Wordsworth the poet. For the Spectre of Urthona is every prophet's own Jonah, in full flight from vision for reasons more than adequate to our unhappy yet still not unpleasant condition as natural men. Though the Spectre of Urthona had his genesis, in Blake's work, as an initially menacing figure, he is very appealing in *Jerusalem*, and Blake's critics (myself included) have erred in slighting this appeal, and thus diminishing the force of Blake's extraordinary artistry. The Spectre of Urthona *is always right*, if the reductive truth of our condition as natural men be taken as truth. Nor is the poor Spectre unimaginative in his reductions; they are exuberant by their unqualified insistence at knowing by knowing the worst, particularly concerning the self and the sexual wars of the self and the other. What is most moving about the Spectre's reductive power is its near alliance with his continual grief. We are repelled by his "mockery & scorn" and his "sullen smile," but each time we hear him we see him also as one who "wiped his tears he washd his visage" and then told the terror of his truths:

> The Man who respects Woman shall be despised by Woman
> And deadly cunning & mean abjectness only, shall enjoy them
> For I will make their places of joy and love, excrementitious.
> Continually building, continually destroying in Family feuds
> While you are under the dominion of a jealous Female
> Unpermanent for ever because of love & jealousy.
> You shall want all the Minute Particulars of Life

The form of prophecy cannot sustain such reductive, natural truths, for in the context of prophecy they are not true. When we listen to the Spectre of Urthona we hear a bard, but not a prophet, and the bard belongs to Blake's own literary age, the time of Sensibility or the Sublime. Blake's lifelong critique of the poets to whom he felt the closest affinity— Thomson, Cowper, Collins, Gray, Chatterton—culminates in *Jerusalem*. The Spectre of Urthona descends from the Los of the Lambeth books, and the Bard of Experience of the *Songs*, but is closer even than they were to the archetype Blake satirizes, the poet of Sensibility, the man of imagination who cannot or will not travel the whole road of excess to the palace of wisdom.

Martin Price, studying "the histrionic note" of mid-eighteenth-century poetry, emphasized the poet as both actor and audience in "the theatre of mind." Precisely this insight is our best starting-point in understanding the Spectre of Urthona, who is so unnerving because he appears always to be "watching with detachment the passions he has worked up in himself." The grand precursor of this histrionic kind of bard is the Satan of the early books of *Paradise Lost*, whose farewell to splendor, upon Mount Niphates, sums up the agony that makes so strange a detachment possible:

> . . . to thee I call,
> But with no friendly voice, and add thy name
> O Sun, to tell thee how I hate thy beams . . .
>
> Me miserable! which way shall I flie
> Infinite wrauth, and infinite despair?
> Which way I flie is Hell, my self am Hell;
> And in the lowest deep a lower deep
> Still threatening to devour me opens wide,
> To which the Hell I suffer seems a Heav'n.

A detachment that can allow so absolute a consciousness of self-damnation has something Jacobean about it. What a Bosola or a Vendice sees at the end, by a flash of vision, Satan must see continuously and forever in the vast theater of his mind. There exists perpetually for Satan the terrible double vision of what was and what is, Eternity and the categories of mental bondage, the fallen forms of space and time. This twofold vision is the burden also of the Bard of Sensibility, but not of the prophet who has seen the *Merkabah*, or even studies in hope to see it, as does the Blake-Los of *Jerusalem*. Freedom for the prophet means freedom from the detachment of the histrionic mode; the prophet retains a sense of himself as actor, but he ceases to be his own audience. A passage from solipsism to otherness is made, the theater of mind dissolves, and the actor stands forth as orator, as a warner of *persons* (Ezekiel 3:17–21). Should he fail to make this passage, he is reduced to the extreme of the histrionic mode, and becomes the singer-actor of his own Mad Songs, one of the "horrid wanderers of the deep" or a destined wretch "washed headlong from on board." I take the first of these phrases from Cowper's powerful, too-little known poem, *On The Ice Islands* (dated 19 March 1799) and the second from the justly famous *The Castaway* (written evidently the following day). A year later and Cowper died, his death like his life a warning to Blake during his years at Hayley's Felpham (1800–1803) and a crucial hidden element in both *Milton* and *Jerusalem*, where Blake fights desperately and successfully to avoid so tragically wasted a death-in-life as Cowper's.

In *On The Ice Islands* Cowper translates his own Latin poem, *Montes Glaciales, In Oceano Germanica Natantes* (written 11 March 1799). The ice islands are "portents," with the beauty of treasure, but apocalyptic warnings nevertheless as they float in "the astonished tide." They appear almost to be volcano-births, yet are Winter's creations:

> He bade arise
> Their uncouth forms, portentous in our eyes.
> Oft as, dissolved by transient suns, the snow
> Left the tall cliff to join the flood below,
> He caught and curdled with a freezing blast
> The current, ere it reached the boundless waste.

This is, to Blake, his Urizen at work, a methodical demiurge who always blunders. In Cowper's phantasmagoria, this is the way things are, a Snow Man's vision, a violence from without that crumbles the mind's feeble defenses. To it, Cowper juxtaposes the creation of Apollo's summer vision:

> So bards of old
> How Delos swam the Ægean deep have told.
> But not of ice was Delos. Delos bore
> Herb, fruit, and flower. She, crowned with laurel, wore
> Even under wintry skies, a summer smile;
> And Delos was Apollo's favourite isle.
> But, horrid wanderers of the deep, to you,
> He deems Cimmerian darkness only due.
> Your hated birth he deigned not to survey,
> But, scornful, turned his glorious eyes away.

One remembers Blake's youthful *Mad Song*, written at least twenty years earlier:

> Like a fiend in a cloud
>   With howling woe,
> After night I do croud,
>   And with night will go;
> I turn my back to the east,
> From whence comforts have increas'd;
> For light doth seize my brain
> With frantic pain.

Late in his life, long after the Felpham crisis, Blake looked back upon Cowper's madness. We do not know when Blake annotated Spurzheim's *Observations on . . . Insanity* (London, 1817), and we perhaps cannot rely on the precise wording of the annotations as being wholly Blake's own rather than Yeats's, since the copy from which Yeats transcribed has been lost. But, to a student of Blake, the wording seems right:

SPURZHEIM: . . . the primitive feelings of religion may be misled and produce insanity . . .

BLAKE: Cowper came to me & said. O that I were insane always I will never rest. Can you not make me truly insane. I will never rest till I am so. O

that in the bosom of God I was hid. You retain health & yet are as
mad as any of us all—over us all—mad as a refuge from unbelief—from
Bacon Newton & Locke

Spurzheim cities Methodism "for its supply of numerous cases" of
insanity, and Blake begins his note by scrawling "Methodism &." The
Spectre of Urthona has the same relation to Blake's Cowper that Los has
to Blake's Ezekiel, and we will see more of the Spectre than we have seen
if we keep in mind that he is both a poet of Sensibility and a kind of
sin-crazed Methodist. Cowper ends *On The Ice Islands* by desperately
warning the "uncouth forms" away:

> Hence! Seek your home, nor longer rashly dare
> The darts of Phoebus, and a softer air;
> Lest you regret, too late, your native coast,
> In no congenial gulf for ever lost!

The power of this, and of the entire poem, is in our implicit but
overwhelming recognition of Cowper's self-recognition; he himself is such
an ice island, and the uncongenial gulf in which he is lost is one with the
"deeper gulfs" that end *The Castaway*:

> No voice divine the storm allayed,
> No light propitious shone,
> When, snatched from all effectual aid,
> We perished, each alone:
> But I beneath a rougher sea,
> And whelmed in deeper gulfs than he.

Though Cowper's terror is his own, the mode of his self-destruction
is akin to that of the Bard of Sensibility proper, Gray's Giant Form:

> "Fond impious Man, think'st thou yon sanguine cloud,
> Rais'd by thy breath, has quench'd the orb of day?
> To-morrow he repairs the golden flood,
> And warms the nations with redoubled ray,
> Enough for me: with joy I see
> The different doom our fates assign.
> Be thine despair, and scept'red care,
> To triumph, and to die, are mine."
> He spoke, and headlong from the mountain's height
> Deep in the roaring tide he plung'd to endless night.

That is not the way the Spectre of Urthona ends:

> Los beheld undaunted furious
> His heavd Hammer; he swung it round & at one blow,
> In unpitying ruin driving down the pyramids of pride

> Smiting the Spectre on his Anvil & the integuments of his Eye
> And Ear unbinding in dire pain, with many blows,
> Of strict severity self-subduing, & with many tears labouring.
>
> Then he sent forth the Spectre all his pyramids were grains
> Of sand & his pillars; dust on the flys wing; & his starry
> Heavens; a moth of gold & silver mocking his anxious grasp.

Cowper and the Bard drown to end an isolation, whether terrible or heroic; the theater of mind dissolves in the endless night of an original chaos, the abyss always sensed in the histrionic mode. The Spectre of Urthona is both shattered and unbound, his anxious grasp of self mocked by his selfhood's reduction to a fine grain, to the Minute Particulars of vision. Because he cannot face the hammering voice of the prophetic orator, the Spectre is at last divided "into a separate space," beyond which he cannot be reduced. The theater of mind is necessarily a Sublime theater of the Indefinite, but the prophet compels definite form to appear.

Jerusalem's quite definite form is the form of prophecy, Blake's mythologized version of the story of Ezekiel, even as the form of Revelation is demonstrated by Austin Farrer to be Saint John's mythologized rebirth of Ezekiel's images. When the visionary orator steps forward, he shares the courage of Gray's Bard, but goes further because his words are also acts. Emerson, in one of his eloquent journal broodings upon eloquence, fixes precisely this stance of Blake's Los:

> Certainly there is no true orator who is not a hero. His attitude in the rostrum, on the platform, requires that he counter-balance his auditory. He is challenger, and must answer all comers. The orator must ever stand with forward foot, in the attitude of advancing. His speech must be just ahead of the assembly, ahead of the whole human race, or it is superfluous. His speech is not to be distinguished from action.
>
> (Journal, June 1846)

Speech that is act cannot be reconciled with excessive self-consciousness; the prophetic mind is necessarily a mind no longer turned in upon itself. The man of Young's Night Thoughts ("I tremble at myself/ And in myself am lost!") is succeeded by prophetic Man, the "identified" Human Form, as Blake exaltedly wishes him phrased. This transition, from representative man as poet of Sensibility, inhabiting the theater of mind, to prophetic Man, a transition made again in Wordsworth and in Shelley, is in Blake at least founded upon biblical precedent. What drew Blake to Ezekiel is the denunciation, first made by that prophet, of the entire spiritual tradition of collective responsibility. As Buber remarks, "Ezekiel individualizes the prophetic alternative." The larger covenant has broken down, because the collectivity of Israel or Albion is no longer a suitable covenant partner.

For the theater of mind, though an Ulro-den of self-consciousness, is founded upon a collective Sublime. The man of Burke, Young, Gray, Cowper, is still the universal man of humanist tradition, still the man Pope and Johnson longed to address. Wordsworth is enough of a Burkean to retain the outline of such a figure, but Blake knows that continuity to be broken down, and forever. Blake's God, like Ezekiel's, sends a "watchman" to admonish individuals, and Los, as that watchman, delivers a message that no collectivity is capable of hearing. The Sublime terror, founded as it is upon a universal anxiety, is dismissed by Blake as the Spectre's rhetoric, his deception of others, while the Sublime transport is similarly dismissed as the Spectre's sentimentality, or self-deception. "Los reads the Stars of Albion! the Spectre reads the Voids/Between the Stars." To see the Burkean Sublime is to see: "a Disorganized/And snowy cloud: brooder of tempests & destructive War."

The bounding outline, or organized vision, Blake rightly found in Ezekiel and the other prophets, who gave him the harsh but definite form in which *Jerusalem* is organized, perhaps even over-organized. The form of prophecy, particularly fixed in Ezekiel, is the unique invention of the writing prophets who sustained the destruction of the Northern kingdom and the subsequent Babylonian exile. Since the *nabi*'s teaching emphasizes return, or salvation by renovation, the form the teaching takes emphasizes a process of return, the *Merkabah*'s fire-bursts from within itself, a declaration that is also a performance. For the *Merkabah*, to surmise largely, is a giant image for the prophetic state-of-being, for the *activity of prophecy*, though it presents itself as something larger, as the only permitted (if daring) image of the divine imagelessness. If we think back to the first of the writing prophets, the sheep-breeder Amos, we find the *situation* of the *Merkabah* without its image. Prophecy comes among us as a sudden onslaught from a stranger, a divine judgment in a storm of human speech, circling in until it addresses itself against the house of Israel. The image favored by Amos is not the storm of the rushing chariot's own splendor, the wind that is the spirit, but the waters of judgment, a more Wordsworthian emblem than Blake could care to accept.

In the writing prophets between Amos and Ezekiel, the image of judgment or form of prophecy departs more and more from the natural. Hosea's emphasis is upon the land, but the land's faithlessness, the wife's whoredoms, presented as unnatural, rather than all-too-natural, as they would be by Blake. Isaiah's vision of God's radiance, his *kabod* (wealth and glory), moves toward the vision of the *Merkabah*, subtly juxtaposing as it does the Divine Throne and the dethroned leper king Uzziah. Micah, a more vehement *nabi*, emphasizes the image of the glory's departure from the sanctuary, and is thus the true precursor of Jeremiah and Ezekiel, and through them of Blake. Jeremiah's great image, the potter's wheel upon which clay is molded into vessels, and marred vessels broken into clay again, is associated unforgettably with the prophet's own afflictions, an association which introduces into the prophetic form a new emphasis upon the *nabi* as person, but only insofar as the person is a vessel of God's message. In Ezekiel, the potter's wheel is taken up into the heavens in the wheels within wheels of the *Merkabah*, whose departure is at one with the advent of the prophet's inner afflictions, his intense personal sufferings.

Blake, a close and superb reader of the prophets, knew all this, better than we can know it because he knew also his election, following Milton, to the line of prophecy. But his immediate poetic tradition was the theater of mind, and he struggled throughout his writing life first partly to reconcile Sensibility and prophecy, and at last largely to disengage the lesser mode from the greater. In *Jerusalem*, the Bard is identified with the Spectre of Urthona, and the *nabi* not with Los or Blake, but with the Los-Blake-Jesus composite who achieves unified form at the poem's close. Cowper's suffering is not redressed, but rather is cast away, for Blake is concerned to distinguish it sharply from the suffering of the prophet, the more fruitful afflictions of Jeremiah and Ezekiel. And, since *Jerusalem* is even more purgatorial than *Milton*, the poem's main concern is to outline firmly the distinction between the two kinds of suffering *in Blake himself*. It is his *own* Spectre of Urthona who must be overcome, though the self-realization necessary for such harsh triumph depends upon his recognition that precisely this psychic component won out in the spirit of Cowper, and in other Bards of Sensibility.

Hayley, who patronized Cowper as he did Blake, extended his interest in what he took to be the "madness" of Bards to the *Jubilate Agno* of Smart, as we know from his correspondence with the Reverend Thomas Carwardine. We do not find in *Jerusalem*, with its powerful control of Blake's emotions, a pathos as immense and memorable as Smart's. The pathos of the Spectre compels a shudder more of revulsion than of sympathy; we are not humiliated by Smart's fate, or Cowper's, but we are by the Spectre's anguish. For the Spectre is rightly associated by Blake with Ezekiel's denunciation of "the dross of silver," the impure to be cast into the terrible refining furnace of Jerusalem-under-siege. Blake is singularly harsh toward the Spectre in *Jerusalem*, not only because it is at last wholly his own Spectre and so most menacing to him, but also because he is turning at last against some of his own deepest literary identifications,

and so attempting to free himself from a poetic attitude powerfully attractive to him, whether in Cowper, Gray, Chatterton—whom he had
admired overtly—or in lesser figures of the Sublime school.

But to cross over from Bard to *nabi*, from the theater of mind to
the orator's theater of action, was not wholly a liberation for Blake's
psyche. A different, a subtler anxiety than is incarnated by the Spectre,
begins to manifest itself in *Jerusalem*. This is Blake's version of the anxiety
of influence, which he had labored heroically to overcome in *Milton*.
Jerusalem is not less in the Shadow of Milton (which Blake identified with
Ezekiel's Covering Cherub) than *Milton* was, and is also in what we could
call, following Blake, the Shadow of Ezekiel. To see and state clearly the
hidden problem concerning Blake's degree of originality in his definitive
poem, we need first to achieve a firmer sense of the poem's psychic
cartography than is now available to us.

Freud, in *The Problem of Anxiety*, distinguished anxiety from grief
and sorrow, first by its underlying "increase of excitation" (itself a reproduction of the birth trauma) and then by its function, as a response to a
situation of danger. Anxiety, he adds, can be experienced only by the
ego, not by the id as "it is not an organization, and cannot estimate
situations of danger." As for the superego, Freud declines to ascribe
anxiety to it, without however explaining why. In Blake, the id (fallen
Tharmas, or the Covering Cherub) does experience anxiety, and so does
the superego (fallen Urizen or the Spectre of Albion, the Spectre proper).
But Blake and Freud agree on the crucial location of anxiety, for the
Blakean ego is Los, fallen form of Urthona, and the Spectre of Urthona is
Los's own anxiety, the anxiety of what Yeats calls the faculty of *Creative
Mind*. Yet Blake does distinguish the ego's anxiety from that of other
psychic components. The Spectre of Urthona is neither the anxiety of
influence, a peculiarly poetic anxiety that belongs to the Covering Cherub,
with its sinister historical beauty of cultural and spiritual tradition, nor the
anxiety of futurity, that belongs to fallen Urizen. Nor is it the sexual
anxiety Blake assigns to Orc, the tormented libido burningly rising to a
perpetual defeat. Los's anxiety is larger and more constant, resembling
Kierkegaard's Concept of Dread, which must be why Northrop Frye ironically calls the Spectre of Urthona the first Existentialist. A desire for what
one fears, a sympathetic antipathy, or walking oxymoron; so Kierkegaard
speaks of Dread, and so we learn to see the Spectre of Urthona. To
Kierkegaard, this was a manifestation of Original Sin; to Blake this
manifests the final consequence of being one of Tirzah's children, a
natural man caught on the spindle of Necessity.

If we combine the insights of Freud and Kierkegaard, then we approach the Spectre of Urthona's condition, though without wholly encompassing it. The missing element is the anxiety endemic in the theater of mind, or the ego's dread that it can never break through into action. To be fearful that one's words can never become deeds, and yet to desire only to continue in that fear, while remembering dimly the trauma of coming to one's separate existence, and sensing the danger (and excitation) of every threat to such separation: that horrible composite is the Spectre of Urthona's consciousness. Blake, who had known this internal adversary with a clarity only the prophets achieve, turns *Jerusalem* against him even as *Milton* was directed against the Covering Cherub, and as *The Four Zoas* identified its antagonist in fallen Urizen. But even the prophets must be all-too-human. Blake triumphs against his ego's Dread, and wards off again the Urizenic horror of futurity, yet becomes vulnerable instead throughout *Jerusalem* to the diffuse anxiety of influence, the *mimschach* or "wide-extending" Cherub. This baneful aspect of Poetic Influence produces the form of *Jerusalem*, which is the form of Ezekiel's prophecy twisted askew by too abrupt a swerve or *clinamen* away from Blake's model.

Ezekiel is both more methodical in arrangement and more prosaic in style than the writing prophets before him. Rabbi Fisch, in his Soncino edition of Ezekiel, notes the even balance of the prophet's divisions, between the siege and fall of Jerusalem and destruction of the kingdom, and the vision of a people's regeneration, twenty-four chapters being assigned to each. Blake might well have adopted this balance, but chose instead a darker emphasis. Ezekiel ends Chapter XXIV with God's definitive establishment of His prophet as a sign, to those who have escaped destruction. "Thou shalt be a sign unto them; and they shall know that I am the Lord." At the close of XXV this formula is repeated, but as a prophecy against the Ammonities, with a grimly significant addition: ". . . and they shall know that I am the Lord, when I shall lay my vengeance upon them." For the prophet has moved from the fiction of disaster to the hope of renovation, a hope dependent upon the downfall of his people's enemies. He moves steadily toward comfort, and the vision of a rebuilt City of God. Blake's directly parallel movement is from Plate 50, end of Chapter 2, to Plate 53, start of Chapter 3 of *Jerusalem*. Plate 50 concludes with an antiphonal lament, of Erin and the Daughters of Beulah, imploring the Lamb of God to come and take away the remembrance of Sin. But Chapter 3 begins with Los weeping vehemently over Albion, and with our being reminded again that this lamenting, still ineffectual prophet is himself "the Vehicular Form of strong Urthona," that is, the *Merkabah* or Divine Chariot still in departure, still mourning in exile.

Throughout *Jerusalem*, no prophetic hint from Ezekiel is adopted if it might lead to what Blake could regard as a premature mitigation of fallen travail. I do not mean to question Blake's harshness, the necessity for his augmented sense of the prophet's burden. But the bitterness of presentation, the burden placed upon even the attentive and disciplined reader, may surpass what was necessary. At the close of Plate 3, addressing the Public, Blake declares his freedom from the "Monotonous Cadence" of English blank verse, even in Milton and Shakespeare:

> But I soon found that in the mouth of a true Orator such monotony was not only awkward, but as much a bondage as rhyme itself. I therefore have produced a variety in every line, both of cadences & number of syllables. Every word and every letter is studied and put into its fit place: the terrific numbers are reserved for the terrific parts—the mild & gentle, for the mild & gentle parts, and the prosaic, for inferior parts: all are necessary to each other.

Parodying Milton's defense of his refusal to use rhyme, Blake indicates his passage beyond Milton to the cadence of Isaiah and Ezekiel, the form of a true Orator. The defense of Blake's cadence has been conducted definitively by a formidable prosodist, John Hollander, in his essay on "Blake and the Metrical Contract," to which I can add nothing. In the passage above, Blake emphasizes, as against Milton, the prosody of the King James Version, which he does not distinguish from the Hebrew original. There is evidence that Blake, remarkably adept at teaching himself languages, had some Hebrew when he worked at *Jerusalem*, but his notions as to the variety of biblical poetic numbers seem to go back to Lowth, as Smart's notions did also. This gave him a distorted sense of the metrical freedom of his great originals, a distortion that was an imaginative aid to him. Whether his distortion of larger prophetic forms was hindrance or action is my concern in the remainder of this essay.

Blake shies away from certain symbolic acts in Ezekiel that earlier had influenced him quite directly. It has never, I think, been noted that Blake's *London* has a precise source in Ezekiel:

> I wander thro' each charter'd street,
> Near where the charter'd Thames does flow.
> And mark in every face I meet
> Marks of weakness, marks of woe.

And the glory of the God of Israel was gone up from the cherub, whereupon he was, to the threshold of the house. And he called to the man clothed with linen, which had the writer's inkhorn by his side;

> And the Lord said unto him, Go through the midst of the city, through the midst of Jerusalem, and set a mark upon the foreheads of the men that sigh and that cry for all the abominations that be done in the midst thereof.
>
> (Ezekiel 9:3–4)

> How the Chimney-sweepers cry
> Every blackning Church appalls,
> And the hapless Soldiers sigh,
> Runs in blood down Palace walls.

Those that sigh and cry are to be marked and spared, but those in Church and Palace are to be slain, as God pours out his fury upon Jerusalem, and upon London. Between Ezekiel and himself Blake is more than content to see an absolute identity. But, a decade or more later, the identity troubles him. If we contrast even the serene closes of Ezekiel and *Jerusalem*, where Blake directly derives from his precursor the *naming* of the City, we confront an identity straining to be dissolved:

> And the name of the city from that day shall be "The Lord is there."
> (Ezekiel 48:35)

> And I heard the Name of their Emanations they are named Jerusalem.
> (*Jerusalem* 99:5)

"The Lord is there" because the promise of Ezekiel's prophecy is that the *Merkabah* will not depart again from His sanctuary. Jerusalem receives therefore a new name. Blake's promise is more restricted, and warier; the Judgment will restore London to Jerusalem, but Jerusalem will still be a smelting furnace of mind, subject to the alternation of Beulah and Eden, creative repose and the artist's activity. So the departed Chariot's Cherubim or restored Zoas are not invoked again at *Jerusalem*'s close, as they are by Ezekiel in his final epiphany. For an apocalyptic poem, *Jerusalem* is remarkably restrained. Blake follows Ezekiel throughout, but always at a distance, for he needs to protect himself not only from the natural history of mind (which crippled the poets of Sensibility) but also from the too-rigorous Hebraic theism that would make his apocalyptic humanism impossible. *Jerusalem* does not accept the dualism of God and man, which is the only dualism sanctioned by the prophets, but which to them was less a dualism than a challenge to confrontation. Blake, who had held back from identifying himself wholly with Milton and Cowper, though he saw the Divine Countenance in them, kept himself distinct at last even from his prophetic precursor, Ezekiel, that he might have his own scope, but also that he might not be affrighted out of Eden the garden of God, though it be by "the anointed cherub that covereth."

THOMAS R. FROSCH

Art and Eden: The Sexes

Aproblem that arises in conjunction
with Albion's final awakening is that, reading Blake, particularly the
poetry and prose after *The Four Zoas*, one often gets the impression that
Eden and the experience of art are synonymous, and this identification
can find considerable support. Blake writes in the *Descriptive Catalogue*,
"The artist is an inhabitant of that happy country," or Eden (E533), and
Jerusalem can be read as the story of the making of a single work of art, in
its fullest psychic and social contexts, at the end of which Los is regathered into paradise. In a remarkable passage, Blake asserts that the same
dwelling is available to the artist's public: "If the Spectator could Enter
into these Images in his Imagination approaching them on the Fiery
Chariot of his Contemplative Thought if he could Enter into Noahs
Rainbow or into his bosom or could make a friend & Companion of one
of these Images of wonder which always intreats him to leave mortal
things as he must know then would he arise from his Grave then would he
meet the Lord in the Air & then he would be happy" (V.L.J., E550).
And in an 1801 letter to Flaxman, Blake congratulates the sculptor on the
completion of his "Great Work," as follows: "The Kingdoms of this World
are now become the Kingdoms of God & his Christ & we shall reign with
him for ever & ever. The Reign of Literature & the Arts Commences"
(Oct. 19, 1801, E686). Such statements could be construed to indicate an
identification of Golgonooza and Jerusalem, the city of art and the city of
Eden. Frye is explicit about this: "The totality of imaginative power, of
which the matrix is art, is what we ordinarily call culture or civilization."

From *The Awakening of Albion: The Renovation of the Body in the Poetry of William Blake.*
Copyright © 1974 by Cornell University Press.

Golgonooza is the edifice of human culture, where all the things of life are remade into their fully human and social forms. When it is finished, "nature, its scaffolding, will be knocked away and man will live in it. Golgonooza will then be the city of God, the New Jerusalem which is the total form of all human culture and civilization."

I would suggest, however, that in the discursive passages above Blake is emphasizing a milder vision of the apocalypse than is created by his poetic narratives and imagery. Blake uses the concept of imagination to refer both to the fallen faculty through which paradise is reconstituted and to the reality of Eden, and the relationship between the two is an intricate one. In this section, I wish to review the distinction in light of the final renovation Blake depicts at the end of *Jerusalem.*

The integral body of Albion survives the fall in the shrunken and scattered organs of sense. It survives in full form not as an accepted actuality but as the Divine Vision, kept by the poet-prophet when all others have forsaken it. The vision of Eden is not, however, a peculiar possession of the artist, for imagination exists in all men as the original, universal, and highest phase of our human consciousness, and it makes itself felt in the natural texture of our lives as a divine intercessor: "What is the Divine Spirit? is the Holy Ghost any other than an Intellectual Fountain?" (J. III: 77, E229). The intellectual fountain does not belong to our natural inheritance but is the part of us that falls into the world in our natural birth, to be enclosed in a cavern-like body. Independent of nature, it can only be diminished by memory, experiential wisdom, or any mental process in which a blank space is filled with sensations, information, or ideas from without. Its inexhaustible energy cannot be acquired but is available to all men through inspiration; and inspiration to Blake is at once a generous opening of the mind and the senses and a labor of copying "(Imagination) The Holy Ghost," rather than the "Goddess Nature (Memory)" (E668). "Genius and Inspiration are the great Origin and Bond of Society" (D.C., E518), for in their imaginations all men inhabit a home where everything is equally holy and human. Blake shares with Marx the conviction that community is not a development of man's history but an original mode of relationship, from which history has been a continuing fall into isolation. But this final home is for Blake available only through the uncompromised uniqueness of individual perception. Keats, in the letter to John Hamilton Reynolds of February 19, 1818, beautifully illuminates not only Blake but the way in which English Romanticism tries to see beyond the dualism of the community and the individual that still today conditions our thinking about perception and about politics: "But the Minds of Mortals are so different and bent on such diverse Journeys that it may at first appear impossible for any common taste and fellowship to exist between two or three under these suppositions— It is however quite the contrary—Minds would leave each other in contrary directions, traverse each other in Numberless points, and [at] last greet each other at the Journeys end." Blake would go even farther, for at the end of *The Four Zoas* and *Jerusalem* the individual discovers both a full sense of community and a full sense of particularity, neither of which can exist without the other.

The imagination, as opposed to the perspective of the mind's eye, is the true universalization; it is a unific, although infinitely various, world for all men, and thus a sphere of absolute truth: "All Forms are Perfect in the Poets Mind. but these are not Abstracted nor Compounded from Nature (but are from Imagination)" (Ann. to Reynolds, E637). In the *Laocoön*, Blake writes: "The Eternal Body of Man is The Imagination. that is God Himself The Divine Body. . . . It manifests itself in his Works of Art" (E271). And since all art potentially opens a path to the same universal home, Eden, there is ultimately no value hierarchy of artists or art-works: "To suppose that Art can go beyond the finest specimens of Art that are now in the world, is not knowing what Art is; it is being blind to the gifts of the spirit" (D.C., E535). Blake can carry this understanding of art to startling lengths; it would seem, for example, that in his inspired work, in vocalizing his vision of Eden, the poet necessarily speaks truth, as if "truth" were by definition the content of enthusiastic poetic song: "I am Inspired! I know it is Truth! / For I Sing" (M.I: 13: 51, E 107).

Thus Blake says far more than that the imagination is one of our valid powers, with its own laws and its own species of knowledge. Imagination is, rather, our whole power, the total functioning interplay of our capacities. The work of the artist is to actualize this innate cooperation as an environment for all men. Since the fall consists in a division of paradise into the spiritual and bodily portions of Divine Vision and organs of perception, the restorative work consists in rebuilding the connections between the two, or expanding the latter to the fullness of the former. That art should be the agency of this rapprochement is not surprising, for it is quite orthodoxly conceived of as a mode of knowing that participates simultaneously in soul and body, a mental work of the senses and feelings. However, Blake finds in the very nature of art, with its distinctly sensuous and affective mode of consciousness, an apocalyptic potentiality.

But the healing possibilities of art are realized only when esthetic pleasure and cognition are conceived of as an acid bath for the natural world, rather than as its complement or decoration, and it is with this purpose that Los builds his great city. Golgonooza is originally constructed in an act of compassion, as a refuge for the imaginative forms which have been exiled from the worlds of single and double vision:

> The stones are pity, and the bricks, well wrought affections:
> Enameld with love & kindness, & the tiles engraven gold
> Labour of merciful hands: the beams & rafters are forgiveness.
>   (see J.I: 12: 30–37, E154)

Here, in the realm of fallen art, natural objects are transformed into poetic percepts. Golgonooza is the imaginative version of the fallen city of man, a "Spiritual fourfold London," and within its scope things are seen in their relation to man and walls are not slabs of stone but "faces." The building of the city, constantly assaulted by all that is not yet art, is a labor akin to the writing of the one great poem to which, says Shelley, all poets are contributors; and the force of art, once it recognizes its own subversive nature, is incremental, eventually assuming the proportions of a counter-creation.

Golgonooza, as noted above, is founded on "London Stone," depicted as the world-center, the omphalos, or nexus with another mode of being. That fallen art, built in nature, does annex us by a new kind of consciousness to something more than the world of our natural perception and natural reason, suggests that it is potentially the point of entry to a new world. But Blake is quite explicit about what Golgonooza does not contain: "Go on, builders in hope: tho Jerusalem wanders far away, / Without the gate of Los: among the dark Satanic wheels" (J.I: 12: 43–44, E154). And in describing the fourfold directionality of the city, Blake writes: "But that toward Eden is walled up, till time of renovation" (52). Both Jerusalem and paradise are outside the dimension of the fallen art form. We know of their existence through art, and, Blake says, the more trust we place in the works of the poetic imagination, the firmer our conviction of an Edenic possibility becomes. But Albion's final reunion with the departed emanation and his actual re-entry into the paradisaical state of human integration is not achieved within the limits of fallen art. Fallen art, in Blake, always occupies an ambivalent position, at once sharing the horizons of the fall and liberated from them, both fundamentally opposed to all our limitations and finally subject to them.

The same passage corroborates the distinction in another way. Blake clearly locates Golgonooza within the world of suffering: "Around Golgonooza lies the land of death eternal; a Land / Of pain and misery and despair and ever brooding melancholy" (13: 30–31, E155). And he goes on to show us Cave, Rock, Tree, and all the terrors of Ulro "on all sides surrounding / Golgonooza." Roughly, Golgonooza is to Jerusalem as Spenser's Cleopolis is to his New Jerusalem. It contains the best of this world and it is a haven; but just as there is a fallen distinction between art and life, so Golgonooza is art within nature. The city Jerusalem, on the other hand, replaces the world of pain, and in Eden the distinction of art and life vanishes. Art, as we know it, is thus not an end but a way. It is able to take its impetus from the world of imagination, the Divine Vision sheltered within, and it is able to open up that world and bring us to the point of entering it; but, in itself, it remains less than Edenic. To suggest, as Hazard Adams and Karl Kiralis do, that the poem *Jerusalem* is written as an example of Divine Vision is, obviously, to open the poem to the kind of attack no human artifact could possibly sustain. What Blake does claim for the poem is precisely that it is a human artifact, made according to the principles of fallen art at its highest, as Blake conceived them, and no more than this.

What separates art from Eden is the closed gate of Tharmas. When it is finally opened in the awakening of Albion, we pass into paradise in our bodies; and in this passage our bodies are resurrected as the unified, fourfold Albion engaged in the fierce and loving Edenic conversations. Now man has recovered the creative potentialities that in the fallen world were only available to art—and even there in limited form. "Even for the visionary who lives in the divine paradise in which creation and perception are the same thing," Frye writes, "the gulf between Pygmalion's human power that conceived a statue and the divine power that brought it to life still exists." But *Jerusalem* insists on a modification of Frye's argument, for there no one can find paradise until all do and the artist is barred from living in Eden until he has completed his task of universal renewal. Once the Western Gate of the body is opened, however, the divine power to create life is exactly what he does possess, if it is understood that the sense of "he" has undergone a radical metamorphosis: Los is no longer a spectral fragment, but, as Urthona, has been reintegrated into Albion, to whom, as a whole, the Edenic creative power is attributed.

In Night IX Blake shows us the difference between fallen and unfallen imagination, between the labor of art and the labor of Eden, in one concise and beautiful image:

> Then Tharmas & Urthona rose from the Golden feast satiated
> With Mirth & Joy Urthona limping from his fall on Tharmas leand
> In his right hand his hammer Tharmas held his Shepherds crook.
> (137: 7–9, E390)

The fallen imagination, as Los, works alone, unsustained by the full unity and creative power of the body; and in the same way Tharmas must function apart from the imagination that could integrate his disorganized faculty. In Generation we have, through our fallen bodies, a limited capacity to transform our environment and our lives according to our desires: the "vegetative body" is the shrunken form of our constitutive power, our ability to literally make the world. But the renovation of tongue and touch which completes the resurrection and gathers the "Parent Power" Tharmas into Albion makes this ability total. Poetry is directly actualized, and the source of poetry is no longer the Divine Vision kept within the fallen imagination, but the body as a whole.

In Blake, the goal of art is the moment at which it becomes unnecessary, because the whole of life has taken on the character of art. Los, poem, and Eden are related to one another rather as are prophet, prophecy, and actualized promise in the Old Testament. It is the job of the fallen artist to reorganize the natural body, to awaken it to its self-induced limitations and its real potentialities, until it regains the capacity to arise and enter Eden by itself. In this transformation, what we now recognize as art disappears: when Albion enters the furnaces, Los drops out of the poem, consumed with all else in his Sublime Universe. Blake's point, it seems, is that it is through one of our fallen fragments that the whole can be regathered; not that one particular fragment is, or is to be taken for, or even stands for, the whole. What Eden is like can be inferred from the experience of artistic work, specifically from those moments in which the images are entered in imagination; it can be inferred from this, but the two are not, judging from the closing plates of *Jerusalem*, identical; for there, in what seems to be Blake's most advanced treatment of the theme, we enter the images in body, in a new life, and together with all other men.

THE SEXES

Another problem raised by the last plates of *Jerusalem* is the status of sexuality in the risen body. Sexuality occupies a difficult position in Blake's myth of renovation, and the Zoa connected with sexual desire, Luvah, is the most complexly ambivalent among Albion's faculties. The problem is underscored by the special prevalence of sexual concern in the final chapter of *Jerusalem* and the gradual increase in tension between spectre and shadow as they approach the apocalypse: "Albion hath entered the Loins, the place of the Last Judgment" (J. II: 44:38, E191).

The difficulty is basically that sexuality, as Blake depicts it, participates in both the given and the desired. In the late work, the words "sex," "nature," and "death" are usually synonymous; and an increasing share of his prophetic outrage is reserved for the sexual temptations of Enitharmon and Vala. At the same time, regeneration always remains an "improvement of sensual enjoyment." The furious opposition to the hypocrisies and the psychic destructiveness of sexual repression is never abated, and the spirit of the *Visions of the Daughters of Albion* survives in full force in the late *The Everlasting Gospel*. To maintain a concept of the late Blake as turning away from the body, one must simply ignore such passages as the following:

> That they may call a shame & Sin
> Loves temple that God dwelleth in
> And hide in secret hidden Shrine
> The Naked Human form divine
> And render that a Lawless thing
> On which the Soul Expands its wing.
>   (E513)

By the time of *Jerusalem*, Blake is well past the vision of Orc, convinced now that Oothoon cannot liberate herself by the sheer force of her desire, or by any isolated acts, but must instead be emancipated by Los. Yet the Jesus of the last epic, while identified in his aspect of savior with Los, is still in his crucifixion and resurrection a manifestation of Luvah. His resurrection is a sexual one, and his new divinity consists in his forgiveness of the acts of man's body, as well as his refusal to submit to a restricted expression of desire, to a ritual of postponement and secrecy, and to the trappings of sin and guilt which deify the virginity of the Daughters of Albion: "If you dare rend their Veil with your Spear; you are healed of Love!" (J. III: 68: 42, E220).

It would seem from the descriptions of the fall of Tharmas in *The Four Zoas* and that of Albion in *Jerusalem* that the ambivalence is inherent in the nature of the sex act itself, for the total sexual experience in each case is one of division. In intercourse the human form and its emanation are split as masculine and feminine sexual partners; but in this case sexuality is not a joining of two distinct natural bodies, but, rather, a schism of the Edenic integrity into two sexually joined bodies. The emanation is finally severed into a separate place, or other body, in the post-coital separation. I will continue the discussion of the original fall in the final section; what is important here is that the loins are established as the place of externalization, the place of the seed of the masculine and the natural birth of the feminine. Thus, images such as that of Albion at Luvah's Gate, "Leaning against the pillars, & his disease rose from his skirts" (J. II: 46: 1, E193), and that of his Affections appearing outside him as his sons, rending a way in his loins and then "ravning to gormandize / The Human majesty" (J. I: 19: 23–24; E162), do not refer to any particular sexual malady, but, on the contrary, to Albion's complete natural health. His disease and the channel of externalization rent in his body, so injuriously that his Giant Beauty is stretched upon the ground in pain and tears, are figures of a specifically reproduction-oriented sexuality. Because of his emphasis on reproduction as a process of naturalization, Blake can answer the primitivists and the deists, with no imputation whatsoever of original sin, that "man is born a Spectre or Satan & is altogether an Evil" (J. II: 52, E198), for the key word here is "born." The natural child is a "vegetated Spectre," and in Blake birth is a cause for mourning because it is an entry into the Body of Death. In addition, reproduction carries with it the aura of meaningless, self-enclosed, and compulsive repetition that characterizes nature as a whole. The fallen world is a "Sexual Machine" (39: 25, E185); and Los says: "I hear the screech of Childbirth loud pealing & the groans / Of Death" (30: 23–24, E175).

Blake understands the binding of sexual energy to natural purposes as a limitation of sexuality to the genitals: "Luvah tore forth from Albions Loins, in fibrous veins, in rivers / Of blood over Europe: a Vegetating Root in grinding pain" (J. II: 47: 4–5, E194). Exiled as a natural seed, the full human energy is imprisoned within a body in which a small part of its range is permitted a fulfillment necessary to the perpetuation of the spectral universe. The remainder of that energy consumes itself and others in the joys of war and destruction, which, the image suggests, replace sensual enjoyment. The following stanza is charged with an intentional and grotesque satire upon the entire social, political, religious, and bodily organization of natural man:

> Albions Spectre from his Loins
> Tore forth in all the pomp of War!
> Satan his name: in flames of fire
> He stretch'd his Druid Pillars far.
> (J. II: 27: 37–40, E171)

The natural man as a whole is reduced to the form of a phallus: Albion has become "a little Grovelling root outside himself." And in the following lines, culminating in two of his richest images, Blake's complete myth seems to resonate from the natural organization of the male and female bodies and the mode of genital sexuality:

Hence the Infernal Veil grows in the disobedient Female:
Which Jesus rends & the whole Druid Law removes away
From the Inner Sanctuary: a False Holiness hid within the Center,
For the Sanctuary of Eden. is in the Camp: in the Outline,
In the Circumference: & every Minute Particular is Holy:
Embraces are Cominglings: from the Head even to the Feet;
And not a pompous High Priest entering by a Secret Place.
(J. III: 69: 38–44, E221)

The centralization of sexuality is, like any other centralization in Blake, a tyranny. And not only is our energy limited to this extent, but the sexual center is for us a secret, hidden place with natural veils and moral restrictions militating against fulfillment. In an added touch, the Spectre of Urthona intensifies the shrinkings of Los and Enitharmon, not only by making the social route to sexual fulfillment devious and self-contradictory, but also by encouraging an emotional ambiguity toward the sexual center itself, making it offensive to the sense of beauty, in its Urizenic reduction as the sense of purity:

The Man who respects Woman shall be despised by Woman
And deadly cunning & mean abjectness only, shall enjoy them
For I will make their places of joy & love, excrementitious.
(J. IV: 88: 37–39, E245)

Blake's idea of genital tyranny might be misconstrued to suggest, by way of emancipation, the technique of *coitus interruptus* or a return to the specific "polymorphous perversity" of the child; but what seems clear in other phases of Blake's imagery, that it is the centralization and not the centralized entity—the tyranny of the separated eye and reason, not eye and reason themselves—that he objects to, should be of help here. The point is that the comminglings—which, as Bloom notes, Blake probably bases on Milton's description of angelic sexuality—suggest that the sense of touch will be improved to the extent that the entire body will be susceptible of the same pleasure that is at present reserved for the genitals. There is no special method in this, nor any act of will, for it can only come about spontaneously as part of the general renovation and decentralization of man's body. For Blake a great subtlety of the Urizenic organization is that the highest degree of bodily pleasure is attainable only through an act which ultimately serves to restrict bodily pleasure. At the same time, a restraint from genitality has as its consequence an entry into Ulro, for this is to abandon the remaining fragment of a fully human sexuality, of which genitality is the diminished form.

But Blake's myth of the sexes reaches beyond the particularities of sexual experience. The unfallen Albion is androgynous; and Jerusalem laments: "O Vala! Humanity is far above / Sexual organization" (J. IV: 79: 73–74, E233). The tearing apart of man into two sexes is the fundamental duality of his life in nature, and Blake sees in it the separation between art and life, desire and act, imagination and love, perceiver and object-world, and all the other fallen schisms. In addition to centralizing sexual energy, then, genital organization perpetuates and stabilizes the primal division of the emanation through the reproduction of natural children, split from the start as male and female. As we have seen in the case of Tharmas, sexual separation is portrayed as a consequence of solipsism and self-will, and it implies mortality, as does any sundering of part from whole:

> The Feminine separates from the Masculine & both from Man,
> Ceasing to be His Emanations, Life to Themselves assuming!

> When the Individual appropriates Universality
> He divides into Male & Female: & when the Male & Female,
> Appropriate Individuality, they become an Eternal Death.
> (J. IV: 90: 1–2, 52–54, E247)

Note that Blake distinguishes male and female, on the one hand, from man, or humanity, on the other: all sexual being is inevitably fragmented. In "To Tirzah," Blake tells us that "The Sexes sprung from Shame and Pride" (E30). The creation of two sexes is inherent in the shock of a primal objectification and, more, in any act of fearful or narcissistic self-reflection; sexual differentiation is a direct materialization of the sense of self.

Blake calls the relationship between the disconnected parts "sexual strife." As soon as Enitharmon separates from the loins of Los, his agony subtly modulates into longing, and the two are consumed by the impossible ambivalences of love and jealousy, "terrified at each others beauty / Envying each other yet desiring, in all devouring Love" (J. IV: 86: 63–64, E243). Los and Enitharmon are Blake's Adam and Eve, and they are also the first natural children, the embodiments, or creative accomplishments, of Tharmas' withdrawal from Enion. In *The Four Zoas* Blake gives us in the story of their growth his fullest exploration of the sexual development of fallen man. Enion bears the children in the infernal landscape in which the schism has abandoned her: "with fierce pain she brought forth on the rocks her sorrow & woe / Behold two little Infants wept upon the desolate wind" (I: 8: 1–2, E300). The place of birth is thus established as Ulro. Blake confirms this in *Jerusalem*: "Such is the nature of the Ulro: that whatever enters: / Becomes Sexual, & is Created, and Vegetated, and Born" (J. II: 39: 21–22, E184).

The children wander away from their mother, who pursues them with "pangs of maternal love," giving them "all her spectrous life." It seems they would be "repelled" by her "Into Non Entity revolving round in dark despair" (F.Z. I: 9: 6, E300). But Eno, a "daughter of Beulah," creates for the lost children Lower Beulah, where the fierce maternity of Ulro is replaced by a gentle and protective one and the ethos of Innocence serves as a refuge from natural conflict, given to the split masculine and feminine until they are sexually able to enter Generation.

The body of Innocence is pregenital, or perhaps prepubescent. But genitality is implicit in it, and in this sense the child's body is a seed, an infant desire eventually to be fulfilled in act. Redeemed, the environment of Innocence is kindly because it encourages the seed to its maturation:

> Where Sexes wander in dreams of bliss among the Emanations
> Where the Masculine & Feminine are nurs'd into Youth & Maiden
> By the tears & smiles of Beulahs Daughters till the time of Sleep is past.
> (J. IV: 79: 75–77, E233)

From this period of latency, a "dark slumberous bliss," youth and maiden eventually wake to the choice that confronts Thel and must decide whether to fully enter, through genitality, the world of mortality and vanishing; or, as Thel, to retreat and attempt to remain in Beulah. Thel is a wish not acted upon, an infant murdered in the cradle, a seed that attempts to take root in the watery dreams of Beulah, rather than the earth of Generation. That earth is the only means of access from Lower to Upper Beulah. In the case of Los and Enitharmon, however, Upper Beulah is not yet available to fallen man; Los himself will have to make it so.

Their life as children appears idyllic on the surface, but since they are separate forms from the start and the powers of the undivided human are split between them, and since too they incarnate the fatal emotions of their parents, they can only act out the new universal power struggle:

> Alternate Love & Hate his breast; hers Scorn & Jealousy
> In embryon passions. they kiss'd not nor embrac'd for shame & fear
> His head beamd light & in his vigorous voice was prophecy
> He could controll the times & seasons, & the days & years
> She could controll the spaces, regions, desart, flood & forest
> But had no power to weave a Veil of covering for her Sins
> She drave the Females all away from Los
> And Los drave all the Males from her away.
> (F.Z. I: 9: 24–31, E301)

Even in this state Los retains an instinct toward renewal; it is again a decisive Blakean theme that everything in Albion's unfallen existence survives the fall in diminished form and, consequently, that the apocalypse is a development of potentialities that are with us now. Here, Los asserts their relationship to the fallen immortals and the primal human integrity, while Enitharmon encourages scorn for them and seeks a separate being. Chafing in the bonds of Los, she sings "a Song of Death! it is a Song of Vala!" Los resists the naturalization Enitharmon prompts, and he violently casts her away, smiting her upon the earth. She calls down Urizen as her champion in the wars of male and female, which are also in the passage the wars of Albion and Luvah for Vala. But Los has struck and cast away a part of himself, and the injury he has given arouses a fatal pity and a desire for the emanation, which is sexually consummated. In the following image, sexual desire itself is an expression of guilt:

> Los saw the wound of his blow he saw he pitied he wept
> Los now repented that he had smitten Enitharmon he felt love
> Arise in all his Veins he threw his arms around her loins
> To heal the wound of his smiting
> They eat the fleshly bread, they drank the nervous wine.
> (12: 40–44, E303)

Their sexuality is a devouring of secret bread and a consuming of the Human Form; the body of Innocence becomes a body of flesh and nerves through a mistaken act of reconciliation between the fragments. The marriage that follows is a mere amalgamation of the split parts, a deadly wedding of mind and nature in which the prophetic heritage of Urthona is betrayed; and the first consequence is that Los, formerly accused by Urizen as a "visionary of Jesus," can now only see the Divine Vision in the distance, high above him: Albion, clothed in Luvah's robes of blood, shines down "on the misty earth," while, beneath him, Luvah and Vala are suspended in the bloody sky, "unable to avert their eyes from one another." Los's nuptial feast is a nightmarish inauguration of Urizen's reign and a parody of the apocalyptic banquet of Luvah; its spousal songs call not for the Divine Breath to go forth over the landscape, but for war and blood; and Urizenic bards compose proverbs of Heaven: "The Horse is of more value than the Man" (15: 1, E304).

Once the Spectre of Urthona enters the description of Los's relationship to Enitharmon, the force of desire for the separate feminine is generally localized in Los's natural selfhood; and it is the promptings of the Spectre to regard the objectified emanation with a self-consuming and other-consuming hunger that the prophetic aspiration must resist:

> Thou Knowest that the Spectre is in Every Man insane brutish
> Deformd that I am thus a ravening devouring lust continually
> Craving & devouring but my Eyes are always upon thee O lovely
> Delusion & I cannot crave for any thing but thee.
> (F.Z. VIIa: 84: 36–39, E352)

In *Jerusalem* the difficult rebellion of Los against the religion of Female Love is pitted against his Spectre's obsession with the fully vegetated and idolized female, Vala. The separate emanation is now a demoness, who embodies society and nature at their most destructive:

> Her hand is a Court of Justice, her Feet: two Armies in Battle
> Storms & Pestilence: in her Locks: & in her Loins Earthquake.
> And Fire. & the Ruin of Cities & Nations & Families & Tongues.
> (J. III: 64: 9–11, E213)

The bliss she promises is no longer of Generation, but of Ulro:

> She cries: The Human is but a Worm, & thou O Male: Thou art
> Thyself Female, a Male: a breeder of Seed: a Son & Husband: & Lo.
> The Human Divine is Womans Shadow, a Vapor in the summers heat
> Go assume Papal dignity thou Spectre, thou Male Harlot! Arthur
> Divide into the Kings of Europe in times remote O Woman-born
> And Woman-nourished & Woman-educated & Woman-scorn'd!
> (12–17)

Los recognizes in her

> The Sexual Death living on accusation of Sin & Judgment
> To freeze Love & Innocence into the gold & silver of the Merchant
> Without Forgiveness of Sin Love is Itself Eternal Death.
> (22–24)

But his Spectre draws Vala into his bosom and they become a dark Hermaphrodite, the assimilation that signals the triumph of nature and the end of sexuality in the final totalitarian body of the Covering Cherub.

Percival puts it well when he writes that the fall into sex is presented as a descent into chastity. It is clear that as natural sexuality develops it moves further and further away from sensory enjoyment and is increasingly dominated by ulterior motives. Luvah's energy has left the loins, and Blake suggests that the joys of fallen sexuality have more to do with mind, heart, and eye than with the body. Finally, in the depths of Ulro, the energy that is denied by the forbidding Druid priests and the virginal Daughters of Albion is released in violence and destruction. The promises, lures, and postponements of the courtly rite send man off to war to find a perverse joy, to win the favor of his mistress, and to consume the energy that would otherwise rend the veil. The aggregate form of the Virgins is the Great Whore Rahab, whose fulfillment parodies that offered by Jerusalem. Men, brought to a final deification of her through the dynamics of denial and accused pleasure, pay for her with their lives, and their satisfaction is to wholly lose their individual outlines and to be absorbed into her. Rahab is described as

> A Religion of Chastity, forming a Commerce to sell Loves,
> With Moral Law, an Equal Balance, not going down with decision
> Therefore the Male severe & cruel filld with stern Revenge:
> Mutual Hate returns & mutual Deceit & mutual Fear.
>
> (J. III: 69: 34–37, E221)

In the inversion of the angels, Rahab appears pure and holy, while the spontaneity of Jerusalem becomes prostitution. But for Blake the true harlotry is the internally and externally idolized chastity that deflects an infant desire from its growth and achievement and reifies love as a promise, a reward, a compensation, or a merchandise. In its harshest phase, love becomes a murderous and gratuitous usage of the other, in which even the quest for power and the pleasures of sadism seem almost secondary to the mechanical continuation of an absurd complex of habits. Gwendolen, one of the Daughters of Albion, proclaims:

> I have mockd those who refused cruelty & I have admired
> The cruel Warrior. I have refused to give love to Merlin the piteous.
> He brings to me the Images of his Love & I reject in chastity
> And turn them out into the streets for Harlots to be food
> To the stern Warrior.
>
> I have destroyd Wandring Reuben who strove to bind my Will
> I have stripd off Josephs beautiful integuement for my Beloved,
> The Cruel-one of Albion: to clothe him in gems of my Zone
> I have named him Jehovah of Hosts. Humanity is become
> A weeping Infant in ruind lovely Jerusalems folding Cloud:
> In Heaven Love begets Love! but Fear is the Parent of Earthly Love!
> And he who will not bend to Love must be subdued by Fear.
>
> (J. IV: 81, E236)

Considered in isolation, such passages might be misleading, for Blake's point is that the priests of accusation and the virgins of denial are empowered by the male enjoyment of the rites of Female Love, of the enticements of distance, of the substitution of purity for beauty as the object of desire, and of the pleasures of theft, secrecy, and possession. In Vala's chaste world, man has been desexualized by making sexual desire an absolute in itself. Fulfillment becomes subtly irrelevant as feeling, abstracted from the body, is pursued for its own sake, so that even torment is eroticized. Virgin, priest, and warrior are Eternal Characters within the naturalized souls of every man and woman, and their paradise is a world of pure emotion, of relationship without objects. Blake's anti-mysticism is nowhere clearer than in his critique of fallen sexuality.

In *The Gates of Paradise*, Blake suggests that sexual organization need not follow the development outlined above:

> When weary Man enters his Cave
> He meets his Saviour in the Grave
> Some find a Female Garment there
> And some a Male, woven with care
> Lest the Sexual Garments sweet
> Should grow a devouring Winding sheet.
> (E265)

The Sexual Garments of Generation are sweet when love does not appropriate universality: "The Imagination is not a State: it is the Human Existence itself / Affection or Love becomes a State, when divided from Imagination" (M. II: 32: 32–33, E131). To take any State as an end in itself is to enter Ulro. The idolization of the genitality of the fallen loins, or the reason of the fallen brain, or the feeling of the fallen heart, or, for that matter, even the art of the fallen imagination, is a self-denial that closes one's energy into the Druid forests. But sexual organization, as well as the most apparently inalienable manifestation of our divisions, is also the primary condition of renewal. Stripped of guilt and of ulterior motivation, sexual love points in the direction of Albion's wholeness, and in this awareness Los makes available to fallen man in Upper Beulah the reality of Oothoon's vision of the innocent, enlarging, and internally and externally unifying pleasures of fulfillment. Genital consummation is a shrunken center, and like every center in Blake it has an expansive inward being; sexual enjoyment is outside the dimension of the natural body, just as imagination is outside that of the mental ratio:

> There is a Grain of Sand in Lambeth that Satan cannot find
> Nor can his Watch Fiends find it: tis translucent & has many Angles
> But he who finds it will find Oothoons palace, for within
> Opening into Beulah every angle is a lovely heaven
> But should the Watch Fiends find it, they would call it Sin
> And lay its Heavens & their inhabitants in blood of punishment.
> (J. II: 37: 15–20, E181)

Here, beneath Earth's central joint, the Shadow of Jerusalem finds shelter among Erin and the Daughters of Beulah; the emanation, in this form, is always available to generative men and women whenever they can free themselves from the torments of love and jealousy to find their pleasure in the sense of touch itself. At the close of *Jerusalem* the Body of Death is awakened to "Life among the Flowers of Beulah," for in Upper Beulah it awakes to another awareness of time and space, another mode of relationship to the other, another sense than the visual, and another body than that of the cavern.

Four modes of sexuality can then be distinguished in Blake, four states of the sense of touch and of Tharmas as the complete body in its erotic activity: in Ulro, the abstention from touch or the hostile tactility of violence; in Generation, genital sexuality in its reproductory phase, the channeling of energy into the maintenance of the cyclical World of Death, and the secrecy, fears, and jealousies which become the true objects of sexual pleasure and for which, indeed, sex serves as a pretext; in Beulah, the realized touch of affection, genital sexuality in its aspect of pleasure, but pleasure entirely free from any conviction of sin; and in Eden, the complete commingling of the risen activity. What Blake shows us as Eden is a community of human forms embracing through their activity. Now tongue and touch are unified and are, together, reintegrated with the other senses, with the effect that the risen activity is a kind of speech, an utterance of the whole man. It would appear that the Edenic conversation and the erotic commingling are identical, the transfigured tactility of the reorganized body, now acting as a whole. This is like no sexuality we know, nor any modification of it, for when Albion awakes, Enitharmon vanishes and there are no longer two sexes. There should be no danger of misconstruing Blake to suggest that the delights of mental endeavor are greater than the delights of natural sexuality, for the distinction between the two only obtains in the separation of male and female, or man and nature. In the fallen world, mental endeavors produce "weak visions of time & space," and bodily pleasure is a shadow of what it might be. But in the resurrection, spiritual and sexual are indistinguishable; indeed the risen body subsists in their new identity. In the following description of Edenic intercourse, Blake opposes the stolen joys and secret bread of natural sexuality to a bodily pleasure incomparably greater:

> When in Eternity Man converses with Man they enter
> Into each others Bosom (which are Universes of delight)
> In mutual interchange. and first their Emanations meet
> Surrounded by their Children. if they embrace & comingle
> The Human-Four-fold Forms mingle also in thunders of Intellect
> But if the Emanations mingle not; with storms & agitations
> Of earthquakes & consuming fires they roll apart in fear
> For Man cannot unite with Man but by their Emanations
> Which stand both Male & Female at the Gates of each Humanity
> How then can I ever again be united as Man with Man
> While thou my Emanation refusest my Fibres of dominion?
> When Souls mingle & join thro all the Fibres of Brotherhood
> Can there be any secret joy on Earth greater than this?
>
> (IV: 88: 3–15, E244)

This is a difficult passage, and line 11 is capable of supporting contradictory interpretations. Each man might have four gates, for instance, as paradise does, and his emanations might be "both Male & Female," or themselves androgynous. As I understand the lines, however, the suggestion seems to be that each Edenic Humanity emanates what we would consider to be two sexual persons, a male and female, at its points of communcation with other human forms, as if each Edenic being, then, appeared to others as a deeply and radically unified couple.

It is in its creative power, however, that the human body is most strikingly transformed. While the genitally organized natural body creates life in the form of reproduction, the children of the Edenic commingling are the visionary forms that thunder from the tongue. The implication is that the process of reproduction now ceases; like Godwin, Blake imagines an end to the births of Ulro and the cycle of the generations. The creativities of art and nature are reintegrated as the Loom is returned from Enitharmon to Luvah, and man emanates the entire world in which he lives, including, as the passage above shows, his own sexual garments. Such an increase in creativity depends upon a reorganization of the relationship between art and sexuality. The dictum in *The Marriage* that all forms of energy are from the body is relevant at this point, as is the strange Memorable Fancy in which Blake describes the printing house of Hell:

> I was in a Printing house in Hell & saw the method in which knowledge is transmitted from generation to generation.
>
> In the first chamber was a Dragon-Man, clearing away the rubbish from a caves mouth; within, a number of Dragons were hollowing the cave,
>
> In the second chamber was a Viper folding round the rock & the cave, and others adorning it with gold silver and precious stones.
>
> In the third chamber was an Eagle with wings and feathers of air, he caused the inside of the cave to be infinite, around were numbers of Eagle like men, who built palaces in the immense cliffs.
>
> In the fourth chamber were Lions of flaming fire raging around & melting the metals into living fluids.
>
> In the fifth chamber were Unnam'd forms, which cast the metals into the expanse.
>
> There they were receiv'd by Men who occupied the sixth chamber, and took the forms of books & were arranged in libraries.
>
> (15, E39)

The process begins with the sexual widening of the doors of perception by the monsters of energy, who renew the senses by sweeping them clean of habitual and institutionalized restrictions. At this excess, the Viper attempts to bind the sexual body, to keep it within the natural context and, by producing all the allurements of a natural existence, to celebrate the sufficiency of sex as an end in itself. In opposition, the Eagle of imagination, the "portion of Genius" of the "Proverbs of Hell," rises from the feeling of freedom and unrestricted possibility that results from the cleansing in the first chamber. Next, the Lions of prophetic wrath, in accord with the teachings of Ezekiel in the earlier banquet scene, resist present ease and gratification and melt down the non-human beauties of nature into the primal substance of a new being. The formless fluids are committed to a chamber of the new and the unknown, whose workers, themselves nameless, or unformed, cast them into the human world, where, received by men, as the Prolific imagination by the Devouring rational consciousness, they appear as books.

In this account the artistic process begins with an upsurge of sexual fulfillment and culminates, by means of an enlarged awareness of bodily pleasure, in a poem. The process can be read, loosely, as analogous to the making of Eden, in which the responsibility of man for his life as a kind of poetic work and the final products are no longer books but realized human lives. In Blake sexual desire is ultimately a desire for a non-natural paradise; and through the artistic work of Los, who combines the functions of Eagle, Lion, and Unnamed Form, the progression from Generation to Upper Beulah to Eden is gradually accomplished. What the progression depends upon is a rise from genitality, which cannot be called a sublimation because it is a rise from genital satisfaction and even seems to be inspired by it. Lawrence, I think, is particularly close to Blake when he describes in *Fantasia of the Unconscious* a sense of renewal following the individual "commingling of sex," a new energy and enthusiasm that stimulates us to "the great purpose of manhood, a passionate unison in actively making a world. This is a real commingling of many." We should bear in mind, however, that the naturalistic Lawrence would probably have approved of Blake's description of Edenic sexuality not as a literal potentiality of the senses but as an allegory of collective work, thereby reducing the new heaven and earth of *Jerusalem* to the redeemed nature of *Milton*.

It seems that the total human activity in any State of Being is simultaneously a sexual and a creative activity; the themes of sensory improvement, production and reproduction, and the relationship of male and female always refer to both. The distinction between art and sexuality is maintained, however, until the final transformation, when both, as we know them, drop out; in their place is the commingling of the risen body, an interplay of faculties with each other and with the total environment they delineate, in which imagination and sexual love reassume their identity, just as soul and body or perception and creation. Then the word "body" once again signifies the "real man" and the "whole man," as well as "all men"; and the fiery lineaments of a finally gratified desire are perceived in the tactility of a complete human speech.

THOMAS WEISKEL

Blake's Critique of Transcendence

In "Circles," Emerson speaks of man's "continual effort to raise himself above himself, to work a pitch above his last height," and finds his image for such ceaseless sublimating in the "generation of circles, wheel without wheel." The soul moves outward, bursting over each concentric orbit of limitation. But since the soul's self-transcendence is without term, the generation of circles itself succumbs to the circularity of succession: this is "the circular or compensatory character of every human action . . . the moral fact of the Unattainable . . . at once the inspirer and the condemner of every success." It is true that in "Compensation," Emerson excepts the soul—unjustifiably, it seems to me—from the universal "tax" or "penalty" of compensation. But the debt returns to be partially paid in "Circles," in the relativity of ceaseless supersession, if not in the proportional contraction of perception that we have argued. Because time will not relent, the ultimate form of activity in the egotistical sublime is circular. The negative sublime, on the contrary, suggests an infinite parallelism in which the perception of an object *as* sublime is a kind of parallax.

Readers of Blake will be tempted to recognize in Emerson's "generation of circles, wheel without wheel" and also in Stevens's "the going round / And round and round, the merely going round" Blake's central imagery of fallen limitation, the circle of destiny or the mills of Satan. Emerson propounds an exuberance without a determinate object, so that the prolific soul of "Circles" seems more solipsistic than creative, and it is always subject to time. And repetition, however large the scope of its acts, is tantamount to disaster for Blake. "The same dull round even of a univer[s]e would soon become a mill with complicated wheels" (E, 2). Blake's central conviction, dramatized in the career of his character Urizen, is that solipsism and the rational alienation of perception into mechanical regularity both result from the same imaginative disease. Blake is equally acute in diagnosing the negative sublime, of which Urizen is also in some respects the type. Both versions of transcendence are reduced, in Blake's radical therapy of culture, to one malaise of perception. Blake learned from Milton, if not from life, that the Fall is immensely and necessarily overdetermined and that any definitive explanation is likely to turn into justification. What looks like indecision in the matter of a cause of the Fall is really the result of a technique in which distinct but correlative motives are superimposed. And about the results of the Fall Blake is definitive, though very complicated; best of all, he offers all the advantages of a perspective truly outside the Romantic sublime.

And some disadvantages as well. Blake is not, with all the distinguished scholarship, getting any easier to read. I used to think he was: with a little diligence the system could be mastered; the difficulty seemed conceptual, the very thing to engage the energetic compulsions of an ever-intellectualizing critic like the author of this book. But then I found myself at crucial points left outside the charmed circularity of Blakean hermeneutics, even playing with the vulgarity, Will the real Blake please appear? It would be ungenerous to cavil at the commentary, which nevertheless now illuminates and surrounds Blake like a hovering cherub. Blake has a way of turning his critics into apologists, and we still await the study at once fully informed, (a major project now), free from prejudice, *and* written from the proper distance. But it is not in the conditions of Blake's recent and spectacular academic success that the difficulty lies. The question is how to read Blake exoterically. He was certainly an ironic poet, rarely to be caught speaking in his own person; so there is an essential problem of tone which cannot be resolved by the application of a schematic calculus, however authentic. The emotions of his text look simple enough: pity, fear, grief, rage, jealousy, pain, joy—elemental stuff. But their permutations seem to make sense only conceptually. More rarely in Blake than in any other major poet does one have the sense that one has been there, at just that point of feeling. Or have we read him wrongly?

Consider the Zoas. One doesn't get far thinking of them exclusively as faculties or psychic agencies correlative to some other system such as Freud's. Each of the Zoas is a character in the specific sense that

each is endowed with consciousness, whereas in Freud's system consciousness is ascribed only to a portion of the ego. The Zoas are states of mind
and feeling as well as figures in a design. It is true that behind what seems
to be an arbitrary turn in the careers of the Zoas, we nearly always find an
analytic insight and not a realized moment of consciousness. But perhaps a
subtler ear could discern the experiential correlative of the insight. We
ought in any case to dispense with all the talk of "on one level" or the
other; it's a tired metaphor that now stands in the way. I think the next
great leap in the reading of Blake will come when we devise an interpretative language for the obscure contiguities of schematization and consciousness. At what point does a schema begin to be "lived"? Conversely, where
does experience schematize itself or merge into the design it unconsciously
plays out? This, in a sense, is our problem with Kant, whose concepts we
are beginning to personify in the hope of finding a deeper structure
beneath the subreptions of his logic.

     After all this beating of the drum my reader will rightly hope for
more than the confrontation of Blake and Kant which is our current
agenda. Unfortunately, an authentic sounding of Blake lies outside the
scope of this book, if not indeed of its author, for our subject is the
Romantic poetics of sublimation, which Blake, quite literally, as the story
goes, could not stomach. Yet I shall attempt to uncover something of
Urizen's felt predicament in the moment of his fall, for it seems to me a
version of the sublime moment. To the contemporary method of reading
Blake entirely in his own terms I can only oppose a somewhat tendentious
effort to think through, by way of Kant, the experience of self-consciousness
which attends reason in the crisis of the sublime. A strong case can easily
be made for Blake's enmity to the Romantic sublime on the "level" of art
theory, and although this is not how we would engage Blake, his opinions
as an aesthetician are worth a passing look as an introduction to his
powerful concern with perception. Blake's views on the sublime as an
aesthetic category are perfectly clear in his annotations to Reynolds's
Discourses. He found Reynolds's work to be grounded on Burke's treatise
on the sublime and the beautiful, which in turn was founded on the
opinions of Newton and Locke, with whom Blake always associated
Bacon. Reading all these men, he felt "Contempt and Abhorrence," for
"They mock Inspiration & Vision" (E, 650). Blake uses the word sublime
as a general honorific and obviously had no use for the distinction,
fashionable after Burke (1757), between the sublime and the beautiful.
His sublime is not the Romantic sublime. What piqued him most in
Reynolds was praise of general conceptions and disdain of minuteness.
And Burke's recommendation of obscurity seemed to him disastrous.

Minute Discrimination is Not Accidental All Sublimity is
founded on Minute Discrimination

A Facility in Composing is the Greatest Power of Art & Belongs
to None but the Greatest Artists, i.e. the Most Minutely
Discriminating and Determinate

The Man who asserts that there is no Such Thing as Softness in
Art & that every thing in Art is Definite & Determinate has not
been told this by Practise but by Inspiration & Vision because
Vision is Determinate & Perfect & he Copies That without Fatigue
Every thing being Definite & determinate Softness is Produced
Alone by Comparative Strength & Weakness in the Marking out of the
Forms

Without Minute Neatness of Execution. The. Sublime cannot Exist!
Grandeur of Ideas is founded on Precision of Ideas.

Singular & Particular Details is the Foundation of the Sublime

Distinct General Form Cannot Exist Distinctness is Particular
Not General

Broken Colours & Broken Lines & Broken Masses are Equally
Subversive of the Sublime

Obscurity is Neither the Source of the Sublime nor of any
Thing Else

(E, 632–47)

As an annotator, Blake is delightfully sure of himself and gives no
quarter. What seems perverse is his insistence that only when vision is
determinate, minute, and particular does it conduct to or contain infinity.
The eye which would "see a World in a Grain of Sand" (E, 481), must be
a "Determinate Organ" (E, 627). Infinite perception must be distinguished
from the perception of the "indefinite," which is Blake's version of
mental hell. Blake is not merely wittily inverting the terms of contemporary
aesthetic discourse. "It is not in Terms that Reynolds & I disagree. Two
Contrary Opinions can never by any Language be made alike" (E, 648).
Nor is he, with Kant and the philosophers, worrying the phenomenological ambiguity of infinity. He conceived perception to be the fundamental
index of consciousness, subsuming the primary and secondary degrees as
formulated by Coleridge. It is an activity of which both object and image
are merely phases or products. We have seen how the Wordsworthian
"fade-out" signals a sublimation in which the formal properties of what is
seen are dissolved and the residual otherness of the thing is alienated as
indefinite substance. Here, for Blake, is the very crisis of man's Fall. In his
view, the positive and negative sublimes turn out to be not genuine contraries but two versions of the same lapse, itself the negation of visionary
perception. Blake's myth of the Fall is an analytic critique of sublimation.

THE PSYCHOPOLITICS OF REASON

What then can Blake tell us about the anxiety we suppose to be at work behind sublimation? We recall the defeat of the sensible imagination or phenomenal intellect in Kant's theory of the sublime. The nearest analogue in Blake to the "understanding" of the philosophers is Urizen, whose fall in Night III of Blake's manuscript epic *The Four Zoas* is suggestively parallel to the mind's self-alienation in Kant. Here first is Kant, at his most psychological, describing the crucial moment; the delight in the sublime is *negative*:

> that is to say it is a feeling of imagination by its own act depriving itself of its freedom by receiving a final determination in accordance with a law other than that of its empirical employment. In this way it gains an extension and a power greater than that which it sacrifices. But the ground of this is concealed from it, and in its place it *feels* the sacrifice or deprivation, as well as its cause, to which it is subjected.

The imagination is evidently in an ambivalent position. It deprives itself "by its own act," and yet it passively receives its orders for this self-deprivation from the law of reason. As a proponent of sublimation, Kant would have it that the gain is greater than the sacrifice, but this is certainly not how it feels from the imagination's point of view. The imagination is here the victim of superior forces, and its self-mutilation can be explained only by the "cause"—fear. The text goes on to assert that

> the *astonishment* which borders on terror, the awe and thrill of devout feeling, that takes hold of one . . . is not actual fear, but rather only an attempt to enter into it [fear] with the imagination, in order to feel the power of this faculty in combining the movement of the mind thereby aroused with its serenity, and of thus being superior to the nature within us, and therefore also to external nature, so far as the latter can have any influence upon our feeling of well-being.

(Pp. 120–21; 5, 269)

The passage is not perspicuous; Kant's personification gets cloudy. It seems the imagination is exposed to fear in order to arouse its power, but this fear is at the same time sublimated or internalized in the wider consciousness of the mind as a whole. Thus, in its converted, ego-form, the power is lost to the imagination (hence the feeling of sacrifice and deprivation), but further, it is directed back against the imagination (the "nature within us") as a superior force. Kant's sublime celebrates the ingenious capacity of the ego to live off the energy and labor of another, who is kept ignorant of what is going on. The imagination can share in the power only by identifying with its superior and hence depriving itself by its own act.

I have gradually modulated into a Blakean politics of the psyche by intensifying Kant's hints of personification. Blake takes his psychopolitical schemata much further into a properly mythopoeic dimension, a fact which may signal the presence of conceptual antinomies which the myth expresses without resolving. The Zoas fall into an obsession with power and face each other in a shifting series of master-slave confrontations. Urizen falls spectacularly when he rejects his emanation Ahania in a fit of what is now called male chauvinism. Schematically, the original condition of Ahania might be said to represent the unselfconscious unity of mind and object which attends creative intellectual work and that is the pleasure without which nothing of real value ever gets articulated. Ahania's own fall directly precedes and precipitates Urizen's and may be understood in a preliminary way as the well-known decline of such work into an alienating activity, so that its results confront the mind as an estranged reality over which the mind has no control and to which it must submit in a constant and fruitless sacrifice of mental energy. (Blake's doctrine of the emanation may be interpreted—apart from its esoteric provenance—in the analogous terms of the early, humanist Marx; indeed, the alienation of labor is a conspicuous theme in Romantic writers and is prominent in Schiller, Shelley, and of course Hegel.) As the third night of the *Four Zoas* opens, Ahania attempts to rescue her lord from the catastrophe engulfing his colleagues. She pleads with him to "Resume [his] fields of Light," apparently hoping, though she fears the worst, that the mind can retain its playful, creative powers in a world devoted to rack. Her plea is eloquent and far-sighted, but Urizen fails to understand and responds defensively:

> She ended. [From] his wrathful throne burst forth the black hail storm
>
> Am I not God said Urizen. Who is Equal to me
> Do I not stretch the heavens abroad or fold them up like a garment
>
> He spoke mustering his heavy clouds around him black opake
>
> Then thunders rolld around & lightnings darted to & fro
> His visage changed to darkness & his strong right hand came forth
> To cast Ahania to the Earth he seizd her by the hair
> And threw her from the steps of ice that froze around his throne
>
> Saying Art thou also become like Vala. thus I cast thee out
> Shall the feminine indolent bliss. the indulgent self of weariness
> The passive idle sleep the enormous night & darkness of Death

Set herself up to give her laws to the active masculine virtue
Thou little diminutive portion that darst be a counterpart
Thy passivity thy laws of obedience & insincerity
Are my abhorrence. Wherefore hast thou taken that fair form
Whence is this power given to thee! once thou wast in my breast
A sluggish current of dim waters. on whose verdant margin
A cavern shaggd with horrid shades. dark and cool & deadly. where
I laid my head in the hot noon after the broken clods
Had wearied me. there I laid my plow & there my horses fed
And thou hast risen with thy moist locks into a watry image
Reflecting all my indolence my weakness & my death
To weigh me down beneath the grave into non Entity
Where Luvah strives scorned by Vala age after age wandering
Shrinking & shrinking from her Lord & calling him the Tempter
And art thou also become like Vala thus I cast thee out.

                                                (42:18–43:22; E, 322)

Urizen's error is complex, as his defensive incoherence attests. He associates Ahania with weakness, but this is pure projection, an unconscious attempt to externalize and thereby to expel his own mental trouble. For it is Ahania who has called him to activity and lamented his paralysis. By gazing on futurity, in which he descries the dread Orc, Urizen has already lost the capacity for "present joy" (37:10); hence his very recollection of former pleasure is poisoned into a memory of "A cavern shaggd with horrid shades, dark and cool & deadly." Thinking is no longer even conceivably fun, for the pleasures of determinate intellect fall to the status of a "nature within us," which is erroneously identified with external nature, or Vala. Under the pressure of immense and unfamiliar anxiety, which springs from a fear of the future, the intellect is trying to concentrate—by concentrating itself. But this effort, heroic and pathetic at once, is doomed because Ahania is the source of all intellectual energy which does not emanate from anxiety. "Whence is this power given to thee!" asks the exasperated Urizen, as if he sensed that the very power he needs is being cut off by this self-mutilation. In this drastic sublimation, the determinate intellect or understanding aspires to superiority by alienating the "objective" imagining on which it is based. After this, the "King of Light" falls "down rushing, ruining, thundering, shuddering" into the state of generation. Blake locates ruin in precisely the same mental event that Kant would celebrate.

Blake's analytic of sublimation is shrewd enough to wrinkle the brow of any self-conscious literary intellectual. We stand to be valuably instructed, if not converted, by his spiritual economics, which are as severe as Freud's and yet argue for a vigorous mental activity not based on the paradox of reductive sublimation—the ceaseless contraction of "lower" into "higher" forms. On the whole, American intellectual culture is devoted to the ideology of the active ego, which can, so marvellously it seems, convert experience into the capital of power. In this context, Blake still has an antinomian aura, especially for those who take his rhetoric for his logic. There are many accounts of the Fall in Blake, and several critiques of sublimation in its sexual, political, and properly artistic guises. Each Fall involves a lapse, a failure or weakness like Urizen's weariness, and also an unjustified usurpation, an arrogation of exclusive power to one agency or faculty. Weakness releases the stuff of perception into an indeterminate otherness (as a refractory emanation) which is thus open for possession by another, and mental activity descends into a violent struggle for power jealously guarded and exercised. Blake fits the traditional and Miltonic theme of prideful usurpation into a psychological calculus of gain and loss, a law of compensation that runs through Generation. When any part of us is less creative than it could be, it immediately attempts to be more than it should, thereby becoming less than it was.

Consequently, we find the same ambiguity of cause in Blake's critique of the sublime that we found in Kant's analytic. There are several phases to Urizen's presumption, which is in each case proportionate to Albion's mental weariness. In Night I, Albion proposes to abandon the proper realm of thought (the South) to Luvah and announces his intention to invade the North, the domain of Urthona ("Earth-owner"), presumably in order to achieve an ownership to which he is originally not entitled; when Luvah objects, he departs secretly into the North anyway (21:16–35; 22:1–10; 32–37). The conflict between Urizen and Luvah is the immediate cause of Urthona's fall (22:16–31). Urizen aspires to the total possession or comprehension of the earth in the logical categories of the understanding—even at the cost of surrendering perceptional clarity to the passions. So, in Kant, the understanding and its correlative, the sensible imagination, attempt to comprehend in *one* intuition a multitude of discrete intuitions, even at the risk of an overextension of faculties and a consequent frustration, a feeling of sacrifice and deprivation. Kant's *Vernunft* ("higher reason") is a rich repository of indefinables, as its transmogrifications in subsequent idealism attest. To some extent it suggests both Urthona and the unfallen Tharmas, a principle of integration, but since it is conceived almost exclusively in negative terms, it is primarily what Blake logically calls a "Negation" or Spectre, a "Holy Reasoning Power" that "Negatives every thing" (E, 151). In Kant, as in Blake, Reason is obsessed with superiority and holiness, and demands awe.

In the moment of his fall, Urizen is turning into the Spectre as he "negatives" Ahania into Vala and abstracts himself from her. Ahania's attempt to forestall their mutual ruin is doomed not only by Urizen's defensiveness but also by her own naiveté, which must be explicated briefly if we wish to understand the negative sublime as a moment of feeling. Ahania presents a version of Albion's fall as a warning to Urizen, but she fails to see—in one of Blake's masterly ironies—how Urizen is already implicated in that fall.

> Then O my dear lord listen to Ahania, listen to the vision
> The vision of Ahania in the slumbers of Urizen
> When Urizen slept in the porch & the Ancient Man was smitten
>
> The Darkning Man walkd on the steps of fire before his halls
> And Vala walked with him in dreams of soft deluding slumber
> He looked up & saw thee Prince of Light thy splendor faded
> [*But saw not Los nor Enitharmon for Luvah hid them in shadow*]
>
> [*In a soft cloud Outstretch'd across, & Luvah dwelt in the cloud*]
>
> Then Man ascended mourning into the splendors of his palace
> Above him rose a Shadow from his wearied intellect
> Of living gold, pure, perfect, holy; in white linen pure he hover'd
> A sweet entrancing self delusion, a watry vision of Man
> Soft exulting in existence all the Man absorbing
> Man fell upon his face prostrate before the watry shadow
> Saying O Lord whence is this change thou knowest I am nothing
> And Vala trembled & covered her face, & her locks were spread on the
>   pavement
>
> I heard astonishd at the Vision & my heart trembled within me
> I heard the voice of the Slumberous Man & thus he spoke
> Idolatrous to his own Shadow words of Eternity uttering
> O I am nothing when I enter into judgment with thee
> If thou withdraw thy breath I die & vanish into Hades
> If thou dost lay thine hand upon me behold I am silent
> If thou withhold thine hand I perish like a fallen leaf
> O I am nothing & to nothing must return again
> If thou withdraw thy breath, behold I am oblivion
>
> He ceasd: the shadowy voice was silent; but the cloud hovered over their
>   heads
>   (39:12–40;19; E, 320–21)

The uncorrupted Urizen may be dozing, but his Spectre is very much at work in this shadow in which the living gold of his unfallen form is draped in spectrous white. Just as in Kantian or "negative" thinking, from the defeated, "wearied intellect" rises a perfect, holy image of ultimacy, a "watry vision" without determinate outline—for, says Kant, the "inscrutability" of Reason's ideas "precludes all positive presentation." The Slumberous Man is made to echo the self-abnegating Psalm 143—"And enter not into judgment with thy servant; for in thy sight shall no man living be justified"—and also Psalm 104:

> thou openest thine hand, they are filled with good.
> thou hidest thy face, they are troubled:
> thou takest away their breath, they die
> and return to their dust.
>
> (Vs. 28–29)

These very verses are quoted by Hegel as the consummate example of the negative sublime.

Ahania hopes that Urizen will reject the idolatry perpetrated while he "slept in the porch," but unknowingly she has exposed his project. (All of her vision may of course be understood as Urizen's moment of self-recognition, but so deeply is the original Urizen split that this further reduction has only theoretical significance at this point.) Urizen is dismayed at Ahania's vision (41:5–9,18; 42:7–8), not because it recapitulates the fall, but because it reveals a countermyth to his own version of the fall—a myth which highlights his own role with an ingenuous clarity the more dangerous for being unconscious. In Urizen's view, Man fell because he became intellectually lazy and his "active masculine virtue" succumbed to Vala, "the feminine indolent bliss. The indulgent self of weariness"—what he hopes to avoid by casting out Ahania. Pleasure undermined self-discipline; in short, Man failed to sublimate. But Ahania's account of the fall suggests that sublimation is itself a creation of intellectual weariness (40:3), which in turn results from Man's commerce with Vala "in dreams of soft deluding slumber." From this point of view, Urizen's myth of the fall is totally incoherent because it proposes as a saving alternative the very sublimation which is the idolatrous result of mental failure.

Blake's irony is such that neither Urizen nor Ahania understands fully what is happening to the "Darkning Man." Ahania hopes naively that the intellect has retained its freedom and is not yet compromised in Man's fall; Urizen, however, refuses to see the fall for what it is and rejects its clear consequence even as he fails to take responsibility for his own role. His actions are secretive; they are concealed from the Darkning Man in just the way that the operations of the Kantian reason were hidden from the understanding. As Ahania's tale of the fall continues, the ironies, dramatic and allusive, rapidly thicken. Down from the shadowy cloud drops—unexpectedly—Luvah:

And Lo that Son of Man, that shadowy Spirit of the Fallen One
Luvah, descended from the cloud; In terror Albion rose
Indignant rose the Awful Man & turnd his back on Vala

And Luvah strove to gain dominion over the mighty Albion
They strove together above the Body where Vala was inclos'd
And the dark Body of Albion left prostrate upon the crystal pavement
Coverd with boils from head to foot. the terrible smitings of Luvah

Then frownd the Fallen Man & put forth Luvah from his presence
(I heard him: frown not Urizen: but listen to my Vision)

Saying, Go & die the Death of Man for Vala the sweet wanderer
I will turn the volutions of your Ears outward; & bend your Nostrils
Downward; & your fluxile Eyes englob'd, roll round in fear
Your withring Lips & Tongue shrink up into a narrow circle
Till into narrow forms you creep. Go take your fiery way
And learn what 'tis to absorb the Man you Spirits of Pity & Love

O Urizen why art thou pale at the visions of Ahania
Listen to her who loves thee lest we also are driven away.
                                        (41:2–4; 41:13–42:8; E, 321)

The allusion to Job identifies Luvah with Satan; as Satan is
licensed by God to try Job, so Urizen is ultimately responsible for Luvah's
descent, which fills Albion with terror—and then, significantly, with
indignation. In Job's case, the boils come "from the sole of his foot to the
crown of his head": Blake's reversed "from head to foot" nicely indicates
the Urizenic nature of the affliction. The boils, traditionally signs of
venereal disease, are identified in *Jerusalem* (21:3–5) as the "disease of
Shame," which also covers from head to foot; Blake's illustration of the
text in the Job series (VI) shows Satan pouring his vial on Job's head, while
Job's wife has custody of his feet and is ignored. Actually, we are informed
by the excised lines ("*& Luvah dwelt in the cloud*") that the "watry vision
of Man" which Albion worships is from the start a compound of Urizen
and Luvah; its full explication, which is unnecessary here, would lead us
to the heart of Blake's brilliant reading of Job—the claim that the
demonic Satan and the jejune God of that text are both aspects of Job's
erroneous theological imagination.

What Ahania's vision reveals is that the perceptional error of the
Fallen Man is also a sexual crisis. This is a fundamental insight into the
psychology of the negative sublime. The Fallen Man responds to sexual
guilt by expelling his passional life into a grotesque naturalization. It now
becomes possible to state the entire sequence of the fall, even at the risk
of some reduction. The Darkning Man first conceives a slumberous passion for Vala; so the subject of the sublime is caught up by an appearance

or prospect "out there" to such an extent that his faculties cease to function energetically and soon feel dwarfed and humiliated. From his "wearied intellect" rises an indeterminate image of perfection or totality; it is a negative projection, but since its origins are concealed from the imagination, the man worships it in self-abnegating awe. At this point Kant's account left unexplained the way in which consciousness rather suddenly ceased to inhabit the plight of the imagination and identified instead with the idea of totality, thereby recovering its self-respect by alienating the "nature within us." In Blake's vision this recovery has the look of an oedipal crisis "successfully" resolved—the very type of sublimation.

Luvah's presence in the cloud is not merely a function of wearied intellect but is also a fantasy which compensates for the passional frustration—the sacrifice and deprivation—which Man feels: it is an image of power. This power is, however, under Urizenic aegis, and it is now directed *against* Man; we remember how in Kant the reason used fear to induce awe for itself. In psychological terms, the passional force is introjected and felt first as fear and then as sexual guilt. "In terror Albion rose / Indignant rose the Awful Man & turned his back on Vala." Albion's struggle with Luvah is not a competition for Vala but Man's attempt to suppress the passion he feels as shame. Ironically, Albion's inability to suppress shame leads him to expel desire itself (Luvah) and its object (Vala)—so that he may be "superior to the nature within . . . and therefore also to external nature." It is clear that this latter feat on Man's part is not quite what Urizen had in mind, for he is disturbed to hear it told: "Then frownd the Fallen Man & put forth Luvah from his presence / (I heard him: frown not Urizen: but listen to my Vision)."

The reader may share Urizen's perplexity over what looks like Albion's sudden reassertion of control over Luvah, but the sequence is psychologically true. In his indignation and struggle against the "Spirits of Pity & Love," Albion has in fact *over*identified with the holy specter he worshipped. Urizen is in the position of a father who, merely by trying to be perfect and godlike, has enforced a more drastic oedipal resolution upon his son than could have been anticipated—a common psychological pattern. Urizen wanted only to be worshipped by both Man and nature ("And Vala trembled & covered her face, & her locks were spread on the pavement"), and Luvah's mission (provocatively identified with the parousia in the epithet "Son of Man") was designed only to insure Albion's self-abrogation in nature. But because the power of the specter is derived as much from frustration as from a dream of totality, Albion's suppression of passion in effect accomplishes a negation more extreme than Urizen had realized was necessary. His response to Ahania, "Art thou also become like Vala. Thus I cast thee out," is in a sense an attempt to catch up with what Albion has already done. Ahania's vision reveals consequences to a Urizen who is still somewhat innocent—he hasn't yet wholly fallen, we remember.

Blake's analytic of sublimation is richly suggestive at a number of points. It helps us to fill in the affective mortar of Kant's structure and to account for some curious facts which emerge as we study speculations about the sublime. The peculiar combination of holy innocence and conspiratorial self-aggrandizement which may be detected in the career of Kant's reason is one such fact. The negative sublime begins with an excessive interest in nature and ends with an excessive disdain of nature, and again and again in reading the texts of the sublime—in Schiller, Schopenhauer, and even in the Wordsworth of *The Borderers*—we feel that this movement is compulsive. Reason and its cognates begin as a negative or dialectical alternative to human limitation, but such quasitheological prestige begins to accumulate around the ideas of reason that in the end reason requires a total withdrawal from all natural connection. We shall later meet the pattern of oedipal overidentification as an element in the "daemonic" sublime. The immediate value of Blake's text is that it plays out a logic implicit in discursive theories of the sublime. We can read the affective logic of the sublime partly in Albion's fall and partly in Urizen's complicated state of self-knowledge.

The ultimate protagonist of the sublime in its third phase—the moment of self-recognition—speaks an extraordinary speech, a compound of anxiety and vaunting pride:

> Am I not God said Urizen. Who is Equal to me
> Do I not stretch the heavens abroad or fold them up like a garment
> He spoke mustering his heavy clouds around him black opake
>
> (42:19–21)

We are taken again to Hegel's chief instance of the negative sublime, Psalm 104, where the Lord is addressed as He "who coverest [Himself] with light as with a garment; who stretchest out the heavens like a curtain" (vs. 2). Urizen's role model is Jehovah himself, and the irony of the "heavy clouds . . . black opake" obviously cuts both ways. Urizen is also answering Luvah, who in the first Night had declined conspiracy with the bold claim: "Dictate to thy Equals, am not I / The Prince of all the hosts of Men nor Equal know in Heaven" (1.22:1–2; E, 307). But Luvah is no longer a threat—Albion has done Urizen's work for him—and Urizen has not yet focused his rage on Ahania. The ultimate object of his threatening rhetorical question is Albion. For Albion's drastic sublimation (a disaster from Blake's point of view), like Job's stubborn victory over Satan, in effect appears to accuse Urizen of being a soft god. Albion can turn against the nature within and without with a force that endangers the hegemony of Urizen, who still inhabits Beulah. Awe and terror, it seems, are not enough—because man can master his passions through indignant suppression. Kant in fact speaks directly to this situation. The mind which recognizes its own sublimity will not prostrate itself timorously before the Godhead; it will identify with that Godhead.

For Urizen this means that his original project—exploiting Man's passive turning outward to nature so that it yields a "watry vision of perfection"—is naive and is endangered by Man's withdrawal from any engagement with nature. The mind convinced of its own sublimity cannot in fact experience the awful or sublime moment, which is a discovery, a movement between two states: the overcoming of sense is necessarily predicated upon an engagement with the sensible. Unlike the positive sublime, whose ultimate form is repetitive and circular, the negative sub-lime theoretically aims toward a unique disillusionment—the unmasking of the "subreption" by which an object seems sublime. Ahania's narrative exhibits in the form of myth the tendency of the positive sublime to yield to the polarizing pressure that results in the negative sublime. Albion, of course, is not a real threat; he doesn't have the respect for himself that Urizen supposes; nothing suggests that he knows that "sweet entrancing self delusion, a watry vision of Man" is in fact "his own shadow." Albion is already worshipping Jehovah before Urizen has quite grown into his role. Albion lacks the self-consciousness of a potential protagonist of the sub-lime. This situation parallels the way reason operated on two levels of consciousness in Kant, the concealment which enables reason to discover its own power in an attitude of awe.

From an affective point of view, the salient feature of Ahania's vision is the coincidence it establishes between the obscuring of the Darkning Man's perception and the suppression of his desire. Blake's text enables us to confront a question that our own discussion has pretty much begged: are the two kinds of sublimation, perceptional and passional, really one, as we have implicitly claimed? Man's idolatrous awe changes to terror with the appearance of Luvah, "that Son of Man," whose arrival suggests (in addition to the oedipal introjection we have remarked) the realization of the judgment Man feared ("O I am nothing when I enter into judgment with thee"). Terror, we may surmise, is consistent with the Spectre's design, insofar as he is a separate will. (The subsequent indigna-tion is Man's own contribution, a further fall into self-righteousness.) Urizen is not yet Jehovah until Man in effect makes him so. In Blake's technical terms, the Spectre represents a Pahad phase of God—the fifth "eye" which immediately precedes Jehovah. *Pahad* is translated "fear" or "terror" in the King James Version. He is invoked by Eliphaz, one of Job's comforters, in a passage cited by Burke as proof of his contention that obscurity is a cause of the sublime:

> But let it be considered that hardly any thing can strike the mind with its greatness, which does not make some sort of approach towards infinity; which nothing can do whilst we are able to perceive its bounds, but to see an object distinctly, and to perceive its bounds, is one and the same thing. A clear idea is therefore another name for a little idea. There is a passage in the book of Job amazingly sublime, and this sublimity is principally due to the terrible uncertainty of the thing described. *In thoughts from the visions of the night, when deep sleep falleth upon men, fear came upon me and trembling, which made all my bones to shake. Then a spirit passed before my face. The hair of my flesh stood up. It stood still,* but I could not discern the form thereof; *an image was before mine eyes; there was silence; and I heard a voice—Shall mortal man be more just than God?* We are first prepared with the utmost solemnity for the vision; we are first terrified, before we are let even into the obscure cause of our emotion; but when this grand cause of terror makes its appearance, what is it? is it not, wrapt up in the shades of its own incomprehensible darkness, more aweful, more striking, more terrible, than the liveliest description, than the clearest painting could possibly represent it?

We have already met Burke's argument in its sophisticated Kantian form. What is indistinct is phenomenologically in-finite, and this leads to a hypostasized infinitude. Burke is not aware, although it would rescue his argument from a dubious premise of causality, that the "fear and trembling" is itself the indistinct spirit, i.e., Pahad. Blake's illustration of the text in the *Job* series (IX) shows Pahad with his arms bound and concealed, which suggests most simply that he is powerless to judge right from left, right from wrong. Job is looking upward calmly at the nightmare invoked by Eliphaz, who is not looking at (i.e., reseeing) his own vision; the other comforters are frightened. In the margins are the forests of night (error) and the verses: "Shall mortal Man be more just than God? Shall a Man be more Pure than his Maker?" The irony is clear: Eliphaz's rhetorical questions, intended to frighten Job, have become for Job genuine questions. If this is God, then mortal man may well be more just and pure. Job's own error is a self-righteousness based on fallen categories. His state is closely analogous to what Urizen fears to be the case with Albion, who, as we have seen, is identified with Job in the third Night. Urizen is threatened to observe in Albion's expulsion of Luvah and Vala a man more just than God, purer than his Maker. Luvah-Satan having failed (ironically by conquest) to execute Urizen's naive design, Urizen must, like the God of *Job*, thunder his own anxiously rhetorical questions: "Am I not God . . . Who is Equal to me."

The point to be grasped in this confluence of texts is that the obscure image is terrible only to him who is conscious of guilt. It is a feeling of guilt that Eliphaz wishes in vain to force upon Job. Albion is already guilty with Vala, and the indistinct image of perfection arises to punish him. He feels this guilt, succumbs to a conviction of its justice, but then is able to suppress it by removing all desire (Luvah) and all occasion for desire (Vala). Like Kant's reason in its ultimate phase of self-congratulation, Albion is no longer exposed to terror. But the cost is great, for this sublimation dooms, among other things, natural religion and any connection to nature. The Kantian therapy is a drastic one; it logically ends in mental suicide. Behind the phenomenology of the sublime moment we begin to descry an immense and fascinating psychodrama, which now invites our attendance.

SUSAN FOX

"Milton": Beulah

The Bard's Song has four distinct parts, a myth of creation, an account of a pivotal action, a judgment on that action, and an act of contrition for it. The first section of Book II is also a prologue in four parts, each directly comparable to its counterpart in the Bard's Song. The first, 30:1–31:7, is a myth of creation; the second, 31:8–63, details the result of the action in the Bard's Song; the third, plate 32, is a judgment necessitated by that action; the fourth, plate 33, is a complicated act of contrition promoted by that judgment.

The first part of the Book II prologue begins with what is probably the most astonishing tonal shift anywhere in Blake's poetry. The warnings and contentions of Book I, with their ominous culminating passage on "the veil of human miseries," have yielded suddenly to a gentle satisfaction:

> There is a place where Contrarieties are equally True
> This place is called Beulah, It is a pleasant lovely Shadow
> Where no dispute can come. Because of those who Sleep.
>
> Beulah is evermore Created around Eternity; appearing
> To the Inhabitants of Eden, around them on all sides.
> But Beulah to its Inhabitants appears within each district
> As the beloved infant in his mothers bosom round incircled
> With arms of love & pity & sweet compassion. But to
> The Sons of Eden the moony habitations of Beulah,
> Are from Great Eternity a mild & pleasant Rest.
>
> (30:1–3, 8–14)

From *Poetic Form in Blake's Milton.* Copyright © 1976 by Princeton University Press.

From Golgonooza to Beulah, from time to the emanation of eternity, from a prophesied end to a remembered beginning: Blake's vision expands to comprehend a reality beyond that of vegetated life. He has reached, by passing inward to Golgonooza, not only vision, but the well-spring of vision. He can see now and describe the "Realms of terror & mild moony lustre" whose regents he invoked at the start of his poem as the "Muses who inspire the Poets Song." Thus Beulah becomes for him and for us, as well as for the eternals for whom it was created, a place of rest.

Although this description breaks drastically with the tone of what preceded it, it retains not only dramatic but also thematic continuity. That great world of Los with which Book I ends is a direct copy of this eternal world pictured now for the first time. The pattern for Golgonooza surrounded by Allamanda is Eden surrounded by Beulah, "Poetic Inspiration" (identified with Eden in 30:19) surrounded by its social source of nourishment and protection; both eternal and temporal complexes rest on Ulro. As Los modeled Urizen's fallen body after the anatomy of Albion's, so he modeled his temporal world after the geography of the eternal. By maintaining eternal forms in time, Los has kept open a potential communication between the realms. He has provided fallen reality with a pattern of eternity, a lifeless form that need only be invested with eternal vision to be revived.

How we see Beulah is a function of where we stand. From Generation it may seem "Realms of terror," for it is the source of inspiration, which is a fearful gift. From Eden it is the surrounding region, simply part of the landscape. But from inside its bounds it seems a compassionate maternal bosom, encompassing and sustaining. So every aspect of reality changes with our perspective on it, seeming, like the vortex that governs perspective, geometry or benevolent friend according to the way we choose to see it. Blake's vision now places him in Beulah, and his poetry will reflect the "love & pity & sweet compassion" of this idyllic realm.

As the first part of the Bard's Song chronicled the creation of Urizen's form and of Golgonooza, the first part of the prologue of Book II relates the creation of Beulah. The emanations, frightened by the mental strife of Eden, beg of Jesus "a Temporal Habitation" (30:29) where they may rest from it.

> So spake the lovely Emanations; & there appeared a pleasant
> Mild Shadow above: beneath: & on all sides round,
> Into this pleasant Shadow all the weak & weary
> Like Women & Children were taken away as on wings
> Of dovelike softness, & shadowy habitations prepared for them
> But every Man returnd & went still going forward thro'

> The Bosom of the Father in Eternity on Eternity
> Neither did any lack or fall into Error without
> A Shadow to repose in all the Days of happy Eternity. . . .
> (30:32–31:7)

The creation of Beulah is thus, like the creation of Golgonooza, an act of salvation, Los's of the fallen masculine forms and Jesus' of the failing feminine forms. The emanations have pled, "Give us a habitation & a place" (30:24), begging of Jesus the very act Los performs in building Golgonooza, in "Giving to airy nothing a name and a habitation" (28:3). The parallel offers a potential renovation of one of the grimmest images in the poem, the opaque shadow that is the consolidation of error: Los's city of art is the redemptive epitome of the shadowy Mundane Shell even as Beulah, which Blake four times in the quoted passage alone calls "shadow" or "shadowy," is a benevolent refuge for faltering beings. Los, and through him the Bard, Milton, and Blake, is identified in his act of creation with the ultimate Reprobate Redeemer, Jesus.

As Milton descended into his shadow, Ololon descends into "this pleasant Shadow Beulah," and the second part of the prologue begins. Part one defined the relationship of Beulah and Eden; part two defines that of Beulah and Generation:

> And the Shadows of Beulah terminate in rocky Albion.
>
> And all Nations wept in affliction Family by Family
> Germany wept towards France & Italy: England wept & trembled
> Towards America: India rose up from his golden bed:
> As one awakend in the night: they saw the Lord coming
> In the Clouds of Ololon with Power & Great Glory!
>
> And all the Living Creatures of the Four Elements, wail'd
> With bitter wailing . . .
> Orc howls on the Atlantic: Enitharmon trembles: All Beulah weeps. . . .
> (31:11–27)

Beulah weeps as Ololon weeps, and all Generation laments with them, for it is the time of weeping, the moment of the loosing of Orc. As the Bard prophesied, the Elect meet the Redeemed, Germany weeping toward the Latin lands, England toward America. The conflict that has tormented all levels of reality, setting Los against Urizen, Milton against Satan, has engulfed the lowest level of reality and become the final conflict, the battles of apocalypse.

All Beulah weeps, but to us in Generation the lamentation is a lyric promise of new birth; for those embroiled in corporeal miseries, even the anguish of a higher state must seem a respite and a joy. Instead of

explicitly defining this vital difference in perspective, as he did throughout Book I, Blake simply illustrates it here with a corresponding shift in
style. The description of vegetated war yields abruptly to a celebration of
natural peace (31:28–63). The progression forms an ironic counterpart to
the second part of the Bard's Song: in Book I this segment is one of
deliberate and disastrous action, of Satan's usurping the harrow and the
ensuing havoc; in the parallel section of Book II, all contention gives way
to a sublimely delicate pastoral hymn. Eden is a place of strife, Beulah of
gentle repose. Yet even in its repose Beulah prophesies the doom of time.
That sublime hymn is not a denial of the conflicts of nations and families,
but a consummation of them. This is the only way gentle Beulah can
describe apocalypse, but it does describe apocalypse.

In Book I Blake defined time and space in matching twenty-three-
line stanzas. In Book II he describes the heralds of the end of time and
space in matching eighteen-line stanzas. The interinvolvement of the
time and space stanzas is repeated in the second pair, which reflect and
complement each other and, not incidentally, amplify their Book I counterparts as well.

Time and space are cosmic artificialities. The harbingers of their
destruction are two humble natural beings, the lark and the wild thyme,
heralds of morning and of spring.

In Book I we learned that the Mundane Shell "finishes where the
lark mounts" (17:27); now the significance of that cryptic image begins to
come clear:

> Thou hearest the Nightingale begin the Song of Spring;
> The Lark sitting upon his earthly bed; just as the morn
> Appears; listens silent; then springing from the waving Corn-field! loud
> He leads the Choir of Day! trill, trill, trill, trill,
> Mounting upon the wings of light into the Great Expanse:
> Reecchoing against the lovely blue & shining heavenly Shell:
> His little throat labours with inspiration; every feather
> On throat & breast & wings vibrates with the effluence Divine
> All Nature listens silent to him & the awful Sun
> Stands still upon the Mountain looking on this little Bird
> With eyes of soft humility, & wonder love & awe.
> Then loud from their green covert all the Birds begin their Song
> The Thrush, the Linnet & the Goldfinch, Robin & the Wren
> Awake the Sun from his sweet reverie upon the Mountain:
> The Nightingale again assays his song, & thro the day,
> And thro the night warbles luxuriant; every Bird of Song
> Attending his loud harmony with admiration & love.
> This is a Vision of the lamentation of Beulah over Ololon!
>
> (31:28–45)

It is not only where the lark mounts that the Mundane Shell ends, but when he mounts: the instant of these lines is the apocalyptic instant of the entire poem, the instant in which the sun, stilled for the length of the moratorium day, is awakened by the chorus of inspiration, the instant when spring and fall are united (the nightingale begins the Song of Spring, but the lark in response arises from autumn's "waving Corn-field"), when the birds of night and day sing together. This is the instant when Ololon's lamentation was heard in Eden and "Providence began" (21:24), but now, instead of drowning her song, the clarions of day echo it throughout Generation.

The structure of the passage is, like the structure of the time passage, cyclical; it opens and closes with the song of the nightingale. Again, the structure is a perfect analogue of the meaning: the nightingale, having inspired the lark, falls silent, only to join finally the chorus all birds of song must join. So John Milton, to whom this passage is surely a tribute, wrote and died, only to be resurrected later in the song of Blake, the lark whose humbler voice he inspired. The unity of the songbirds is the unity of the prophetic poets in Book I, of the Bard and Milton and Blake and Los. Their singing together fulfills the prayer of Moses that is the motto of *Milton*: "Would to God that all the Lords people were prophets." The instant in which all men are prophets, in which all voices sing together, is the instant of apocalypse.

The circular rhetoric of the lark and time passages is a device Blake uses throughout the poem to emphasize key passages and to unify the often contradictory impulses that comprise the passages. Milton's first speech, beginning and ending "I go to Eternal Death," begins in hatred of satanic selfhood and ends by embracing that selfhood (14:14–32); Rintrah and Palamabron castigate Los for his pity at the beginning and end of their fearful speech (22:29–23:30), counseling wrath to avenge the destruction of the merciful; Blake himself will address Ololon in a brief speech beginning and ending with a plea for comfort for his emanation, but meanwhile concerned with his own affliction (36:27–31). The device of circularity is not new in *Milton*; Blake used it throughout his career, from "The Tyger" through the Argument to *The Marriage of Heaven and Hell* to the more diffuse version of it in the reflecting actions of Nights One and Nine in *The Four Zoas*. But it has a special force in this poem about the mutuality of contraries, reinforcing insistently the identity of the polarities it circumscribes.

In the instant of the lark's song the second of Los's early-rising messengers awakes. To the song of all the birds the wild thyme leads a dance of all the flowers, a dance that may recall the terrifying dance of

Los himself in the *Book of Urizen* and *The Four Zoas*, or of Urizen after his binding in the Bard's Song; though here, described in the language of the Song of Songs with echoes of *Lycidas*, the motion is "all in order sweet & lovely":

> Thou percievest the Flowers put forth their precious Odours!
> And none can tell how from so small a center comes such sweets
> Forgetting that within that Center Eternity expands
> Its ever during doors, that Og & Anak fiercely guard[.]
> First eer the morning breaks joy opens in the flowery bosoms
> Joy even to tears, which the Sun rising dries; first the Wild Thyme
> And Meadow-sweet downy & soft waving among the reeds.
> Light springing on the air lead the sweet Dance: they wake
> The Honeysuckle sleeping on the Oak: the flaunting beauty
> Revels along upon the wind; the White-thorn lovely May
> Opens her many lovely eyes: listening the Rose still sleeps
> None dare to wake her. soon she bursts her crimson curtaind bed
> And comes forth in the majesty of beauty; every Flower:
> The Pink, the Jessamine, the Wall-flower, the Carnation
> The Jonquil, the mild Lilly opes her heavens! every Tree,
> And Flower & Herb soon fill the air with an innumerable Dance
> Yet all in order sweet & lovely, Men are sick with Love!
> Such is a Vision of the lamentation of Beulah over Ololon. . . .
>
> (31:46–63)

After both of these idyllic passages Blake has had to remind us that they are "a Vision of the lamentation of Beulah over Ololon," for they are so gracious and so fair that they erase all sense of the horror they entail. The end of time they signal may sound in the soft tones of gentle Beulah an instant of harmony and love, but it is an instant to be achieved in Generation only by agony and devastation. These two passages reflect not only the time and space passages of Book I, with their exalted sense of the constructs of Los's world, but also two far less reassuring passages in the Allamanda section: on plate 27 Blake described the creatures around the wine-press of war on earth, the venomous insects and the stinging weeds; what are they but the dread obverse of lark and thyme? The wasp and hornet, nettle and thistle are the mundane forms of those creatures that, imaginatively realized, are called lark and wild thyme, messengers of Los. Neither wasp nor lark is the whole emblem of the apocalyptic instant, for that instant comprises both anguish and release, both poison and song. The wasp is what we see in Generation, the lark what Beulah celebrates; the man who perceives their identity renovates in his imagination both Generation and Beulah.

The space stanza refined earlier definitions of the vortex by relating them to individual mortal experience. It reaffirmed also the ability of every individual mortal being to discover eternity within himself, for "every Space smaller than a Globule of Mans blood. opens / Into Eternity" (29:21–22). The wild thyme stanza refines those conceptions further: "opening a center," which is what one does when he passes within himself from the temporal to the eternal vortex, yields the joys of eternity not only to the explorer himself but to those around him. The "precious Odours" released from the eternal centers of the flowers can inspire us all to seek that center. The seeking, of course, is not easy; the center is guarded: "Bowlahoola & Allamanda are placed on each side / Of that Pulsation & that Globule," according to the space stanza; Og and Anak guard the center of the wild thyme.

Both time and the lark seem more active, more progressive than the stationary space and wild thyme. This parallel is given more force by a key alignment in the Book II passages: the lark by his singing is identified with the sense of hearing, whereas the flowers are identified with all the other senses. They are fragrant and visually gorgeous; they are "downy & soft" and they open to the sun and dance voluptuously. Together, lark and thyme symbolize all the fallen senses. The most potent sense, the one through which inspiration acts to renovate the others, receives a symbol and a stanza to itself; as the other senses respond to it they are given a corresponding symbol and stanza. This is precisely the relationship between time and space; they are mutual factors of fallen reality, yet only one is independently mobile and can thereby act to renovate them both.

We have seen the interrelatedness of time and space, and the interrelatedness of their emblems, lark and thyme. The identification of a mobile bird with the active male regents of time and of a stationary flower with the passive female regents of space seems standard enough. But the particular flower Blake chose for this otherwise unpuzzling iconography creates a significant confusion within that iconography: "Wild Thyme" irresistibly suggests a punning identification not with space, but with its contrary. This aural identification is, of course, hardly inappropriate: even the names of the emblems he designates indicate what was for Blake the necessary mutuality of contrary principles.

Time and space are the totality of fallen experience; lark and thyme represent our ability to perceive them. The former are abstract, the latter concrete, the former cosmic, the latter personal. Each pair is appropriate to its book, for as Book I dealt with a myth of creation-fall-redemption, Book II will describe the relevance of that grand myth to every fallen person.

In the second part of the Bard's Song Satan usurped the harrow and divided fallen man. The corresponding segment of Book II interprets Satan's action in terms of our fallen reality ("Nations wept in affliction Family by Family"), and offers an antidote to it: by renovation of the senses, fallen people can be united and restored to eternity. The third section of Book II's prologue, plate 32, also interprets and redresses its counterpart. The parallelism of the two third sections is unmistakable: each takes place around a couch of the dead (Albion's, Milton's), each is concerned with Satan's division of the nations. In Book I we see the fall and division itself; we see Satan's new opacity and the creation of female space. In Book II we learn, in a passage of that impassioned technicality that is now a familiar rhetorical device, of the meaning of that division to our fallen universe, and of its imminent resolution.

Plate 32 is a conversation of Milton's eternal portion with the Seven Angels. It opens with Milton's discontent:

> I have turned my back upon these Heavens builded on cruelty
> My Spectre still wandering thro' them follows my Emanation
> He hunts her footsteps thro' the snow & the wintry hail & rain
> The idiot Reasoner laughs at the Man of Imagination
> And from laughter proceeds to murder by undervaluing calumny. . . .
>
> (32:3–7)

This is a curious speech, an unsettling one because it disrupts our perspective in order to redefine it. The heavens from which Milton turns away are the heavens we have seen him enter, the "heavens of Albion" of the invocation, "the heavens beneath Buelah" which constitute Ulro-Generation. How, if he has voluntarily entered those heavens, has he turned his back on them? This is the paradox of the vortex: Milton does exist simultaneously on several levels of reality. That his various portions are not in agreement underscores the basic conflict of the poem, the contention of Milton and his spectre. This particular version of that conflict offers a necessary counterbalance to our usual conception of the natures of the combatants. Milton's tone here borders on elite disdain; he could hardly care less what happens to that nasty spectre. The spectre, on the other hand, is performing, with whatever perverted motives, the necessary constructive function of Milton himself, seeking out Ololon. There is, we must understand, positive value in the spectrous portion of a divided being, and destructive error in the immortal part. The Elect not only needs but deserves preservation. Milton's Edenic portion has recoiled from the action it set in motion itself; it disowns its own shadow. Until it embraces that shadow and renovates it, Milton will remain a divided self. That we have already seen Milton embrace his spectre Urizen in Book I indicates the position of this speech in the action "sequence" of the poem: it is a close-up analysis of the instant of Milton's descent, a study from a different angle of Milton's division into Edenic, Beulaic, and Ulroic portions (15:1–20). In Book I we saw that division as the first phase of a process without duration, a process concluded by the driving of Milton's eternal vestiges into Ulro by the outraged eternals (20:41–50). Now in Book II we return to the first phase again; we see Milton on his couch with his comforting angels, as we saw him earlier, but this time we recognize in his spectrous part the internal causes of his division. Here, as in the Book I death-couch passage, the end of the division is imminent: the angels will soon tell Milton that he is "a State about to be Created / Called Eternal Annihilation" (32:26–27): his immortal portion is about to descend into his satanic shadow.

The Seven Angels dispel Milton's hesitation. Using their own dual nature as an object lesson, they warn him that his spectre yet contains a portion of his living individuality, and may not be abandoned.

> We are not Individuals but States: Combinations of Individuals
> We were Angels of the Divine Presence: & were Druids in Annandale
> Compelld to combine into Form by Satan. . . .
> Distinguish therefore States from Individuals in those States.
> States Change: but Individual Identities never change nor cease:
> You cannot go to Eternal Death in that which can never Die.
>
> (32:10–12, 22–24)

States are the means by which the eternals salvaged the fallen Elect. The space created by Enitharmon, in the form given to it by Los and the duration authorized for it by the eternals, is divided into "Twenty-seven Churches" (32:25), the units of the Mundane Shell. Each of those units shelters a collection of fallen individuals, who pass successively from unit to unit, "state" to "state," until they may pass beyond states altogether, until they reattain Eden. To return thus to imaginative reality the identity must be whole, its parts fully integrated; vortical multidimensionality does not exist in eternity. Milton's spectre pursuing Ololon through the deeps is compound both of error and of Milton's human individuality. Milton cannot abandon him without abandoning a part of himself, and thus his hope for return to Eden.

The difference between immortal Milton and his spectre is the difference between Angels of the Presence and druids in Annandale, between freedom and tyranny. Joined "in Freedom & holy Brotherhood" the spirits are human; "Compelld to combine into Form by Satan" they are "Shapeless Rocks" (32:12–17). So Milton in free union with spectre and emanation is human ("they and / Himself was Human," 17:5–6), while in bondage to his oath he is the rock Sinai (17:14). "Los's Mathematic power" redeems (29:38); Satan's condemns (32:16–21). The process by which tyranny is converted to freedom, spectre to living identity, is the annihilation of what makes it tyrannous in the first place. But that "Selfhood" cannot be vanquished from without; it must truly be converted, informed so fully by its own humanity that it ceases to exist as selfhood. It cannot perish any more than Jesus will permit Satan to perish, but it can be changed, and therefore cease to exist as it was known.

In part three of the Bard's Song Eden passed judgment on Satan; in the corresponding part of Book II, the Seven Angels tell Milton to "Judge then of thy Own Self" (32:30). They have taught him to preserve his identity, annihilating only the created states that contain and restrict it. To judge of his self is to liberate his spectre and recreate it human, to fulfill the judgment of Eden that Satan "must be new Created continually moment by moment" (11:20). This we have seen him do in building Urizen anew with red clay.

Part four of the Bard's Song describes the female response to part three; the corresponding section in the second book presents a feminine counterpart to the doctrine of states and individuals. As the fallen male form is divided, so is his female portion; Milton has his spectre, Ololon her shadow Rahab. The spectre is no more terrifying than the female shadow, and his recreation is no more crucial than hers. Plate 33, the last part of the Book II prologue, describes the renovation of the shadowy female Elect, who must "be continually Redeem'd / By death & misery of those [she loves] & by Annihilation" (33:12–13).

Beulah chants Jesus' castigation of Babylon, shadow of his emanation Jerusalem, whose vegetated jealousy has "Cut off my loves in fury till I have no love left for thee" (33:7). This is the prototypic male-female conflict, the cycle of jealousy and fear reflected in the relationships of Orc and the Shadowy Female and Milton and Ololon. But Jesus foresees an end to the cycle. Milton's descent will cause Ololon/Rehab to repent of her jealousy, and that in turn will bring Babylon to return Jerusalem to Jesus. The parallel of Ololon and Jerusalem in his speech and the contingency of Babylon's redemption on Rahab's remind us once again of the identity of eternal and temporal beings, and of the dependence of the once eternal on the temporal for resurrection.

The final segment of the prologue is the same in each book of *Milton*: the errant female will, Leutha or Ololon, recognizes her guilt and repents. Leutha's repentance in Book I brings the Bard's prophecy of reconciliation: the Elect shall meet the Redeemed in love and forgiveness. Ololon's repentance, prophesied by Jesus and implicit in the chanting of that prophecy not only by Beulah but by Ololon herself (we have heard, it seems, the divine voice in "the Songs of Beulah in the Lamentations of Ololon" [33:24]), promises reconciliation, too, and by the same terms the Bard established: Ololon shall bring "maidens" to her lord as Elynittria brought Leutha to Palamabron. As Milton descended to find Ololon after Leutha's lament in the Bard's history, so Ololon descends to find Milton after the divine promise in her own lamentation. Each of these crucial laments thus prepares the way for the reunion of Milton and Ololon in Generation.

All four parts of the Book II prologue interpret their parallel parts in the Bard's Song, and offer antidotes to its gloom. If the fallen universe had to be created in anguish and bitterness, still there is hope for it because its model is fair Beulah, a providential place of ease and revitalization. If Satan perverted the true order of existence and brought still more anguish and bitterness, which we see now in the strife of nations in our fallen world, yet we may, by purifying our senses and thereby understanding these dread conditions, end them. If the judgment against Rintrah caused Satan in his pride and Los in his wrath to be closed up in Canaan, a judgment against what is annihilable in the self can end the imprisonment and return all its victims to eternity. If Leutha's repentance was vain because Satan would not respond, Ololon's repentance will fulfill the Bard's prophecy, for Milton has already turned to seek her.

Thus the first four plates of Book II are clearly related structurally and thematically to the Bard's Song. Their relation to the rest of Book II is the relation of the Bard's Song to the body of Book I. They form, like the Bard's Song, a prologue to the action of their book, though at first they may seem simply a part of that action. Part one, the story of the creation of Beulah, is clearly antecedent, but the laments of part two seem merely an amplification of the action itself. They accompany the descent of Ololon, and that descent is the action. But they take Ololon only as far as Beulah, and Beulah is, after all, as natural and familiar a setting for her as Eden; it is Ololon's descent "to death in Ulro among the Transgressors" (21:46) that is the book's significant action, action decided upon and in fact taken in Book I. A lament as she passes Beulah is, after plate 21, past history. Part three is antecedent by much the same logic: the Angels' injunction anticipates Milton's self-judgment, but by the time we read that injunction he has already judged of himself and descended. The tone of the fourth part is what makes it antecedent: the disapproval in the divine voice suggests that at the time of the speech Ololon had not yet repented, although Jesus prophesies that she will; but we heard her repent twelve plates before. The four parts of the prologue of Book II predate the action of the book and underscore its motives and its urgency just as the Bard's Song operates in Book I.

LESLIE BRISMAN

"The Four Zoas": First Things

It is possible to approach the special
character of the version of first things in Night VIIA by projecting back
on the author of this extraordinary episode something that the student of
it must feel. If one has read through *The Four Zoas* one knows that the
version in Night VIIA is the temporally definitive one—in the sense that
the remaining Nights, VIII and IX, do not offer still another version. On
the other hand, the perspectivism of previous versions challenges the very
idea of a definitive account, and the larger problem—how to bring so
continually climactic a poem to a single climax—finds a focal point in the
repetition of the story of Albion's fall.

That a final turn to beginnings should bring the poem to its climax
and help precipitate the end suggests the critical approach (and the
attempt to discover its equivalent for the creating poet) called "deconstruc-
tion." The term implies climactic, if not destructive, finality, while
actually referring to the project of searching out underlying or originatory
metaphysical assumptions on the basis of which a literary or philosophical
work has been built. Derrida writes of Husserl's phenomenology that the
whole system is based on the categorical distinction between primordial
presentation and representative re-production: "Properly speaking, Husserl
is not *led* to recognize this heterogeneity, for it is this which constitutes
the very possibility of phenomenology. For phenomenology can only make
sense if a pure and primordial presentation is possible and given in the
original." The categorical distinction that Derrida "comes to" is the point
that Husserl may be said to "come from." I turn to this illustration because

it seems to me more than an analogy or metaphor for poetry. Blake's work cannot be reduced to a pure phenomenology; and not enough sense can be made of Urizen, Luvah, and Urthona if their actions and stances—let alone their emanations—are simply the constitutive elements of a transcendental psychology. Blake is in the position of Husserl's critic, exposing the "absolute heterogeneity"—or rather expanding the heterogeneity of presentation and representation to fill the space of his poem.

To be sure, it is impossible to recapture the burden of awareness Blake assumed in revising Night VII of *The Four Zoas* and presenting the poem's story of first things for the last time. But to represent the retrospective consciousness that surveys the heterogeneous presentations of the past and sets out to re-present the story in a way that will free it from first-and-last, I borrow from Derrida this summary of his argument with Husserl: "Perception does not exist . . . what is called perception is not primordial . . . somehow everything 'begins' by 're-presentation' (a proposition which can only be maintained by the elimination of these last two concepts: it means that there is no 'beginning' and that the 'representation' we were talking about is not the modification of a 're-' that has *befallen* a primordial presentation)." We could call such critical insight the fruit of what Blake terms, in Night VIIA, "The Tree of Mystery," for in taking it in one's eyes are opened, one's illusions about the primordial are demystified, and the nakedness of the text's assumptions is exposed. What Blake finds left to do is to reconstruct on the basis of such a deconstructive awareness, to reimagine his Giant Forms in terms of a story that will express the consciousness of illusion otherwise burdensome. He requires both a recovery and a re-covering: a return to imaginative health (finding a medium for expressing the otherwise oppressive consciousness of illusion) and an act of covering once more (as Adam and Eve did their generative parts, as Wallace Stevens finds the poet must do to the primordial rock) by refictionalizing the story of original generation.

Consciousness of fictionality may be expressed in terms of an original fiction by transforming the literal and figurative elements of an old tale. In Night VIIA, Blake goes back to the Genesis story of a tree of knowledge and, by a triumphant displacement, makes the undermining of that fiction stand for the consciousness of his own fictions about first things. "Undermining" is perhaps not quite the right word because it is not quite literal enough. Blake gets to the ground of the old fiction by re-presenting his old characters *on the ground* of the old fiction, "Beneath the Tree of Mystery among the leaves & fruit." Genesis describes fallen Adam and Eve hiding *bitoch etz hagan* (within the tree[s] of the garden), which the Vulgate preserves in the singular (*in medio ligni paradisi*).

Literalism in the reimagining of this event leads to such imaginative achievements as Milton's banyan tree and Chaucer's pear—with Damian and May up in it. Blake no doubt draws on the tradition when he conceives of the tree of knowledge—like Jesus' cross, said to be of the same wood—as a synecdoche for the world of nature in which the fallen imagination is bound. But he goes further in questioning the ground of these imaginings and returning his characters to the literal ground in which these metaphysical trees take their root. More precisely, he does not return the old characters to the newly literalized ground but reimagines the old characters in terms of shadows that represent them and whose very reimagining stands for consciousness of representation. In place of Los and Enitharmon we find, beneath the tree of mystery, the Spectre of Urthona and the Shadow of Enitharmon. These two shadow forth their counterparts in the world above, and when they present the story of Albion's fall once more they not only "present it" in the sense of making it present to one another and to us; they re-present it, for they are characters whose very existence and whose setting acknowledge the fact that there is no presenting but in re-presencing.

The Shadow of Enitharmon and the Spectre of Urthona tell the story to one another, in itself a fact that acknowledges fiction because conversation or dialogue demystifies the potentially absolute status of myth as revealed by one speaking voice. The phenomenological aspect of previous versions of Albion's fall depended on the transcendent dignity of the individual voice. Derrida points out that the special status of voice for phenomenology depends on "the fact that the phenomenological 'body' of the signifier seems to fade away at the very moment it is produced; it seems already to belong to the element of ideality." When Blake presents two speakers, for neither of whom individually the original myth has the "immediate presence" it gains in their dialogue, the "body" of the signifier seems to be apprehended not in the fading but in the making. The limits of phenomenology are transcended because dialogue ventures "outside ideality, outside interiority of the self-present life." Previous versions have taken into account the situation of speaker and auditor—in Night III particularly, where what Ahania has to say about Urizen is intricately dependent on the fact that she is speaking to him and registering his reactions while attempting to change them. Nevertheless the story has at that point a self-presence to Ahania that it does not to the Shadow of Enitharmon in Night VIIA.

Here are the portions of the exchange that together constitute the new version of our story. First the Shadow of Enitharmon to the Spectre:

Among the flowers of Beulah walked the Eternal Man, & saw
Vala, the lily of the desert: melting in high noon
Upon her bosom in sweet bliss he fainted. Wonder seized
All Heaven: they saw him dark; they built a golden wall
Round Beulah. There he revelled in delight among the flowers.
Vala was pregnant & brought forth Urizen, prince of light,
First-born of generation. Then behold, a wonder to the eyes
Of the now fallen Man, a double form Vala appeared! A male
And female, shuddering pale: the fallen Man recoiled
From the enormity, & called them *Luvah & Vala*, turning down
The vales to find his way back into Heaven—but found none,
For his frail eyes were faded & his ears heavy & dull.
Urizen grew up in the plains of Beulah. Many sons
And many daughters flourished round the holy tent of man,
Till he forgot Eternity, delighted in his sweet joy
Among his family, his flocks & herds & tents & pastures.

But Luvah close conferred with Urizen in darksome night
To bind the father & enslave the brethren. Nought he knew
Of sweet Eternity: the blood flowed round the holy tent, & riven
From its hinges, uttering its final groan all Beulah fell
In dark confusion. Meantime Los was born & Enitharmon,
But how I know not; then forgetfulness quite wrapped me up
A period, nor do I more remember, till I stood
Beside Los in the cavern dark, enslaved to vegetative forms,
According to the will of Luvah who assumed the place
Of the Eternal Man, & smote him.

Forgetfulness covers part of the story (precisely the facts of
Enitharmon's generation), but this Spectre recovers and re-presences the
tale of generation. Los, Enitharmon, and the Spectre of Urthona emerge
as the de-generated components (degenerate, and one generation later) of
the original Urthona:

                                              One dread morn—
Listen, O vision of delight—one dread morn of gory blood
The Manhood was divided, for the gentle passions, making way
Through the infinite labyrinths of the heart & through the nostrils issuing
In odorous stupefaction, stood before the eyes of Man,
A female bright. I stood beside my anvil dark; a mass
Of iron glowed bright, prepared for spades & ploughshares: sudden down
I sunk, with cries of blood issuing downward in the veins
Which now my rivers were become, rolling in tubelike forms
Shut up within themselves, descending down I sunk along
The gory tide even to the place of seed, & there dividing
I was divided in darkness & oblivion. Thou an infant woe,
And I an infant terror in the womb of Enion.

As dialogue, this exchange suggests that the myth recounted has been naturalized, or recast in terms of the way people talk about their backgrounds. David Wagenknecht says of the Shadow and the Spectre here that "they while away the time before coitus like young people at a dance, telling each other where they come from." But I doubt whether young people at a dance often get this much "into" one another's histories, for as dark and self-serving as these characters are they appear to be conversing with, not just talking at, one another. It is a common history they speak, dividing between them the recitation of its parts. The Shadow's account expands on other versions of Albion's dalliance and outlines the events given by the messengers from Beulah in Night I, lines 179–213 of Stevensons's text. The Spectre follows with the equivalent of lines 214–229.

Some of the differences between the messengers' account and this one need to be specified. In Night I, the Spectre is a minor meteor breaking off from the celestial body of Urthona, and so the difference between "Beside his anvil stood Urthona dark" (I.214) and "I stood beside my anvil dark" (VIIA.280) is more than a shift from third to first person—even acknowledging the dramatic re-placing of the mysterious adjective. One could say that in Night VIIA the speaking "I" is proleptically the Spectre of Urthona, or simply that the Spectre identifies himself with his unfallen form. Both these formulations belie the way the Spectre's account belies his generation. The difference between the "I" identified with Urthona and "I an infant terror" is unlike the temporal difference between the "I" I was yesterday and the "I" I am today. Memory connects my past with my present self; but when the Spectre remembers himself as Urthona, he re-members the self that has been broken apart into separate members—Los, Enitharmon, and the Spectre. Urthona has been dismembered; he is not yet re-membered and only anticipates such union: "then shall we unite again in bliss." As a sign of this union to come, Enitharmon and the Spectre embrace now. The pre-coital conversation thus must be seen as a sign of a sign, with the fitting together of their narrative parts standing metaleptically for the more corporeal fitting together to come. That, in turn, stands for the final, less corporeal fitting together—the reunification of Spectre and Los which in time stands for and works toward the ultimate union of Spectre, Los, and Enitharmon to reconstitute Urthona.

The number of *in turns* necessitated here points to the episode as a turning point. Surely we approach a nadir reading about the Shadow of Enitharmon, "Bitterly she wept, embracing fervent / Her once-loved lord, now but a shade, herself also a shade." But this literal apophrades or return of the dead has these shades, at the same time, shadowing forth the apocalyptic union to come. Here is one of Blake's shadiest episodes confronting itself as such, playing with all senses of shade (*le jeu des différences*) and discovering in such self-consciousness about how one episode shadows forth another a point of regeneration. Derrida writes, "If language never escapes analogy, if it is indeed analogy through and through, it ought, having arrived at this point, at this stage, freely to assume its own destruction and cast metaphor against metaphor. . . . It is at the price of this war of language against itself that the sense and question of its origin will be thinkable." We can say of Spectre and Shadow that they are metaphor cast against metaphor. The product of their union (a metaphor for metaphor confronting itself) is a form of Vala, who is Veiled Meaning or Analogy (Nature as metaphoric vehicle) incarnate.

Two details help authenticate the revelations of the Night VIIA version as more than play with the idea of language. One is that Vala is not named as such when Enitharmon brings forth "a wonder horrible." When this wonder is named later in the poem it is renamed Rahab. Error is thus consolidated, not left to the mild mistakes of metaphoric language and the circularity of coming up with (coming back to) Vala. The other detail is that Vala *is* named in the Shadow's account, which literalizes the doubling nature of analogy when Vala is seen splitting into Luvah and Vala. From the psychologizing perspective of previous accounts we could say that "a double form Vala appeared" refers to the doubling of the mind in the presence of a sexual object. More precisely, in response to an object of desire absent to the mind because *out there* in external nature, a man (or a woman, mutatis mutandis) creates the Form of Desire present to the mind—an imago-vision of the ideal (to which no lady can match up) or a vision of the external object as metaphoric (no lady can threaten *as* a lady). Such Presences are forms of Vala. But one also idealizes oneself as desirable and desiring, and one can be dwarfed by this shadow's superior form and purity of desire. We encountered the creation of such an overshadower in Night III: he is Luvah, who appears when Vala splits, when sexuality alienates Albion from the basic self-presence in which one recognizes one's desire and one's object of desire as one's own.

Yet at the center of this version of first things we are beyond psychology—or rather at a core of pure psychology we might better label semiology. The turn from Albion "saw / Vala" to "a double form Vala appeared" is a return from the interpersonal possibilities of sexuality to intrapersonal sign creation. The Shadow's account concerns the way we make shadowy presences and signs that do not simply refer to external reality but differ from it, defer our involvement with it, and finally debar us from it. When Adam named the animals he knew a creative power that preceded fall. But when Blake's Albion "called them Luvah & Vala" he read the signs, as it were, that barred his way back to paradise. The Shadow's account insists on this primordial relationship between metaphor-making and sexuality. Her opening lines present sexuality in especially literary, even biblical, terms: "Among the flowers of Beulah walked the Eternal Man, & saw / Vala, the lily of the desert" (The fall into metaphor is the fall into Generation—the equation of sexual attraction with the forms of generated nature.) Any freshness accompanying the turn to such meta-phors is dispelled by the haste and the deadness of the metaphors that follow: "melting in high noon / Upon her bosom in sweet bliss he fainted." Time (noon) is distempered, place (bosom) displaced in such language, and the distance implied by language is literalized in the building of a wall around Beulah. But semiology is not simply topology—metaphors do not simply substitute one place for another; they temporally displace meaning, and the Shadow's greatest variation on the story of the Fall involves a reworking of the fall into time.

It has the ring of the pristine, almost a Biblical genealogy: "Vala was pregnant & brought forth Urizen, prince of light, / First-born of genera-tion." We have met other acts of generation in which one of Blake's Giant Forms "takes in" and gives birth to another; Enion, for example, harbors Enitharmon and Los and delivers them into this world of Generation. But this is the first time one of the "original" four Zoas is imagined as generated, and the lines challenge the idea of an original, atemporal state. Derrida says of speech that what distinguishes it from other modes of signification (like pictures) is its temporality: "And this temporality does not unfold a sense that would itself be nontemporal; even before being expressed, sense is through and through temporal." The situation in Night VIIA of one disembodied shadowy voice addressing another focuses on the nature of their account of first things as speech and reminds us that sense itself is temporal, that the forms that Shadow and Spectre re-present make no sense outside time, and that an unfallen Urizen is (as yet) inconceiv-able. Out of this awareness the fallen Urizen could be said to be "conceived."

Psychologically, the fallen Urizen appears to be something like the superego, so that one idea of a deferred or generated Urizen rather than an original Zoa could correspond to the generation of an internalized author-ity figure out of the confrontation of the id with externality. But the semiological cast of Night VIIA suggests that we reformulate the temporal difference in terms of what Husserl calls the phenomenology of internal time consciousness, and consider Urizen not as a parental Presence but as the arch denier or evader of the present. Husserl calls our awareness of the present "primal": "The primal impression is the absolute beginning of this generation [of the sense of time]—the primal source, that from which all others are continually generated. In itself, however, it is not generated; it does not come into existence as that which is generated but through spontaneous generation. It does not grow up (it has no seed): it is primal creation." That is just what Urizen cannot recognize and cannot "be." All anxiety and futurity, Urizen must now be conceived "as that which is generated." The Shadow's account continues, and Urizen's collusion with Luvah in rebellion against Albion takes on something of the quality of the Freudian primal scene: it reminds us of the first sons' tribal slaying of the father. This reminder tags the fall, for the very turn to psychology marks a falling away from purer concern with signs. The account of the Shadow of Enitharmon makes manifest the nature of Generation by naturalizing the story, turning the Zoas, who ought to be seen as faculties of the individual psyche, into children rebellious against a parental authority. This naturalization is a central error within a Blake story, just as nothing could be more invidious than the mode of interpretation that would argue Blake's interest in regeneration to be a displacement based on the failure of Blake-the-man to generate biological children. Biographical criticism *naturalizes*, and finds not first things but fall, not even psychology—the study of the soul—but biology, the study of the world of nature. Los and Enitharmon, children of the fall, may be said to be generated when they are mentally (and, in terms of the myth of Enion, physically) conceived as children. Yet confronted *as metaphor*, biological generation is essential. Night IX will rejuvenate the parental metaphor, and rejuvenate man: he will "rise from generation free," but in an innocence expressed or organized into generational terms. And to rejuvenate the generational metaphor is to see generation as image of regeneration.

That formula (Blake uses it in the opening of *Jerusalem*) discovers something not just about the nature of a generational image but about metaphoric language generally. In Night VIIA, to see Urizen as generated is to see that our "primary" sense of time—the one that "pre-occupies" us most—concerns the anxiety produced by the presence of shadows of the past and the fore-shadowed presence of the future. "I think, therefore I am" may be true in the sense that my "first" thought is logically the thought that I am thinking. But that was no child's first thought, and no functioning adult's most stimulating (generative) thought. We live in and think about not a world of what Husserl calls "the spontaneous generation of the awareness of presentness," but a world of Generation, a world of delayed gratifications and delayed symbol-making. We learn to describe our world metaphorically, knowing that the very use of metaphoric language marks a falling away from presentness.

The tree of mystery, beneath which these revelations take place (are given a place in Blake), could thus be called the tree of metaphor-making. God planted many trees and one big metaphor in the first garden—or, more precisely, two metaphors, a metaphor of metaphor-making (the tree of knowledge) and a metaphor of presentness (the tree of life-without-the-temporalizations-of-metaphor). In Blake's revision of the Biblical archetype, the fruit of the tree of knowledge still opens the eyes to an awareness connected with sexuality, but now the knowledge could be said to concern just how metaphoric "tree," "opening the eyes," and sexuality itself really are, and how dependent on covering, delaying, and hiding in the tree we really are. The lure of knowledge posed in the Biblical story by the serpent properly belongs to the Spectre in Night VIIA, and like the serpent the knowledge he has must first be seen as a piece of psychology or psychological strategy before it can be abstracted into knowledge about the nature of representation.

By presenting Urizen as born from the union of Albion and Vala, the Shadow of Enitharmon suggested that parental possessiveness may be basic to sexual desire. Ending her speech with that tantalizing note of obscurity and fascination about her genesis ("Los was born & Enitharmon, / But how I know not"), she gives the Spectre his cue for the parental reading of the history of psychic division. In his account, Albion's sexual fall causes a division felt as a descent into generation: "I was divided in darkness & oblivion. Thou an infant woe, / And I an infant terror in the womb of Enion." Perceiving that the fallen female is attracted to the image of a father, he comes up with just the history that makes him seem, though "so horrible a form," sexually attractive:

> My masculine spirit scorning the frail body issued forth
> From Enion's brain, in this deformed form leaving thee there
> Till times passed over thee; but still my spirit returning hovered
> And formed a male to be a counterpart to thee, O love.

I do not know what authority that last line has as history of the Eternals, but its effect on the Shadow of Enitharmon is clear. Claiming to be Los's "father," the Spectre presents himself as what the lady really wants. The sexuality is nasty but incisive, and might be deemed the counterpart of the pedestrian nastiness which sees a man as being really attracted to the Mother Nature he sees in potentia in a given lady; woman is attracted to that in a man which seems not of woman born. Something in a wife not only prefers her father-in-law (spiritual form of man of whom the son is de-generated shadow) but desires the destruction of the natural husband who stands in the path of spiritual union with that idealized form. I may look like deformity and lust, the Spectre argues, but "I am as the spectre of the living," and will take you beyond natural appearances back through the "gates of Eternal life."

That much is Spectre psychology, and like Milton's Satan, who takes his clues from Eve, the Spectre depends for his knowledge on the Shadow's blindness to the fact that her tale of generation contains the seed of the answer the Spectre elaborates. But what begins as psychology or a naturalized drama of sexual temptation emerges in our eyes—and, more especially, in the eyes of Los, who "reads" this episode—as a drama about the nature of metaphoric representation. The Shadow cannot re-member the facts re: generation; the Spectre re-members and re-generates the Zoas, and re-presents the present confrontation in a stark I-Thou relationship that, incidentally, shows just how much Blake can do with his dramatic verse: "Thou an infant woe, / And I an infant terror in the womb of Enion." What seems nothing less than miraculous is that this literal or biological regeneration points the way to spiritual regeneration. Their unified story of generation—of themselves as infants—which "stands for" and impels their union and generation of an infant horrible, leads to the regeneration of Los and Urizen. Night VIIA closes triumphantly with a metaphor of generation as Los comes to see Urizen aright: "he beheld him an infant / Lovely."

The Night VIIA version of first things is thus distinguished not only by its subtlety but by the way this narration moves us closer to the return to Eternal life. The old story is regenerated (refurbished for the occasion); it now concerns re-generation (seeing the Zoas reemerge as infants, the next generation); and it regenerates the poem (giving Los, and ultimately the poet, the burst of energy to fabricate embodied sem-blances). Though the rebirth of Luvah as Orc and the rebirth of Vala as Rahab are not themselves redemptive reworkings, they increase the mo-mentum of regeneration that produces the vision at the end of Night VIIA of Urizen as an infant, and, ultimately, in Night IX, of Tharmas and Enion as little children. More immediately, the recitation of the story of the fall sends reverberations into the larger plot stalled at that point. The labor pains of the Shadow of Enitharmon produce sighs and groans each of which "bore Urthona's Spectre on its wings." Pity, which divides the soul, also humanizes its spectrous forms, turning them from objects of fear and distance into objects of identification.

One can summarize the achievement of the Night VIIA account of first things by pointing to the relationship of a story re: generation and one of regeneration, or by noting that a story about origins becomes a story about originating stories about origins—a story about originality. But such formulas belie the *poetic* achievement of Blake and the way metaphoric language transcends any statement language can make about metaphor. Consider the wondrous innocence of the Shadow of Enitharmon as she declares herself in the dark about her origins: "Meantime Los was born & Enitharmon, / But how I know not; then forgetfulness quite wrapped me up / A period, nor do I more remember." Such little oblivions are the special province of poetry and help it to the same transcendence of formulaic thought that the whole creative mind has over pure consciousness. Forgetfulness covers not just the birth of Enitharmon but the relationship between Enitharmon and the Shadow of Enitharmon speaking. When the Spectre hails her, "Listen, thou my vision, / I view futurity in thee," he collapses in the appositive "my vision" just the temporalizing difference that is allowing this whole episode to take place. "My vision" could be said to mean, literally, "she whom I now see." It also means "she in whom I foresee," or "she with whom I foresee." If the Spectre made clear just what he would lose through clarification, his statement might go something like this: "You are the one through whom (granted the awareness I have but can lay aside that you are 'lovely / Delusion') I can create."

Stalled on the level of Los and Enitharmon, the narrative has plunged beneath the tree of mystery to confront shade with shade. This expressed awareness of metaphoricity is no stumbling block but almost a condition of creativity, which so often in Blake—and in revisionary poetry generally—depends on taking what was literal metaphorically or vice versa. When this awareness of metaphoricity is projected on the Shadow herself it produces this beautiful pause: "Bitterly she wept, embracing fervent / Her once-loved lord, now but a shade, herself also a shade." When the awareness of metaphoricity is projected back on the spatialized distinction between Enitharmon and her shadow in the world "below," it produces the vision Los sees: "She lay the image of death, / Moved by strong shudders till her shadow was delivered." In some literal or pseudoliteral way these lines describe two characters, one so in sympathy with the other that one's labor pains are felt by the other as deathly agonies. While metaphoric language is being used the effect of perceiving Enitharmon as the "image of death" seems to be to make—for a moment— Death a reality with Enitharmon Death's shadow, and the Shadow of Enitharmon the Shadow of a shadow. But this is a mistake of metaphormaking, for the "reality" taken away from Enitharmon in making her an "image" belongs not to Death but to the Shadow, whose woes Enitharmon is reflecting. What is required to separate these terms more clearly is not a topology of upper and lower worlds, not a spatial but a temporal distinction, which is precisely what Blake offers in describing Enitharmon as the image *till* her shadow was delivered. Blake's subject is less immediately the delays of gratification needed for any labor (genetic or literary) than it is the deferral needed for any sign to perform the function of representation by giving as "present" something not (yet) there.

Blake dismisses the Shadow of Enitharmon, which has done him good service (foreshadowing and bringing about the regeneration of Enitharmon) but which he no longer needs; he puts the Shadow (the Shadow's child?) far off—giving it charge over the world of the dead till the time of the resurrection. Metaphoricity is replaced by the mutuality of present affection, and we have only to contrast with the complexities of the account we have heard the radical simplicity, "Enitharmon told the tale / Of Urthona" (ll. 334–35) to see how far we have come. Summarily, the events of generation are recounted from the perspective of regeneration, and not only recounted but redeemed. "The whole *proprium* or self-hood of man," wrote Swedenborg, "is in the will, and this *proprium* is evil from his first birth, and becomes good by a second birth." The search for origins—the curiosity about natural or first birth as such—is for Blake the indulgence of the selfhood. Perhaps for this reason Blake leaves Los blind to the birthpangs of Enitharmon's Shadow, sympathetic to the agonies of Enitharmon but oblivious of the actual facts of generation: "nor could his eyes perceive / The cause of her dire anguish." Los's business will be to "see" generation as an image of regeneration, and for such prophetic vision a little literal blindness is a help.

A new understanding of the nature of image or metaphor is a new burst of imagination. Los sees the Shadow-Spectre union shadowing forth the integration of self that is spiritual regeneration. What must be *first* expressed in external, natural terms comes to be understood in its deferred or metaphoric form as the inner life. Los announces:

> Even I, already, feel a world within
> Opening its gates, & in it all the real substances
> Of which these in the outward world are shadows which pass away.
> Come then into my bosom, & in thy shadow arms bring with thee
> My lovely Enitharmon.

The burden of negativity which afflicts semiological discussions drops away, and Los makes those "shadow arms" seem beautiful (and perhaps gently humorous) just by accepting them for what they are. His words can be taken as a caveat for literary criticism, a humanistic conviction that after all the shadows of literary representation have been deconstructed and revealed as metaphysical or linguistic illusions, they need to be embraced for what they are. Metaphoricity is embraced, metaphorically.

If the danger in perceiving the distance between signs and their significance is that the signs tend to look less appealing (metaphor as a bad mistake—if not as the Fall), Los performs a correction of desire. Knowing the origins of illusion, he does not turn away, but feels a burst of originating power: "Stern desire / I feel to fabricate embodied semblances in which the dead / May live before us in our places and in the gardens of our labour" (ll.435–37). He knows semblances for semblances. But he knows also that they can be made to "live before us," and if "before" cannot mean "anterior to," restoring priorities, it can mean "present to us," restoring a sense of presentness as art best can.

LEOPOLD DAMROSCH, JR.

Los and Apocalypse

Los precipitates the Last Judgment, tearing the sun and moon from the heavens which are then rolled up while the last trump sounds (*FZ* 117:6ff., E390/K377). But he does not create it. The role of art is to make apocalypse possible and then give way. By himself Los is the crippled smith, and he cannot be whole until he reunites in Man—"Urthona limping from his fall on Tharmas leand" (*FZ* 137:8, E390/K377). Apocalypse is internal and individual, though it may also be social and historical, since "whenever any Individual Rejects Error & Embraces Truth a Last Judgment passes upon that Individual" (*VLJ*, E551/K613). Each person must achieve for himself a communion with Eternity like that which Blake experienced when "the Lark mounted with a loud trill from Felphams Vale" (*M* 42:29, E142/K534).

Now, this individualizing of vision places a special strain on the conception of apocalypse. If I am right about Blake's theory of symbolism, reality is not subjective; our visions differ because we build them out of fallen materials, not because the archetypal or eternal Forms are infinitely diverse. "The Last Judgment is one of these Stupendous Visions. I have represented it as I saw it. To different People it appears differently as every thing else does for tho on Earth things seem Permanent they are less permanent than a Shadow as we all know too well" (*VLJ*, E544/K605). In the fallen world, therefore, imagination exists in the spaces *between* experience as ordinarily understood.

An Eternity perpetually created by the imagination is very different from a consummation at the end of historical time, and *Milton* and

Jerusalem are accordingly much more elliptical about the apocalypse than *The Four Zoas*. As Grimes reminds us, Blake's theology escapes history by locating salvation in the interstices between historical events rather than at their culmination. In writing *The Four Zoas*, where apocalypse retains a historical basis and alludes systematically to biblical precedent, Blake evidently came to realize that traditional eschatology was incompatible with his myth; and it is worth considering why this should be so.

In traditional terms man awaits not himself but the king. "I saw in the night visions, and behold, one like the Son of man came with the clouds of heaven, and came to the Ancient of days, and they brought him near before him. And there was given him dominion, and glory, and a kingdom, that all people, nations, and languages, should serve him: his dominion is an everlasting dominion, which shall not pass away, and his kingdom that which shall not be destroyed." Blake will have nothing to do with Christ the King, but he needs a divine agent of the *eschaton*, the "end," who can embody the ending in personal form instead of presiding over it from above.

In a moving passage in the eighth Night of *The Four Zoas*, Los and Jerusalem take down the body of Jesus from the cross and bear it to the sepulchre which Los had hewn for himself in the rock of the fallen world, "despairing of Life Eternal (FZ 106:16, E365/K349). Rahab then cuts off "the Mantle of Luvah from/The Lamb of God," revealing "the Temple & the Synagogue of Satan & Mystery," the whole system of repression concealed in the profane misuse of Jesus in the symbolism of the Anti-christ. (Only the fallen church sees Jesus as dead; the true Christ, dis-guised from fallen eyes by Luvah's robes of blood, is life everlasting.) At this crisis Los appeals to Rahab:

> He answered her with tenderness & love not uninspird
> Los sat upon his anvil stock they sat beside the forge
> Los wipd the sweat from his red brow & thus began
> To the delusive female forms shining among his furnaces:
> I am that shadowy Prophet who six thousand years ago
> Fell from my station in the Eternal bosom. I divided
> To multitude & my multitudes are children of Care & Labour
> O Rahab I behold thee I was once like thee a Son
> Of Pride and I also have pierced the Lamb of God in pride & wrath.
> (FZ 113:44–52, E365/K350)

The Miltonic turn of "love not uninspired" is keenly ironic. Rahab refuses this plea, just as Eve betrayed Adam's love, and unites with Urizen to bring about the final consolidation of Error that precedes apocalypse. What we feel most deeply here is the hopelessness of Los's art unless aided by divine power. Far from being Jesus, he has pierced Jesus, has labored to exhaustion but in vain, and has placed the divine corpse (as he imagines it) in a tomb hewn in despair for himself.

As we noticed in the last chapter, Luvah's robes of blood recall the passage in Isaiah that lies behind the winepress image in Revelation: "I have trodden the winepress alone; and of the people there was none with me: for I will tread them in mine anger, and trample them in my fury; and their blood shall be sprinkled upon my garments, and I will stain all my raiment" (Isa. 63:3). Jesus is at once the sacrifice whose blood takes the place of that of beasts (a contrast made explicit in the Epistle to the Hebrews) and the trampler of the grapes of humanity in the apocalypse. The traditional interpretation of wine symbolizing immortality—casting off the wineskins of mortality—should not blind us to the violence and even sadism in the Dionysiac drunkenness of Luvah's sons and daughters. Blake exploits the rhetoric of revolution, and does not minimize the anguish of the end of the world as we know it.

> The blood of life flows plentiful Odors of life arose
> All round the heavenly arches & the Odors rose singing this song
> O terrible wine presses of Luvah O caverns of the Grave
> How lovely the delights of those risen again from death
> O trembling joy excess of joy is like Excess of grief
> (FZ 135:38–136:3, E389/K376)

Here the apocalypse is still imagined as coming at the end of a narrative sequence, and the real suffering that it entails is fully acknowledged.

In displacing Luvah from the center of apocalypse, Blake considerably alters his vision of its significance. To substitute Los for Luvah is to place a very great, perhaps an intolerable, burden upon the imagination, which must now act as judge, pardoner, and victim all at once. "The blow of his Hammer is Justice, the swing of his Hammer: Mercy./The force of Los's Hammer is eternal Forgiveness" (J 88:49–50, E245/K734). The death of Jesus is an eternally recurring act of unselfishness, not a unique sacrifice that gives meaning to human suffering and identifies the Judge of the *eschaton* with the human beings whom he judges.

> Jesus said, Wouldest thou love one who never died
> For thee or ever die for one who had not died for thee
> And if God dieth not for Man & giveth not himself
> Eternally for Man Man could not exist! for Man is Love:
> As God is Love: every kindness to another is a little Death
> In the Divine Image nor can Man exist but by Brotherhood.
> (J 96:23–28, E253/K743)

Death happens over and over again, eternally, and every act of kindness, since it involves a suppression of selfhood, is a kind of death. In such a system there is not much room left for a decisive apocalypse after which all things will be made new.

Since Los is Time, the implications of this shift in Blake's thought deserve attention. It is of course true that his view of history took on, as Frye says, a Spenglerian pessimism, and that it participates in the widespread Romantic internalization of apocalypse that Abrams has described so well. But it needs to be said also that Blake's ambivalence about the meaning of history reflects a conception of time and eternity that has often surfaced in the Western tradition. From the Old Testament, Christianity inherited an idea of history as linear progression embodying the will of God, in contrast to the endless cycles of Greek and oriental thought. Buber speaks of the prophetic "turning to the future," and since in Blake it is Urizen who broods upon futurity, Bloom rightly reminds us that the prophets "refused to yield up history to the Accuser to the extent that Blake did." But Christian typology drastically altered this pattern by interpreting the events of the Old Testament as symbolic units planted there by God to foreshadow the events of the New, and looked forward to an ending in which history would be gathered up into eternity. In such an eschatology, as Bultmann has said, "The end is not the completion of history but its breaking-off," and the meaning of history is not grounded in events as such, for "in every moment slumbers the possibility of being the eschatological moment." Accordingly, there has always been a strong impulse in Christianity toward a conception of eternity that could liberate man from time by affording a breakthrough out of temporal succession.

It was a frequent theme in Renaissance speculation that eternity, far from being separate from or above the world of time, is fully present in every instant. In phenomenological experience this eternal moment is revealed in the sudden lightning flash of the mystics, Boehme's *Blitz*: "For when the dark anguish . . . receives freedom in itself, it is transformed in the terror, in freedom, into a flash, and the flash embraces freedom or gentleness. Then the string of death is broken." We continue to inhabit the same universe as before, but for the first time we see it truly.

Blake's Los says, "I walk up and down in Six Thousand Years: their Events are present before me" (J 74:19, E227/K714). The cycles of fallen history, Los's handiwork, forever repeat themselves, but Jesus breaks into them and gathers them into eternity.

But Jesus breaking thro' the Central Zones of Death & Hell
Opens Eternity in Time & Space; triumphant in Mercy.
Thus are the Heavens formd by Los within the Mundane Shell
And where Luther ends Adam begins again in Eternal Circle
To awake the Prisoners of Death; to bring Albion again
With Luvah into light eternal, in his eternal day.
(J 76:21–26, E229/K716)

The effect is not so much to end time as to redeem it, freeing man from Urizenic preoccupation with past and future so that he can live each moment in the fullness of eternity. As Wittgenstein says, "If we take eternity to mean not infinite temporal duration but timelessness, then eternal life belongs to those who live in the present." The final vision of the Zoas, conversing in visionary forms dramatic, represents them as "going forward irresistible from Eternity to Eternity," a phrase which we have seen in Boehme and which probably derives from biblical locutions like "from everlasting to everlasting." Eternity is no static nontemporal state, but neither is it the bottomless draining away of atomistic historical moments; it is a succession of fully living moments each one of which embodies or expresses eternity.

Blake never relaxed his lifelong hatred of social injustice, as is obvious in the brilliant attack on factory labor and press-gang militarism in *Jerusalem* 65, or in aphorisms like "The Princes Robes & Beggars Rags/Are Toadstools on the Misers Bags" (*Auguries*, E482/K432). But given his philosophy of time, it is no wonder that he moved toward a political quietism that should make us qualify the usual assumption that he was a fiery radical. The seventeenth-century Antinomians whom he so much resembles were similarly ineffective in (or detached from) the political arena of their equally turbulent times. To a modern Protestant spokesman they may look like "fanatical and violently subversive elements, . . . forerunners of the French Revolution and of Marxism," since their rhetoric was certainly inflammatory enough. But as their historian dryly remarks, "Inexplicable knowledge of the true laws of all happening is not easily translated into workable rules of ordinary political intercourse."

Similarly, Blake after the early 1790s was radical but not political. He was philosophically more radical than the *philosophes*, since he believed that society could not be changed until man himself was changed. But politically he lacked their strong commitment to reform, and wrote as a spectator of history rather than as a participant in it, much as the Old Testament prophets viewed the victories of Assyria or Babylon as expressions of God's will. There is a strong providential element in Blake's thought, and since he awaits the total renovation of man before expecting the renovation of society, he is chiliastic where the Enlightenment was utopian. And the hope of change soon alters into a private and internal form; there can be no apocalypse in the state of bondage that we are accustomed to, which can be escaped only by escaping the body of death. "Many Persons such as Paine & Voltaire with some of the Ancient Greeks say we will not converse concerning Good & Evil we will live in Paradise & Liberty. You may do so in Spirit but not in the Mortal Body. . . . While we are in the world of Mortality we Must Suffer" (*VLJ*, E554/K615–616).

In such a philosophy the relation of the artist to events grows increasingly tenuous. In the third illustration to Gray's *Bard* the bard is shown as a gigantic figure staring down at the doomed king whose fate he weaves in bloody cords, which are also the strings of a gory harp. We are reminded both of the poet's power and of his immersion in the natural world (imaged also by the enraged figures of oak, cave, and torrent in the next illustration but one). We admire the rebel against tyranny but we recognize as well his complicity in the bloodbath that rebellion brings about.

In reinterpreting the apocalypse Blake has thus to deal in a new way with the material of suffering and punishment. It might be said that he retains the imagery but not the meaning of the wrath of God, the Day of Yahweh, *dies irae*. Man is alienated, but from himself only; he dwells in error but not in sin, and the erroneous aspects of himself can be dismissed as Satanic rather than confronted and worked through in a narrative progression (which is one reason why *Jerusalem* has so much less narrative form even than *Milton*, let alone *The Four Zoas*).

> With such a horrid clang
> As on Mount Sinai rang
> While the red fire, and smould'ring clouds out brake:
> The aged earth aghast
> With terror of that blast.
> Shall from the surface to the centre shake;
> When at the world's last session,
> The dreadful judge in middle air shall spread his throne.

Blake has the Judgment but not the omnipotent Judge, the imagery of punishment without its justification.

It would be still truer, however, to say that in retaining traces of the orgiastic drunkenness (see *Milton* 27, E123–124/K513–514), Blake means to remind us of the physical and temporal nature of such a Last Judgment as this. Puritans often rejoiced in the grisly images of the Book of Revelation because they enjoyed the thought of their enemies weltering in blood. Blake's conception is much closer to Boehme's, in which Christ "treads the winepress of the fierceness and wrath, and enters into the wrath as into the center of fire, and extinguishes the fire with his heavenly blood." The wrath of apocalypse is the wrath of the contraries. Christ enters the wrath as he enters the mortal body, and is not himself wrathful except insofar as he takes upon him the wrathfulness of the fallen world. In Blake the apocalypse, like the Incarnation and the Crucifixion, must be inseparable from the misery of the fallen body.

Since Blake's usage differs from the usual Christian connotations of apocalypse, some commentators prefer to use the term "eschatology" or to point out that Blake sometimes contrasts visionary rebirth during the present life with a later entrance into life everlasting, much as Paul does in Colossians. This would imply a fairly traditional view of the *Parousia*, Christ's presence in the believer's soul and his ultimate coming in the apocalypse. But we must be careful not to ascribe to Blake a wholehearted acceptance of the usual interpretations of the familiar "kingdom of God is within you" (Luke 17:21). For if this text often encouraged a "process of de-eschatalogization, whereby the *Parousia* hope was given a completely spiritual content," then Blake's suspicion of the fallen imagination must once again be emphasized.

Leslie Brisman distinguishes usefully between prophetic time, which seeks to create temporal structures against the mere confusion of chaos, and apocalyptic time, the vision of reality as instantaneous and atemporal. Since Los's task is carried out in prophetic time—since in fact he creates and *is* prophetic time—his role is deeply problematic. Even if the time he creates is the mercy of eternity, he inevitably violates the atemporal ideal and participates in the fall. The winepress of Los is inseparable from fallen conflict, and it doubles as the printing press of fallen art:

> This Wine-press is call'd War on Earth, it is the Printing-Press
> Of Los; and here he lays his words in order above the mortal brain
> As cogs are formd in a wheel to turn the cogs of the adverse wheel.
> (M 27:8–10, E123/K513)

Much suffering must be endured before this winepress can produce the wine of eternity. The printing press is a Urizenic machine of "cogs tyrannic" that move each other "by compulsion" and must be contrasted with "those in Eden: which/Wheel within Wheel in freedom revolve in harmony & peace" (J 15:18–20, E157/K636).

Just as art is not apocalypse but a prelude to it, so apocalypse may be a prelude to a new fall. Eden gives way to Beulah, Beulah to Generation and then Ulro. I would interpret "whenever" as meaning "over and over again" rather than "once and for all" in the statement "Whenever any Individual Rejects Error & Embraces Truth a Last Judgment passes upon that Individual" (*VLJ*, E551/K613). No one lives in a perpetual epiphany. And in the fallen world the fearfulness of apocalypse, of the winepress of Luvah and its sadistic torments, is no mere metaphor.

> Loud the Serpent Orc ragd thro his twenty Seven
> Folds. The tree of Mystery went up in folding flames
> Blood issud out in mighty volumes pouring in whirlpools fierce
> From out the flood gates of the Sky The Gates are burst down pour
> The torrents black upon the Earth the blood pours down incessant
> Kings in their palaces lie drownd Shepherds their flocks their tents
> Roll down the mountains in black torrents Cities Villages
> High spires & Castles drownd in the black deluge Shoal on Shoal
> Float the dead carcases of Men & Beasts driven to & fro on waves
> Of foaming blood beneath the black incessant Sky till all
> Mysterys tyrants are cut off & not one left on Earth.
> (FZ 119:3–13, E373/K359)

The vision of rivers of black blood, of men and beasts and cities drowning in it, is obsessive and appalling.

When Blake reimagines the apocalypse in the later prophecies he does not reject these dreadful images but, as always in his symbolism, transvalues them. And the basis for this is present in *The Four Zoas* too, for directly after the passage just quoted we read,

> From the clotted gore & from the hollow den
> Start forth the trembling millions into flames of mental fire
> Bathing their Limbs in the bright visions of Eternity.
> (119:21–23)

Fire and strife in Eternity are symbols of life, not death. What changes in *Milton* and *Jerusalem* is the recognition that history is not the theater of this transformation, which comes instead in an accession of Jesus into the individual imagination. Just as Los enabled Blake to fight free of an obsessive vision of his father and brothers in which "The heavens drop with human gore" (E693/K818), so Jesus liberates man by turning the blood of apocalypse into wine: "Whence is this sound of rage of Men drinking each others blood/Drunk with the smoking gore & red but not with nourishing wine" (FZ 120:11–12, E374/K360). And this is the answer to the torment of the Spectre and of "Female Love"—

> Throughout all Eternity
> I forgive you you forgive me
> As our Dear Redeemer said
> This the Wine & this the Bread.
> (E468/K417)

If apocalypse is a matter of individual (and perhaps temporary) vision rather than of universal Last Things, the function of art must be to urge us toward our own epiphanies and to sustain us during the bleak periods between them, keeping the Divine Vision in time of trouble. The vision of Edenic harmony at the end of *Jerusalem* is just that—a vision, not a condition which the poem has made available to its readers.

> And they conversed together in Visionary forms dramatic which bright
> Redounded from their Tongues in thunderous majesty, in Visions
> In new Expanses, creating exemplars of Memory and of Intellect
> Creating Space, Creating Time according to the wonders Divine
> Of Human Imagination, throughout all the Three Regions immense
> Of Childhood, Manhood & Old Age. . . .
>
> (J 98:28–33, E255/K746)

There are two subjects here, the Eternals' mode of activity and the particular forms which that activity creates. As forms, these serve as "exemplars" for the fallen world. They create time and space (Los and Enitharmon); they appeal to memory as well as intellect (i.e., to a faculty which Blake consistently associates with the fallen state); and they take account of the temporal sequence of human life (childhood, manhood, old age) which has no place in Eternity but is inherent in mortal existence. As readers we overhear the conversation in visionary forms, or possibly (Blake certainly does not make it clear) we are the forms. But what they mean to us is very different from what they mean to the Eternals.

To the Eternals, what matters is the ongoing activity, not the forms that it creates. They enjoy an Edenic wholeness in which the body and its senses are renovated and infinite. As Cusanus describes the paradise that contains the harmony of opposites, "Thou art there where speech, sight, hearing, touch, reason, knowledge, and understanding are the same, and where seeing is one with being seen, and hearing with being heard, and tasting with being tasted, and touching with being touched, and speaking with hearing, and creating with speaking." In such a state the *logos* would be more than an analogue of human speech; every "conversation" would be a poetic making of the most fundamental kind, a making that had no need of the static forms made by Los. The structure would no longer be stubborn because structure as such would cease to have meaning. Jerusalem would be felt rather than seen; in Frosch's eloquent expression, "Now there is no perspectival imagery of any kind, but simply the joyful crying of her name, and she surrounds the perceiver like a sound." For as we saw in our discussion of the female, Blake can come to terms with the Emanation only by seeing it as a mode of activity rather than as a part of the self.

The metaphor of conversation suggests the directness of communication (between eternal beings? between parts of the self?) that Blake sought in vain to achieve in the externalized fallen world. When Albion awakens he is heard "speaking the Words of Eternity in Human Forms" (J 95:9, E252/K742). Words are not signs but living beings, in reminiscence of the sound as of "the voice of speech" that Ezekiel heard the moving "Zoas" make (Ezek. 1:24). And conversation must therefore be more than language as we know it, the stubborn structure of Los. Poetry, painting and music are all together the powers "of conversing with Paradise which the flood did not Sweep away" (VLJ, E548/K609), and just as in the final plate of Job or the song of the heavenly host in the sun, we may imagine that music rather than poetry is the best intimation of Edenic "conversation." The mysterious figure Sotha, who seems to be warfare on earth and music in Eden, suggests that the energies that feed fallen war are translated in Eden into the dynamic interrelations of musical harmony. Contraries are equally true in Beulah; in Eden they interact in continual "strife." Listening to a Bach fugue work itself out, one would not speak of its elements as "equally true" but as developing dynamically one out of another. Even "harmony" may be the wrong word, since Blake preferred the line of melody, just as he preferred outline to coloring; and we know that he composed and sang melodies for his songs which some listeners thought "most singularly beautiful."

In contrast with the rigid forms hammered out by Los, these forms are *dramatic*. They resemble the give and take of conversation or the forward movement of music, not the static shape of an artifact. An idealist philosopher of language declares almost exactly as Blake does, "The 'symbolic form' in which reality is represented or pictured by poetry is always dramatic." But the dramas of the fallen world, like the tragedies that Blake despised for accepting the finality of Experience, constantly degrade this vital interaction.

> What is a Wife & what is a Harlot? What is a Church? & What
> Is a Theatre? are they Two & not One? can they Exist Separate?
> Are not Religion & Politics the Same Thing?
> (J 57:8–10, E205/K689)

A wife and a harlot are the same not only because marriage is institutionalized prostitution, but also because at best they both gratify the desires of Luvah and Vala. A church and a theater are the same not only because religion ought ideally to be communication, but also because it usually degenerates into a transaction between actors and spectators. Blake would hear the voice of Satan in Eliot's remark, "The only dramatic satisfaction that I find now is in a High Mass well performed."

The visionary forms are an ideal to which we can aspire, furnishing "exemplars" for our art; they are not our art. If Aristotelian drama has a beginning, middle, and end, Blake's ideal of spontaneous dramatic speech would be a perpetual beginning with no sense of an ending, a joy that is set free even as it is possessed:

> He who binds to himself a joy
> Doth the wingèd life destroy
> But he who kisses the joy as it flies
> Lives in Eternitys sun rise.
> (E465/K179)

Reshuffle the plates of *Jerusalem* as he might, Blake was still confined to permanent sequences of words on plates of metal, and he could not altogether dispel the image of himself as Urizen writing on books of brass with an iron pen. And *Jerusalem* ends, not with the visionary forms, but with a perpetual return to the world as we know it, where we are sustained by the Beulah-comforts of Albion's Emanation Jerusalem until we can break through into Eden.

> All Human Forms identified even Tree Metal Earth & Stone, all
> Human Forms identified, living going forth & returning wearied
> Into the Planetary lives of Years Months Days & Hours reposing
> And then Awaking into his Bosom in the Life of Immortality.
> And I heard the Name of their Emanations they are named Jerusalem.
> (99:1–5, E256/K747)

If we could speak in visionary forms dramatic we would have no further need of Los and his art. But the apocalypse can never come permanently, for we will always sink in weariness into Jerusalem's bosom; and therefore, lest we fall still further into the Satanic void, Los must rouse himself again and again to keep the Divine Vision and point toward the path of release.

DAVID WAGENKNECHT

Transformations

When Blake wrote in "Night":

> The sun descending in the west
> The evening star does shine.
> The birds are silent in their nest,
> And I must seek for mine,
> The moon like a flower,
> In heavens high bower;
> With silent delight,
> Sits and smiles on the night,
>
>   (E13)

he was very likely thinking of one particular evening in Milton's *Paradise Lost*:

> *Hesperus* that led
> The starrie Host, rose brightest, till the Moon
> Rising in clouded Majestie, at length
> Apparent Queen unvaild her peerless light,
> And ore the dark her Silver Mantle threw.
>   When *Adam* thus to *Eve*: Fair Consort, th'hour
> Of night, and all things now retir'd to rest
> Mind us of like repose. . . .
>
>   (IV. 605–612)

This is interesting for a number of reasons, only the least important of which is confirmation of the suspicion that "Night" is about sexual experience; once retired, our first parents waste no time:

> . . . other Rites
> Observing none, but adoration pure
> Which God likes best, into this inmost bower
> Handed they went; and eas'd the putting off
> These troublesom disguises which wee wear,
> Strait side by side were laid, nor turnd I weene
> *Adam* from his fair Spouse, nor *Eve* the Rites
> Mysterious of connubial Love refus'd.
>
> (IV. 736–743)

What must have interested Blake about this particular night is that, however simplified the rites, there were enough wedding meats to attract one important uninvited guest. The high wall of Paradise is only a single bound to Satan, who enters like a "prowling Wolfe" (183) "into Gods Fould" (192), and seeing immediately that sexuality is the very essence of Eden ("Imparadis't in one anothers arms"; 506), waits patiently to poison with the seeds of the Fall the aftermath of Eve's connubial rites. Milton's angels find Satan

> Squat like a Toad, close at the eare of *Eve*;
> Assaying by his Devilish art to reach
> The Organs of her Fancie.
>
> (IV. 800–802)

Both Blake's night and Milton's have their guardian angels in residence, but beyond this depart from each other so radically that to discuss "Night" in terms of *Paradise Lost*, Book IV, is to pass beyond what we normally recognize as influence and allusion. Nothing could seem further from the dénouement of Blake's poem, with its lion and lamb recumbent together, than the sullenness of the drawn battle between Gabriel and Satan which ends Milton's book. That there does, nevertheless, seem to have been imaginative traffic between the two passages testifies to Blake's intense regard for Milton as well as to his determination to transform Milton to his own purposes.

The basis of the traffic is Blake's idea that Milton's Book IV propounds a "version" of the Fall, looked at from the sexual aspect. The feral animals who prowl the Garden would represent to Blake fallen sexuality and the fact that Man's undoing was as good as accomplished. Milton's lion *is* in fact Satan:

> A Lion now he stalks with fierie glare,
> Then as a Tiger, who by chance hath spi'd
> In some Purlieu two gentle Fawnes at play,
> Strait couches close, then rising changes oft
> His couchant watch, as one who chose his ground
> Whence rushing he might surest seise them both.
>
> (IV. 402–407)

Blake would also have been interested in a remark which Satan's prey, Adam, makes while surveying his Paradise. Still "innocent," Adam notices prominently in the course of a hymn of praise to the Creator what he calls his "one easie prohibition" (433):

> that onely Tree
> Of Knowledge, planted by the Tree of Life,
> So neer grows Death to life.
>
> (IV.423–425)

The remark would have seemed more than casual to Blake, who founds his ambiguous conceptions, Innocence and Experience, on awareness deeper than Adam's of how close to life grows death. With oncoming "Night," the connubial rites therein, and the insinuations of the toad, the gap will narrow to nothing; there will commence at the same moment the confluence of imageries shared by epithalamion and elegy.

Blake records some of these considerations in his poem:

> I can lie down and sleep;
> Or think on him who bore thy name.
>
> (E14)

Both Lyca and Thel (and eventually Milton and Ololon) will want to lie down thus; Blake is associating sleep with fallen sexuality and entering the realm of death. But it is a bit startling to observe that the second line quoted associates contemplation of Christ's sacrifice with loss of innocence. The concluding lines of the poem may be no less subversive:

> For wash'd in lifes river,
> My bright mane for ever,
> Shall shine like the gold,
> As I guard o'er the fold.
>
> (E14)

I have argued earlier that the speaker of "Night" undergoes a metamorphosis, his voice merging with and becoming identical to that of the lion at the end. In terms of the Miltonic analogues, this suggests that Adam in "Night" becomes identified in some sense with Satan. We could translate this suggestion simply: Adam is infected by Satan, he falls. But the lion's vision at the end of "Night" seems positive—unless terribly qualified by its appearance in a consciously maintained fiction—and this means that entrance into Generation, to be "wash'd in lifes river," is positive also. To contemplate a Satan who brings about the Fall and who also brings golden light to a fallen world is to penetrate deeply Blake's developed mythology and his reading of Milton. Blake's mythological figure who embodies aspects of both Adam and Satan is Los (in the unfallen state, Urthona). My reading of these facts will carry us eventually through *Jerusalem*. Immediately it suggests the complexity of Blake's attitude toward Generation.

In Night I of the *Vala/The Four Zoas* manuscript, Urizen (who bears some resemblance to the God of *Paradise Lost*) plans a division of the fallen world with Luvah (who bears some resemblance to Milton's Satan). The proposed division of the world between a god of repressive reason and a god of passionate energy and desire has an obvious bearing on the sexual division of Adam and Eve I have been discussing:

> Thou Luvah said the Prince of Light behold our sons & daughters
> Reposd on beds. let them sleep on. do thou alone depart
> Into thy wished Kingdom where in Majesty & Power
> We may erect a throne. deep in the North I place my lot
> Thou in the South listen attentive.
>
> (21.20–24; E307)

The lines recall Milton (see *Paradise Lost*, V. 666–693; compare IV. 782–783), and they suggest the situation in "Night." Urizen and Luvah are both willing to "smite this dark sleeper in his tent" (22.10), which recalls Satan at the ear of Eve, and when Urizen departs suddenly, as he does, he leaves the sleeper subject to "the rage of Luvah / To pour its fury on himself & on the Eternal Man" (22.36–37; E308). Urizen's defection suggests to David Erdman the Netherlands campaign of 1799, but it might make us think of a Miltonic God whose protection of Adam and Eve is not as effective as it could be: Gabriel's angels arrive at the end of Book IV of *Paradise Lost* only after Satan has had a chance to deliver his message into the soft ear of Eve. How reasonable it is to think of this message in terms of the "rage of Luvah" can be seen in one of the principal metaphorical events of Blake's Night I (10.10–11.2; E301). In this metaphor Luvah assumes directly the role of Milton's Satan: rising from the heart to the brain of sleeping Humanity, he steals the horses of the Light and rises into the Chariot of Day (we recall that Lucifer is the "Son of Morn in weary Nights decline"; E266). Behind him, on Humanity's pillow, he leaves his emanation, Vala. Man's embrace of this emanation or accretion is equivalent to his Fall into what Blake calls Generation. As we shall see, these terms are more Miltonic than they sound.

The magnificent epic poem which Blake never brought to a final, publishable form was to have been called *Vala*, and it will seem logical therefore to associate the development or evolution of that manuscript, and the mental struggles to which it bears eloquent testimony, with Blake's attitude toward Generation. But if the foregoing discussion of

"Night" and *Paradise Lost* points in the direction of Vala, I hope it will also have been seen to point to something even more important, the collision in Blake's imagination of Milton and the idea of transformation. For purposes of discussion it will often be necessary to deal with these two problems separately, but it cannot be emphasized enough that my purpose is to demonstrate neither that Blake is Milton in disguise nor that he is Proteus. Blake said that "Milton lov'd me in childhood & shew'd me his face" (E680), but it is Milton's conceptual importance in the development of Blake's mythology which is of concern here. That importance expresses itself through the astonishing range of transformations and metamorphoses undergone by Milton at Blake's hands (while still remaining recognizably Milton), but the controlling principle of these changes is neither influence nor Blake's astonishing agility, but what I have been calling the idea of pastoral.

I am saying, then, that having observed pastoralism to be alive and well in the *Songs*, largely with the help of Spenser, I am interested now in demonstrating its conceptual importance and developmental role in the longer poems, largely with the help of Milton. But there is a less simple, and I think more important, aspect to this.

As intensive work on Blake continues, it becomes increasingly evident how central and common to all approaches is the idea of transformation. On this common ground meet ways of reading Blake as different from each other (though not necessarily opposed) as Kathleen Raine's and David Erdman's. To read either critic is to observe the rich sea changes undergone in the pages of Blake by, say, Persephone or George III. Whether or not we want to accept a given reading ought to give way eventually to a concern for the principle of transformation itself. Northrop Frye remarks: "As I continued to work on Blake, it became inescapably clear that the kind of thinking the Prophecies displayed was normal and typical poetic thinking." If we apply to the idea of Blake's imagination as a sort of universally effective transformation system Frye's idea of typicality, or normality, we come up with an idea of the poet as one who can include in his poem the whole universe of allusion. And in fact Frye, if we can trust his own genealogy for the *Anatomy of Criticism* as by Blake out of Spenser, seems to have gone on from his study of Blake, probably the best we are ever likely to have, to the idea of literature itself as a total, systematic body—the ultimate body of allusion for the ultimately allusive poet (Frye, *Anatomy*).

The danger to this approach is that the quest for the poet's field of allusion may carry us ever further from a sense of his preferences and purposes. Frye has developed a concept of mythological *displacement* which we can use to expose this problem. Displacement is defined as "the adaptation of myth and metaphor to canons of morality or plausibility" (Frye, *Anatomy*). Frye seems to suppose "that there is such a thing as a pure myth (archetype) the displacements of which can be traced through history." The difficulty with Blake, given his universality, or archetypal quality, is to define or even identify his modes of displacement. For example, Morton Paley has recently demonstrated two instances, the illustrations to Edward Young's *Night Thoughts* and the historical apotheoses of Pitt and Nelson presented in his 1809 exhibition, where Blake's consciousness, or lack of consciousness, of displacement can be very troubling. His technique in the former instance is *tacitly* to undermine Young's meaning by translating the *Night Thoughts* into a system of visual symbols the meaning of which, once understood, can be seen as a consistent attack on the values of the poem being "illustrated." The effect here is of a kind of ironic counterpoint. We have seen him doing something very similar in the *Songs of Innocence*, loading an ostensibly idyllic scene with covert reminders of physical horror. We can see him practicing similar sleight of hand in his illustrations to Ambrose Philips' imitation of Virgil, and have to contemplate his apparent willingness to accept without correction the lyric enthusiasms of Samuel Palmer—Palmer called the illustrations in his notebook "little dells, and nooks, and corners of Paradise"—despite the fact that Palmer's enthusiasms have very little if anything to do with the illustrations Blake achieved. In the case of the historical apotheoses, Blake's apparent unwillingness to descend to displacement accounts not only for the paintings themselves but as well for catalogue descriptions of them which come close to being deliberately misleading. At any rate, nothing like the "meaning" of the paintings has been publicly apparent until, thanks to the efforts of Mark Schorer, David Erdman, and Morton Paley, recent times.

However, to speak of "meaning" in this connection is to beg large questions. Blake has Los say in *Jerusalem*:

> Thou art in Error; trouble me not with thy righteousness.
> I have innocence to defend and ignorance to instruct:
> I have no time for seeming; and little arts of compliment,
> In morality and virtue: in self-glorying and pride.
>
> (42.25–28; E187)

What I have been referring to as "displacement" may have seemed simply "seeming" to Blake; we must remember, moreover, that the illustrations to *Innocence* and to Philips' Virgil imitation, the *Night Thoughts* drawings and the historical apotheoses are all very much *there* for us to see. The artist himself was hardly to blame that so few have chosen to look, and there is something perverse about applying the word "tacit" to Blake's most extensive series of related paintings (the *Night Thoughts* set), 537 watercolors in all.

Nevertheless, we approach here a central problem of Blake's place in recent criticism. Geoffrey Hartman has attacked Frye's conception of displacement, arguing "not that myth is displaced but that it is historical," and that "it comes to us institutionalized from the beginning." Hartman feels that "to Frye's total myth we must therefore add a historical account of the war that myth has waged with myth." Further: "What is true of the realist is true of any writer, as Frye's own theory of displacement has shown: reality is never more than the *plausible* artifice. But in that case the notion of displacement becomes unnecessary except to indicate the direction of human credibility—credibility defining that realm in which contraries are no longer felt." Blake, as we know, was acutely conscious of the problem of plausibility:

> Then I asked: does a firm perswasion that a thing is so, make it so?
> He replied. All poets believe that it does . . .
>
> (E38)

Blake's awareness of the problem, and the peculiar fact that his imaginary interlocutor in this instance is the prophet Isaiah point to an extremely high degree of historical self-consciousness. Just as his meter is a systematically achieved function of his relationship to the traditions of his time, so his election of a prophetic function for poetry represents similar self-consciousness to that of Thomas Chatterton and James Macpherson. Similarly, Blake is often willing to forego "displacement" because of self-consciousness with respect to the platitudinizing of his age. Blake's distrust of the Augustan epigram, as John Hollander points out, was extreme: "Epigrammatic tautology, for Blake, seems to be a kind of death." But this is the problem. Blake's creation of an alternative tradition, of a plausibility more universally founded than that of the Augustans, may seem to us part of his positive achievement, but to literary history it has often destroyed all sense of his vulgar relations and made him seem "an interruption in cultural history" (Frye, *Fearful Symmetry*). Blake lived in an age when the percentage of displacement relative to original myth was very high (as in *The Rape of the Lock*), and to reverse these proportions was to suggest a close identification between displacement and history itself: failure to embrace moral emotions in a sententious time can seem the same thing as withdrawal from history. This spurious identification has always haunted Blake criticism, and every work which did not seem to have a definable relationship to history (and there is much room for debate about the ones which do) could be seen as a vacuum, drawing toward it biographical and historical information. It is no accident that Blake has been more than usually victimized by biographical fantasists. And even on the level of sense and sound scholarship, we can see the danger in contemporary criticism. Kathleen Raine's criticism not only seeks to discover meanings, but to provide a historical and doctrinal home for the poet. Not for nothing is her major study of Blake called *Blake and Tradition*. We can see traces of the same problem in Erdman's criticism. David Erdman's services to Blake scholarship are so manifold that no serious student can not be grateful to him, and certainly his thesis that Blake's poems reflect contemporary history is unassailable, but his anxiety to surround each and every crux of Blake criticism with a solution based upon responses to the progress of contemporary history needs to be vigorously challenged. In the first edition of *Blake: Prophet against Empire* (Princeton, N.J.: Princeton University Press, 1954) Erdman went so far as to suggest that the *Vala/The Four Zoas* manuscript went astray because Blake's thematic purposes were extremely at variance with the current of history. Moreover, Blake was attempting something *foolish*: "In *The Four Zoas* he seems to have allowed his tune to be called by events unfolding as he wrote. The result is as mad as the effort to play croquet in Wonderland with living mallets and balls." My quotation comes from the second, revised edition (1969) of Erdman's book (p. 294), which acknowledges the very severe attack on his thesis by G. E. Bentley, Jr., in his facsimile edition of the manuscript (Bentley demonstrates that Erdman's approach to *The Four Zoas* is based on inaccurate dating of the manuscript) only by a footnote appended to the passage quoted, beginning, "We cannot be sure." Erdman's unwillingness to give in on this and many another point relevant to *The Four Zoas* (see the discussion of Night VII(b) below) seems in part a response to the poet's own self-conscious and enormous repudiations, an act of painful and kind duty, like Milton slapping flesh on the wasted frame of Urizen by the shore of Arnon.

At any rate, we should now be in a position to see the relationship between this question and the principle of transformation, for even when the distance between Blake's lines and a historical situation, or an element of what Miss Raine calls "the tradition," is great indeed, it is no greater than the distance between, say, Blake and Young.

We cannot give up the transformations, for they are there. And I do not mean to imply either that one can dispute either Miss Raine or Mr. Erdman except on the basis of interpretations of specific poems. But perhaps I have said enough to suggest that Geoffrey Hartman is right in this critical instance, and that the "history" we seek for Blake is the history of the war of myth against myth. I believe we can find what we are looking for in the life-long tension between Blake and Milton, but that does not mean that Milton is Blake's myth (as Miss Raine might state this approach), or that Milton is Blake's history—though this is much closer to the truth. The shape of the conflict is determined by the idea of pastoral; but it remains true that the principle of displacement in Blake, the source at once of the world view accommodated to Christian plausibility and of the tension with that view which gives his work its relationship to "canons of morality," is—for the duration of his poetical career anyway—Milton.

DIANA HUME GEORGE

The Feminine in Blake

Although *Jerusalem* contains the final version of Blake's vision of the proper relationship of the sexes and a modification of the identification of emanation with females, it also contains a sharp renewal of distrust toward the negative-feminine, which he finally names in *Jerusalem* as the Female Will. The Female Will is not women, but women are the manifestations of the Female Will. Female Will represents the material world, nature as destructive necessity, and the domination of forces that have been styled feminine over forces that have been styled masculine. In empiricism and "natural religion," Blake saw not the amelioration of humankind's status as sinners in the hands of an angry male god, but the subjection of humankind to natural forces that replaced that god, duplicating or even exceeding his vindictiveness, arbitrariness, and restrictiveness.

For Blake, the emergence of nature as the primary redemptive symbol of romanticism was not a reaction against the Age of Reason, but rather its fulfillment and culmination. Man had always imaged nature as feminine, and Blake perceived that process of symbol formation as one in which man grew not larger but even smaller than he was under the auspices of Christianity. Nor was the Age of Reason itself a reaction against Christian theology as enacted in culture; it was part of the same evolutionary process, one that was increasingly regressive rather than progressive. Man was no longer at the mercy of a spiritual world that was infinite, though that was dismal enough; now he was at the mercy of a material and natural world that was finite. The old religion had at least infinity to recommend it to Blake. The new dispensation appeared to open all the world to man's knowledge, but that world was smaller imaginatively—or if its expanses were granted, they were seen as beyond man's grasp in a manner finally little different from that posited by preceding world views. Man's creative energies were now consumed by his relationships with the object world, which he thought of as external to himself. In this process, Blake saw yet another aspect of the same divisiveness that had characterized other periods of history, one rooted like the others in sexual dialectics. The Female Will was his personified representation of the separateness of nature from man. Nature is things-as-they-are, not things-as-they-might-be, and if man models himself after nature, he can see himself only as finite, even minute.

Blake was so enraged by the process of nature deification in the late eighteenth and early nineteenth centuries that his historical moment accounts for his almost obsessive preoccupation with the Female Will. The Female Will is present as early as *Europe* (1794), in the acts of Enitharmon. In *Europe*, Christian history is portrayed as "a female dream," and man himself is only woman's dream.

> Now comes the night of Enitharmon's joy!
> Who shall I call? Who shall I send?
> That Woman, lovely Woman! may have dominion?
> (*Europe* 6:1–3)

It seems a curious reading of history indeed, for Blake knew very well that Christian culture was patriarchal, and demonstrated that knowledge in many poems, especially in *Visions of the Daughters of Albion*, published the previous year. Throughout his life he objected to man's repression of woman's freedom, expressed primarily through the laws of Urizen, the Old Testament Jehovah. But he saw the process as subversively reciprocal. Woman was taught that her sexuality was unclean and sinful. Therefore, she repressed it and withheld it from herself and from man. That power base, the passive-aggressive, became a comprehensive one in Blake's view. The withholding of sexuality in the name of moral virtue and Christian propriety had been woman's chief function in civilization, to her everlasting detriment and to man's. Woman used her withheld sexuality first as a protection, then as a bludgeon. "Go! Tell the Human race that Woman's love is Sin!" cries Enitharmon.

> That an Eternal life awaits the worm of sixty winters
> In an allegorical abode where existence hath never come.
> Forbid all Joy, & from her childhood shall the little female
> Spread nets in every secret path.
> (*Europe* 6:5–9)

The allegorical abode is the Christian heaven, which is to be attained by a renunciation of pleasure in this world. In the earlier works, Blake carefully balances the fault: Urizen has forced the female, who then becomes complicit in the crime against humanity.

In *Jerusalem*, Blake continues to attempt a balance of causal attribution. The male spectre is the counterpart of the Female Will, and he is meant to appear as destructive and dangerous as the Female Will. Blake made what seems every possible effort to establish that Female Will is not equivalent to woman, but that woman is the manifestation of the Female Will because she is identified with nature throughout history. As he grew older, Blake became more and more convinced that nature worship was the primary manifestation of man's fall in his own time and, correspondingly, his vehemence against it increased. He named his final epic *Jerusalem*, in honor of the redemptive form of woman as liberty, inspiration, and the process of poetry. But any accounting of Blake's values for the feminine is also obliged to come to terms with some peculiarly strong statements in *Jerusalem*.

Los, Blake's own spokesman, cries:

> What may Man be? who can tell. but what may Woman be?
> To have power over Man from Cradle to corruptive grave.
> There is a Throne in every Man, it is the Throne of God
> This Woman has claimd as her own & Man is no more.
> (*Jerusalem* 30:25–28)

Blake is speaking of man's entrapment in physical mortality and his enslavement to nature. As before, Blake's intention is to include the female in the term "man." But in *Jerusalem* it becomes increasingly difficult for Blake and his reader to feel that inclusion. In *Milton*, Blake carefully abstained from using the word "woman" to express his convictions about forces that have been portrayed as feminine. *Milton* reads like a strategic and judicious withdrawal of that term from its overuse in *Europe*. But in *Jerusalem*, woman in the fallen world is repeatedly equated with the Female Will. "O Albion why wilt thou Create a Female Will?" (30:31). The negative aspect of the sexual was in *Milton* more evenly divided between the separated masculine and feminine forms, Satan/spectre/shadow and the sixfold Miltonic female. But in *Jerusalem* the "Sexual Machine" is predominantly female, "an Aged Virgin Form" (39:25). "This World is all a cradle . . ." (56:8). Increasingly, woman in fall is only natural body, only oppressive maternity. Vala, the erring emanation in *Jerusalem*, cries, "The Human Divine is Womans Shadow, a Vapor in the summers heat." He is "Woman-born / And Woman-nourished & Woman-educated & Woman-scorn'd!" (64:16–17). The torture of humans that was accomplished by both sons and daughters of Albion in *Milton* is almost exclusively the function of the daughters in *Jerusalem*.

The description of Beulah is now "Where every Female delights to give her maiden to her husband / The Female searches sea & land for gratifications to the / Male Genius" (69:15–17). Rahab and Vala rage through the pages of *Jerusalem* with their train of daughters and witches, destroying everything in their path. "O who can withstand her power / Her name is Vala in eternity: in Time her name is Rahab" (70:30–31). The intentions of the women are total destruction of the men. Enitharmon decides to "exhaust in War" the "fury of men" so that "Woman permanent remain" (82:35).

Blake reminds the reader periodically that woman's alliance is, after all, with Satan, "the God of this world," and with "the Patriarchal pomp and cruelty," but the reminders read as interludes in a sustained tirade against nature and increasingly, therefore, against woman. The contention of Los and Enitharmon becomes a battle of wills, for "Two Wills they had, and two Intellects." The emanation that before seemed to be a nearly equal partner in the united humanity is now just as often presented as the aspect that must merely capitulate; the emanation "refusest my Fibres of dominion" (88:13). Theoretically, the spectre must also be under the dominion of the humanity, and in these very passages Blake is attempting to break the identification of emanation with woman. But the emanation to whom Los speaks is Enitharmon, who is by definition a female in the fallen world. And she answers him, "This is Womans World," and declares that she will increase her power "Till God himself becomes a Male subservient to the Female" (88:21).

At the same time, *Jerusalem* also contains the most fully developed version of the positive-feminine, the redemptive form of Jerusalem. Throughout *Jerusalem*, she attempts to persuade her negative counterparts to work with her. Blake's rage is against nature, and Jerusalem is not natural but spiritual. "Vala produc'd the Bodies Jerusalem gave the Souls" (18:7). *Jerusalem* ends in the marriage of Jerusalem and Albion, and thereby with inclusion of the feminine principle in humanity. But because Blake believed that "humanity is far beyond sexual organization," he was obliged to seek human relationship other than marriage to symbolize the highest form of communication in Eternity. That relationship evolves in the major prophecies as brotherhood through Christ. "This is Friendship & Brotherhood without it Man Is Not" (96:16). Though "Sexes must vanish & cease to be" in Eternity, Blake describes the relationships of Eternity in gendered language, perhaps because our language is gender-bound and created from that sexual dialectic.

The image of woman in *Jerusalem* solidifies, then, into unfortunate extremes. In *Milton*, Ololon and the sixfold female "represented and contained" all positive and negative aspects of the feminine. In *Jerusalem*, each woman is characterized *only* by extremes: she is either Vala/Rahab or Jerusalem, ravaging destructive principle or redemptive principle. There seems far less room for "real" women here than in Blake's earlier work. That last-minute leap into Eternity—which is technically genderless—must accomplish woman's salvation, for her aspect in the fallen world in *Jerusalem* is uniformly ghastly. There were frequent indications of this development in *Milton*. "But every Man returnd & went still going forward thro' / The Bosom of the Father in Eternity on Eternity" (31:4–5) is a formulation that, whatever its intentions, reads curiously like "patriarchal pomp." But *Milton* is without the tirades against Female Will that threaten to overpower Blake's vision of theoretical equality between sexless sexes in eternity. It would be convenient to redeem Blake's view of woman to accord with what were clearly his intentions, and to do so by emphasizing that the Female Will is not really woman at all. Blake's mythology was highly symbolic, and his symbolism might be brought to his rescue on exactly this issue. An analysis of metaphorical process in Blake, however, compounds rather than simplifies the problem.

Blake's composite portrayal of females and the feminine has been the cause of continuous confusion for his readers. Even the best of his readers seem unable to fathom the situation. Northrop Frye's "Notes for a Commentary on *Milton*" summarize what I read as a contradiction, or at least an immense difficulty, in Blake as well as in his critics. Frye details the structure of the fourfold in Blake's symbolism. In Eden or eternity, "man is one with God, and everything else is part of a divine, and therefore a human, creation. In the natural world, only similarity and separation are perceived. In the imaginative or eternal view, Blake speaks of "Identities of Things."

> A thing may be identified *as* itself, yet it cannot be identified except as an individual of a class. The class is its "living form," not its abstract essence, and form in Blake is a synonym for image, or experienced reality. . . . All Blake's images and mythical figures are "minute particulars" or individuals identified with their total forms. Hence they are "States, Combinations of Individuals," and can be seen in other singular or collective aspects.

In other words, all things are identical with each other. In the imaginative view, all things are within the human form, and all forms or images of that body are identical. Frye argues that such a vision can be expressed only through metaphor, and the metaphor, in its radical form, "is a statement of identification." Everything may be one in "essence" but infinitely varied in "identity." This is surely one of the reasons Blake turns to Christianity, whose language Frye calls "instinctively metaphorical." Christ *is* God and man. *Revelation* expresses a world view in which all things have attained human rather than merely natural form. The divine world, then, is one in which all aspects of infinite and eternal humanity are One God. The human world, from the imaginative point of view, is one in which all men are one man, "expressed in terms of sexual rather than social love, a world in which a Bridegroom and Bride are one Flesh." In Generation, the imaginative and natural visions battle; in Beulah, "nature begins to take on its proper form of a female 'emanation' loved because created. Christianity preserves this symbolism when it speaks of the Church as the Bride of Christ."

On one hand, then, Blake can be defended against accusations of hating women through his tirades against the Female Will precisely because the Female Will is not women. But the Poetic Genius is not that which finds mere similarity; it is that which creates "identification." Blake claimed the status of "vision" for his entire mythology. If women are the manifestation of the Female Will, or the destructiveness of nature, then they *are* the Female Will. The "female" is a "form" in Blake, and thus an image. Female human beings can be identified only as individuals of a class, to follow Frye's formulations. That class is "human beings of the feminine gender." This is the feminine existence, for there is only one essence, which is eternal and not sexual. Blake constantly reminded his readers that they must not mistake an "Individual" for a "State." "Distinguish therefore States from Individuals in those States" (*Jerusalem* 32:22). States are abstractions, and individuals are humanities, not abstractions. Blake always counseled that abstraction was the enemy of mankind, but in his rage at the natural world, Blake forgot his own first rule. Women in the fallen world in *Jerusalem* are not portrayed as "Minute Particulars," but as abstractions of the Female Will, utterly identified with nature. Woman is redeemed in Eternity, but not as woman. In Eternity the female humanity is an "individual identified with its total form," the Human Form Divine. But in Generation she is also identified with her total form, the form of the natural world.

The redemptive form of the feminine must be found, then, in Eternity. Frye has this to say about the nature of gender in Eternity: "In Eden there is no Mother-God. . . . God is always the Supreme Male, the creator for whom the distinction between the beloved female and created child has disappeared." Despite Blake's warnings to the contrary, even so sensitive a reader as Frye has managed to miss Blake's point. But it might also be suggested that Blake missed his own point. How did this state of affairs come about?

Blake was the product of his acculturation. The fact that he could perceive and anatomize the processes of symbol formation in culture did not mean that he was immune to them himself. His representation of nature as feminine was not merely a strategy by which he adopted the historical terminology in order to destroy it or to disclose its true meaning. According to his own analysis of the development of consciousness in the fallen world, the perception of nature as feminine was deeply ingrained in his own thought processes. He was well able to see what that identification had produced in history, but less able, not surprisingly, to perceive the long-range results of his own appropriation of the conventional terminology which eventually restricted his capacity to portray the feminine.

In the Dante series, begun about 1824 and left unfinished at Blake's death, woman is treacherous and delusive. Blake was convinced that Dante had made "the Goddess Nature & not the Holy Ghost" the foundation of his belief. Beatrice, far from being the spiritual inspiration she is in the source text, is instead portrayed as the Goddess Nature, a form of Rahab/Vala. Woman/man configurations in the heavily symbolic *Purgatorio* and *Paradiso* designs are consistently styled as Nature/man confrontations. In "Beatrice Addressing Dante from the Car," Dante gestures in submission to Beatrice, poetic genius subordinating itself to Female Will. Plate 16, "The Goddess of Fortune," portrays a Vala-like figure presiding under twin globes of materialism and rationalism. Above her head, Blake wrote in pencil, "The Hole of a Shit-house. The Goddess Fortune is the Devil's servant, ready to Kiss any one's arse." In their sketchy form, the twin globes are unmistakably a woman's breasts. The large circle in which are drawn Vala and the acerbic remarks are the ample belly and hips of the vegetative female, Nature.

Just as Blake could not stand completely outside history or consciousness, neither could he absent himself from the social arena. The pressures and tensions of sexuality were his own as well as other men's. It is improbable that he could so clearly have understood the process by which men project women as the elusive other, and spend their lives pursuing and attempting to appropriate women, unless he had been the victim of that process himself. Blake resented nature and what he called the Female Will, and he probably also resented real women as embodiments of those forces. It is not merely that history has styled those forces as feminine, but that Blake felt them as feminine also. And that feeling is partly the result of processes that are biologically determined.

We are of woman born. Our bodies die. Blake saw the idea of bodily mortality as pernicious, for it denied another and higher reality. Women are not capriciously chosen by Blake as symbols of the natural world; they are the bearers and first nurturers of humanity. Body means woman, and Blake loved the body, which, when used expansively, was a gateway into Eternity. Bodily birth and death are inevitable, and Blake was ready to make the best of it, but not to acknowledge it as the all. He was a realist who was determined to love the body for its potential, even as he hated its limitations. But he was so hypersensitively aware of the dangers of the body that his early critics may be forgiven for mistaking him as a body hater—they are wrong, but not altogether wrong. It is the natural and mortal body that Blake loved and hated, and though the potential for spiritual regeneration lies in the physical body, the actuality does not. (The actuality is in Eternity.) Blake calls the new body a "spiritual" body. To the extent that he saw the natural body as the enemy of humanity, to almost exactly that extent he saw woman as the enemy of humanity. Woman *as woman* is her own enemy and man's as well. Man *as man* is the same. Body is a positive aspect of humanity when it is used as a gateway out of body or beyond body, in such a way as to include body.

According to his own analysis, Blake is entirely justified in adopting conventional diction to characterize "masculine" and "feminine," for he is describing the historical evolution of those "principles," and he takes care not to equate them with men and women in their human form. "Reason and Energy, Love and Hate, are necessary to Human existence. From these contraries spring what the religious call Good & Evil. Good is the passive that obeys Reason. Evil is the active springing from energy" (*The Marriage of Heaven and Hell*, Plate 3). Though reason and energy, active and passive, are contraries, and both are necessary, active energy is superior to passive reason. By following the conventional meanings of masculine and feminine, Blake associated "reasoning passivity" with the feminine and "imaginative activity" with the masculine. This does not mean that women in Blake do not act. But when they do, they are not being "feminine," but rather female. The feminine is a passive category in Blake, but the Female Will is active in the extreme. Feminine passivity may be either valuable or pernicious, as may masculine activity. But by following historical symbols and then trying to reorient them, Blake became mired in the inevitable identification of female, feminine principle, and woman.

Blake's problems with portrayals of sexuality and of women, as I see it, are problems of symbol formation that express themselves in the limitations of language. If, as Blake posits, consciousness itself is sexual, dialectic, and gender-specific, then the development of language will also be gendered; and this is, of course, the case. Blake's vision of the human form and his idea of the value of being human was constantly rendered problematic by language. He had to try to speak the literally unspeakable. Language and art were his tools for reunification of the Human Form Divine, but the images available to him to communicate his vision of the eternal were necessarily drawn from the repository of the material and natural world. That world—its images and therefore its language—was sexual. Blake wished to portray everything as human, and humans in this world are sexual beings. He was thus compelled to express ultimately genderless human forms in gendered terms.

If "Humanity Is far beyond sexual organization," then it is also beyond language and image. There are, quite literally, no words that will completely express Blake's vision. Poetry and art in the fallen world are keepers of the divine vision, but they must make do with the tools at hand. The major prophecies are Blake's use of those tools, a documentation of his effort to say everything in as many ways as possible, in the visionary hope that the whole would be recognized as more than the sum of its parts. To accomplish this task, he turned in every direction; most of all, to the sexes. Here, where he tried hardest to heal, he was constantly confronted with the wound. Sometimes, ironically, he deepened the wound.

There are, I think, other reasons Blake's prophecies move in directions that are less and less sympathetic to women in the fallen world. The major villains of the earlier works, and especially those of the 1790s, tend to be portrayed as male. The proportion of villainy that falls to the female in the later work is significantly greater. This shift is partly the product of his historical situation. In the earlier works, Blake saw the major historical movement against which he must revolt as the Age of Reason. Because abstract reasoning is a masculine principle in the evolution of culture, it is to be expected that Blake would portray it as male. But in the first decades of the 1800s, romanticism was the spirit of the age, and with romanticism came the deification of nature as goddess. As I have tried to suggest, the two movements and their sexual reflections or symbols are not antithetical for Blake; they are integral developments that grow out of one another. They are not proper contraries at all, but merely negations that duplicate themselves and cancel out any possible progress. The animating spirit of the first is masculine, and the animating spirit of the second is feminine. What appears to be (and in some respect is) a mounting vehemence toward natural women, simultaneously developed with the regeneration of spiritual woman, is a product of Blake's particular moment.

One further mitigating factor remains to be considered in Blake's comprehensive portrayal of the Female Will. It accounts in part for the way in which the Female Will dominates the action of *Jerusalem*. Blake was better able to name and embody the destructive forces exerted by men in history for a simple reason: there were many more names available to him. The qualities he damns in men can be divided among numerous historical personages as well as among his mythical characters. Bacon, Newton, Locke, Voltaire, Titian, Rubens, Dante, Milton: the prophecies are full of their names. But there was no such historical gallery open to Blake when he wished to "give a body to Error" in the female. He was forced to make do with biblical women and his own mythological characters. To make up for the lack, he postulated the Female Will, a name that suffers from abstraction and overgeneralization because her "Minute Particulars" had few familiar names in history.

Blake was able to perceive the limitations of Milton's values for the feminine, and there is some evidence in *Jerusalem* that he was beginning to perceive his own. That he was not able to perceive all of them is not entirely a failure on his part. Rather, the degree to which he valued the feminine is unprecedented. Writing a century and more after Milton, he advanced Milton's thought on the sexes by an immeasurable degree. In apocalypse, "the Hand of Man grasps firm between the Male & Female Loves" (*Jerusalem* 97:15). Jerusalem disappears as an individual character at the end of *Jerusalem* because she has at last awakened and "overspread all Nations as in Ancient Time" (97:2). City and woman, the absolute redemptive form of humanity in her book as Milton is in *Milton*, she suffuses "All Human Forms." Jerusalem is the "name" of all emanations, the ability to move freely between time and space, the impulse to create, and creation itself as living process. Blake preserved more of Milton's "mistaken" vision than I believed he intended, but far less of it than most of his own predecessors and successors.

Milton's idea of what constituted the proper relationship between the sexes was radical and revolutionary—and also conservative and reactionary. He attempted to change the basis of sexual interaction only to a certain degree, and the foundation, feminine inferiority, remained intact. Blake intended to abolish that inequality but, like Milton, found there were assumptions he was unwilling or perhaps unable to part with. Blake battled sexual repression in Milton and in himself. Freud continued the process a century after Blake. It is now nearly another century since Freud first began to write, and culture has not come very far since then. Whatever the limitations of Blake's vision may have been, I cannot fairly fault them. Culture, as opposed to small numbers of individuals within it, has not begun to approach Blake's vision, and it is only beginning to approach Milton's. Blake would be disappointed, but not in the least surprised.

He might be surprised, however, by the kinds of criticism to which his works are increasingly subject in the political climate of this decade. I quote at length from Susan Fox's predominantly excellent analysis, "The Female as Metaphor in William Blake's Poetry," because it illustrates an emergent tendency in Blake criticism which I find troublesome.

> Blake made the chief character of *Visions of the Daughters of Albion* female not just because he admired Mary Wollstonecraft and thought women at least potentially men's equals, but also because he needed a chief character who could be raped and tied down and suppressed with-out recourse—or rather, with the single recourse of giving birth to the revolutionary male force which can end the victimization. *Visions of the Daughters of Albion* has a heroine and not a hero partly because one of the points of the poem is that its central figure, "the soft soul of America," is a slave. Oothoon was chosen for her part not just because she was wise and brave, but also because she was female and thus powerless. Her gender is a trap—just the trap the symbolism of the poem demands. Blake rails against her being trapped, of course—he was never not libertarian. But it is one thing to despise oppression, and another to envision the means of the oppressed to end it. No woman in any Blake poem has both the will and the power to initiate her own salvation—not even the strongest and most independent of his women, Oothoon.

It is important to note that Fox is dealing not with the Female Will, the issue on which Blake is admittedly most open to critical remon-strance, but rather with Blake's most openly feminist poem. I appreciate Fox's motives, but her analysis suffers from the same kind of expectation that characterizes the objections of Freud's critics on the same subject: that description somehow suggests prescription, and/or that description should be succeeded by alternative prescription. The analogy with Freud's critics is more than fortuitous, because Blake's and Freud's perceptions of femininity were very similar. Several significant problems are summarized in this excerpt from Fox's essay.

First, it is indeed important that Blake wrote *Visions of the Daugh-ters of Albion* shortly after he illustrated Wollstonecraft's book of short stories. The works of the 1790s show a conscious occupation of Blake's energies with issues that might be termed feminist. The political allegory is also important for Blake during this period, during which he wrote such less disguised political treatises as *America* and *Europe*. But Fox points out the aptness of Blake's metaphorical use of females in the political allegory as much to castigate as to praise him. She appears to fault Blake for not "envisioning the means of the oppressed to end [oppression]." This judgment effectively removes *Visions* from its context in Blake's career. With the possible and only partial exception of *The Marriage of Heaven and Hell*, the early works are not intended to enact regeneration. They are readings of history as it is, not as it should have been or might be in the future. By selecting a woman to represent America in the political allegory and womanhood in the sociosexual allegory, Blake serves the first purpose of transformation by providing a penetrating analysis. Synthesis will come later, in the major prophecies. I am more sympathetic to criticisms of the ways in which Blake envisions feminine participation in "the means to end oppression" than I am to criticisms that he did not manage it at the beginning of his career. And it is only a half-truth that no woman in Blake initiates her own salvation. For the most part, neither do men, nor can one sex do so without the active cooperation of the other.

Even if *Visions* is less prophecy than history, it does indeed contain prophetic passages that envision the means to end oppression (as we have seen). People cannot escape their tyrants, according to Blake, until those tyrants are exposed. Even in the major prophecies, disclosure is more than the prelude to transformation; it is an integral part of the redemptive process. And Oothoon, a woman, is the speaker of all of the prophetic passages in *Visions*. (Fox's reading of Blake is always knowledgeable and perceptive, and often superb. Even competent readers of Blake will misread him on the feminine unless the complexities addressed here are considered.)

Blake's early characterizations of women are primarily as victims because women were, historically, victims. But for Blake, women were victimizers as well. The symbolic content of the Female Will is perhaps the major problem in Blake's characterizations of the feminine, but it is not the only one. The literal and historical levels on which real men and women interact were a large part of Blake's concern, and women are seldom faultless on those levels. I can most clearly illustrate my points by continuing the parallels between Blake and Freud.

As Juliet Mitchell has shown in *Psychoanalysis and Feminism*, those who condemn Freud for his views on women usually fail to understand that Freud's is an *analysis of* patriarchy. More fundamental still, Freud's critics often do not accept the tenets of psychoanalysis at all. Mitchell's major point is that by dismissing and misjudging Freud, women discard an important ally. They identify him with the facts he discovered, and they do not like those facts; hence, they must not be facts. Freud provides us with the most comprehensive psychological dramatization of patriarchy available. If that dramatization includes some unpleasant things about what the feminine has meant, in culture and in individuals, his critics hold him responsible. This attitude precludes not only an understanding of his worth as cultural historian, but also the use of his findings in the attempt to transform culture. It also effectively precludes, in my view, the possibility of ascertaining the ways in which some of his findings really were culture-specific, and therefore of only very limited use.

I anticipate the same process in Blake criticism. In the case of earlier critiques, the process is already evident. The relationship of masculine to feminine and of man to woman is perceived as the foundation of consciousness by both Blake and Freud. Accurate reading of Blake requires, as fully as does accurate reading of Freud, acceptance of the axioms of psychoanalysis: full acknowledgement of the range of unconscious throught processes and of the role of sexuality in human personality. Infantile sexuality and oedipal configurations, though they appear in considerably modified form, are also implicitly fundamental in Blake.

I do not think that most feminist critics come to Blake with a sympathetic approach to this apparatus. (Most people do not have the slightest inclination to accept the range and significance of sexuality and unconscious thought.) Blake critics, as a group, may be more likely to accept these axioms, or at least to pay them lip service. But, as Mitchell points out, many successful pyschologists, and even some psychoanalysts, do not really accept these dicta. (Mitchell cites Reich as a famous example of an analyst who did not believe in the unconscious.) What has happened in Freudian criticism is, I think, likely to occur in Blake scholarship, from within the circle of aficionados as well as from without. The more widely Blake is read, the more he will be misapprehended, as Freud has been. And there is every evidence that Blake's popularity is still increasing. This era will be as touchily sensitive to Blake's convictions about sexuality as it is to Freud's. Earlier Blake critics tended to misread Blake on women because the subject was not, in particular, an issue for them. Contemporary Blake critics misread him on the same subject because it *is* such an issue for them, and for our time.

One final reason I think this tendency to misread Blake on women and the feminine will increase is based not on his similarity to Freud, but on a clear difference. Freud did little to suggest in what ways women might have contributed to their own denigration. Instead, he simply accepted feminine conditioning as a given imposed upon women. When he protested it, as he often did, he protested against cultural trends, not against people. The supposedly weaker sense of justice in women is attributed by Freud to the weaker foundation of the superego in women. The lack of intellectual distinction in women arises from undue and excessive suppression of the sexual instincts; hence, women have less energy available for the all-important work of sublimation. Freud's critics looked only at the result he presented (in these examples, a weaker sense of justice and a lack of intellection), entirely omitting consideration of the analysis that underlies it, an analysis that admits that society *made* women weaker. It does not occur to such critics that Freud was in some respects right, and that his analysis explains rather than justifies the conditions. (He does, at some few points, attempt to justify such conditions. In either case, that is beside the point.)

Defined as patriarchal society has defined it, intellectual capacity in women, or at least its manifestation in culture, *is* historically weaker in women than in men. So, too, is the sense of "justice," for justice is subjectively masculine, Judaic, and derived from law. If such mistakes of interpretation have been so consistently made in the case of Freud, who saw women almost exclusively as victims, one might expect even greater mistakes in the case of Blake, who saw women as both victims and victimizers. Not content to leave woman nursing her other-imposed neurosis within the confines of the kitchen, Blake analyzed the ways in which women not only submitted to their own denigration but helped it along, and thereby gained power through manipulation in the passive-aggressive mode. Blake's sense of women's significance in the external events of history was also far keener than Freud's, and Blake was as hard on women as on men for the mess that history is.

The need to be free of responsibility for things-as-they-are is, I believe, a disturbing characteristic of the neo-feminist movement, one that implicitly attempts to salvage the exclusive privileges that accrue to the oppressed in a historical scenario in which women are only victims. Blake's prophetic fury fell on women as fully as on men because he did not accept the idea that women are, or ever were, only unwilling innocents. His condemnations of traditional feminine behavior, like Swift's, were rooted in the conviction that woman herself deserved far better—that what appeared to constitute virtue was in fact a profound self-betrayal.

Chronology

1757   Born November 28 in London.

1771   Apprenticed to James Basire, an engraver.

1782   Married to Catherine Boucher.

1783   *Poetical Sketches* published, containing poems written 1769–1778.

1787   Death of Robert Blake, the poet's beloved younger brother.

1789   Engraving of *Songs of Innocence* and *The Book of Thel*.

1790   Writes *The Marriage of Heaven and Hell* at the Christological age of thirty-three.

1791   Printing of *The French Revolution* by left-wing publisher Joseph Johnson, but the poem abandoned in proof sheets.

1793   Engraving of *America* and *Visions of the Daughters of Albion*.

1794   Engraving of *Songs of Experience, Europe* and *The Book of Urizen*.

1795   Engraving of *The Book of Los, The Song of Los* and *The Book of Ahania*.

1797   Begins to write *Vala*, or *The Four Zoas*.

1800   Goes with wife to Felpham, Sussex, to live and work with William Hayley.

1803   Quarrels with Hayley and returns to London.

1804   Is tried for sedition and acquitted after being accused by a soldier, John Scholfield. Blake's epics, *Milton* and *Jerusalem*, are dated by him as of this year, but are believed to have been finished rather later.

1809   Exhibits his paintings, but fails of buyers. A *Descriptive Catalogue*, written for the exhibition, survives, and contains his remarkable criticism of Chaucer.

1818   Becomes mentor to younger painters: John Linnell, Samuel Palmer, Edward Calvert, George Richmond.

1820   Woodcuts to Virgil's *Pastorals*.

1825   Completes engravings for The Book of Job.

1826   Completes illustrations to Dante.

1827   Dies on August 12.

Contributors

HAROLD BLOOM, Sterling Professor of the Humanities at Yale University, is the author of *The Anxiety of Influence*, *Poetry and Repression* and many other volumes of literary criticism. His forthcoming study, *Freud: Transference and Authority*, attempts a full-scale reading of all of Freud's major writings. A MacArthur Prize Fellow, he is general editor of five series of literary criticism published by Chelsea House.

DAVID V. ERDMAN, the dean of Blake scholars, is Professor of English Emeritus at The University of the State of New York, Stony Brook, and is the Editor of Publications of the New York Public Library. He is the major historical and textual authority on Blake, and is the editor of the definitive editions of Blake's writings and of Blake's illuminated books. His *Prophet Against Empire* is the crucial historical study of Blake.

ROBERT F. GLECKNER, Professor of English at Duke University, is the author of *Byron and the Ruins of Paradise* and of two books on Blake, one on *Songs of Innocence and Experience* and the other on *Poetical Sketches*. His many essays include important studies of Blake and Joyce.

NORTHROP FRYE is University Professor Emeritus at the University of Toronto. He is the principal literary theorist of our century. His major works include *Fearful Symmetry*, *Anatomy of Criticism* and *The Great Code*.

W. J. T. MITCHELL is Professor of English at the University of Chicago, where he edits the magazine *Critical Inquiry*. He is the author of *Blake's Composite Art*.

THOMAS R. FROSCH is Professor of English at Queens College of the City University of New York. His work includes poems and essays in critical theory, in addition to his book, *The Awakening of Albion*.

THOMAS WEISKEL taught at Yale until his tragic accidental death. His masterly book, *The Romantic Sublime*, appeared in 1976 with a foreword by Portia Williams Weiskel.

SUSAN FOX is Professor of English at Queens College of New York. She is the author of *Poetic Form in Blake's "Milton."*

LESLIE BRISMAN is Professor of English at Yale University. He is the author of *Romantic Origins* and of *Milton's Poetry of Choice and its Romantic Heirs.*

LEOPOLD DAMROSCH, JR. is Professor of English at the University of Virginia. He is the author of *Samuel Johnson and the Tragic Sense* and *Symbol and Truth in Blake's Myth.*

DAVID WAGENKNECHT is Professor of English at Boston University, where he edits the magazine *Studies in Romanticism.* He is the author of *Blake's Night.*

DIANA HUME GEORGE is Professor of English at Pennsylvania State University, Behrend College. She is the author of *Blake and Freud.*

Bibliography

Adams, Hazard. *Blake and Yeats: The Contrary Vision.* New York: Russell and Russell, 1968.

Ault, Donald. *Visionary Physics: Blake's Response to Newton.* Chicago: The University of Chicago Press, 1974.

Beer, John. *Blake's Humanism.* Manchester: Manchester University Press, 1968.

Behrendt, Stephen C. *The Moment of Explosion: Blake and the Illustration of Milton.* Lincoln: University of Nebraska Press, 1983.

Bentley, G. E., ed. *William Blake's Writings.* Oxford: Clarendon Press, 1978.

————, ed. *Tiriel.* Oxford: Clarendon Press, 1967.

Bloom, Harold. *Blake's Apocalypse: A Study in Poetic Argument.* Ithaca: Cornell University Press, 1970.

Bogen, Nancy, ed. *The Book of Thel.* Providence: Brown University Press, 1971.

Bronowski, Jacob. *William Blake and the Age of Revolution.* London: Routledge and Kegan Paul, 1972.

Curran, Stuart, and Wittreich, Joseph, Jr., eds. *Blake's Sublime Allegory: Essays on the Four Zoas, Milton, Jerusalem.* Madison: University of Wisconsin Press, 1973.

Damon, Samuel Foster. *William Blake: His Philosophy and Symbols.* Gloucester, Mass.: P. Smith, 1978.

Damrosch, Leopold. *Symbol and Truth in Blake's Myth.* Princeton: Princeton University Press, 1980.

Davies, John Gordon. *The Theology of William Blake.* Hamden, Conn.: Archon Books, 1966.

Davis, Michael. *William Blake: A New Kind of Man.* London: Elek, 1977.

Dorfman, Deborah. *Blake in the Nineteenth Century: His Reputation as a Poet from Gilchrist to Yeats.* New Haven: Yale University Press, 1969.

Easson, Kay Parkhurst, and Easson, Roger R., eds. *The Book of Urizen.* Boulder, Col.: Shambala, 1978.

Erdman, David V. *Blake: Prophet Against Empire.* Princeton: Princeton University Press, 1969.

————, ed. *The Complete Poetry and Prose of William Blake.* Berkeley: University of California Press, 1982.

————, ed. *The Illuminated Blake.* Garden City, N.Y.: The Anchor Press/Doubleday, 1974.

————, ed. *The Poetry and Prose of William Blake.* Commentary by Harold Bloom. 4th ed. Garden City, N.Y.: Doubleday, 1970.

Essick, Robert N. *The Visionary Hand: Essays for the Study of William Blake's Art and Aesthetics.* Los Angeles: Hennesy and Ingalls, 1973.

Fisher, Peter F. *The Valley of Vision*. Edited by Northrop Frye. Toronto: University of Toronto Press, 1961.

Fox, Susan. *Poetic Form in Blake's Milton*. Princeton: Princeton University Press, 1976.

Frosch, Thomas R. *The Awakening of Albion: The Renovation of the Body in the Poetry of William Blake*. Ithaca: Cornell University Press, 1974.

Frye, Northrop. *Blake: A Collection of Critical Essays*. Englewood Cliffs, N.J.: Prentice-Hall, Inc., 1966.

―――. *Fearful Symmetry: A Study of William Blake*. Princeton: Princeton University Press, 1947.

―――, ed. *Selected Poetry and Prose*. New York: Modern Library, 1953.

Gallant, Christine. *Blake and the Assimilation of Chaos*. Princeton: Princeton University Press, 1978.

George, Diana Hume. *Blake and Freud*. Ithaca: Cornell University Press, 1980.

Gilchrist, Alexander. *The Life of William Blake*. Totowa, N.J.: Rowman and Littlefield, 1973.

Gillham, D. G. *William Blake*. London: Cambridge University Press, 1973.

Gleckner, Robert F. *The Piper and the Bard: A Study of William Blake*. Detroit: Wayne State University Press, 1959.

Hagstrum, Jean H. *William Blake: Poet and Painter, An Introduction to the Illuminated Verse*. Chicago: The University of Chicago Press, 1964.

Harper, George Mills. *The Neoplatonism of William Blake*. Chapel Hill: The University of North Carolina Press, 1961.

Howard, John. *Blake's Milton: A Study of the Selfhood*. Rutherford, N.J.: Fairleigh Dickinson University Press, 1976.

Jackson, Wallace. *The Probable and the Marvelous: Blake, Wordsworth and the 18th Century Critical Tradition*. Athens: University of Georgia Press, 1978.

John, Brian. *Supreme Fictions: Studies in the Work of William Blake, Thomas Carlyle, Yeats and D. H. Lawrence*. Montreal: McGill-Queens University Press, 1974.

Kazin, Alfred, ed. *The Portable Blake*. New York: The Viking Press, 1946.

Keynes, Geoffrey. *Blake Studies: Essays on His Life and Work*. 2nd ed. Oxford: Clarendon Press, 1971.

―――, ed. *The Letters of William Blake*. 3rd ed. Oxford: Clarendon Press, 1980.

―――, ed. *The Marriage of Heaven and Hell*. New York: Oxford University Press, 1975.

―――, ed. *The Complete Writings of William Blake*. London: Oxford University Press, 1966.

Klonsky, Milton. *William Blake: The Seer and His Visions*. New York: Harmony Books, 1977.

Lindsay, Jack. *William Blake: His Life and Work*. New York: Braziller, 1979.

Lister, Raymond. *William Blake: An Introduction to the Man and His work*. London: Bell, 1968.

Margoliouth, Herschel Maurice. *William Blake*. Hamden, Conn.: Archon Books, 1967.

Mellor, Anne Kostelanetz. *Blake's Human Form Divine*. Berkeley: University of California Press, 1974.

Mitchell, W. J. T. *Blake's Composite Art: A Study of the Illuminated Poetry*. Princeton: Princeton University Press, 1978.

Nurmi, Martin K. *William Blake*. Kent: Ohio State University Press, 1976.

O'Neill, Judith, ed. *Critics on Blake*. Coral Gables: University of Miami Press, 1970.

Paley, Morton D. *Energy and Imagination: A Study of the Development of Blake's Thought*. Oxford: Clarendon Press, 1970.

———. *Twentieth Century Interpretations on "Songs of Innocence and of Experience."* Englewood Cliffs, N.J.: Prentice-Hall, 1969.

Raine, Kathleen Jessie. *William Blake*. London: Thames and Hudson, 1970.

———. *Blake and the New Age*. Boston: George Allen and Unwin, 1979.

Sabri-Tabrizi, G. F. *The "Heaven" and "Hell" of William Blake*. London: Lawrence and Wishart, 1975.

Schorer, Mark. *William Blake: The Politics of Vision*. New York: Vintage Books, 1959.

Seurat, Denis. *Blake and Milton*. London: S. Nott, 1935.

Stevenson, W. H., ed. *The Poems of William Blake*. Harlow: Longman, 1971.

Van Sinderen, Adrian. *Blake and the Mystic Genius*. Syracuse: Syracuse University Press, 1949.

Vogler, Thomas A. *Preludes to Vision: The Epic Venture in Blake, Wordsworth, Keats and Hart Crane*. Berkeley: University of California Press, 1971.

Wagenknecht, David. *Blake's Night: William Blake and the Idea of the Pastoral*. Cambridge, Mass.: The Belknap Press, 1973.

Witcutt, William Purcell. *Blake: A Psychological Study*. Darby, Pa.: Folcroft Library Editions, 1974.

Acknowledgments

"Introduction" by Harold Bloom from *Poetry and Repression* by Harold Bloom, copyright © 1976 by Yale University Press. Reprinted by permission of Yale University Press.

"Blake: The Historical Approach" by David V. Erdman from *English Institute Essays 1963*, edited by Alan S. Downer, copyright © 1963 by Columbia University Press. Reprinted by permission.

"Point of View and Context in Blake's Songs" by Robert F. Gleckner from *Bulletin of the New York Public Library* 61, no. 11 (November 1957), copyright © 1957 by *Bulletin of the New York Public Library*. Reprinted by permission.

"The Keys to the Gates" by Northrop Frye from *Some British Romantics: A Collection of Essays*, edited by James V. Logan, John E. Jordan, Northrop Frye, copyright © 1966 by Ohio State University Press. Reprinted by permission.

"Blake's Composite Art" by W. J. T. Mitchell from *Blake's Visionary Forms Dramatic*, edited by David V. Erdman and John E. Grant, copyright © 1971 by Princeton University Press. Reprinted by permission.

"*Jerusalem:* The Bard of Sensibility and the Form of Prophecy" by Harold Bloom from *The Ringers in the Tower* by Harold Bloom, copyright © 1971 by The University of Chicago Press. Reprinted by permission of The University of Chicago Press.

"Art and Eden: The Sexes" by Thomas R. Frosch from *The Awakening of Albion: The Renovation of the Body in the Poetry of William Blake* by Thomas R. Frosch, copyright © 1974 by Cornell University Press. Reprinted by permission.

"Blake's Critique of Transcendence" by Thomas Weiskel from *The Romantic Sublime: Studies in the Structure and Psychology of Transcendence* by Thomas Weiskel, copyright © 1976 by Johns Hopkins University Press. Reprinted by permission of Johns Hopkins University Press.

"*Milton:* Beulah" by Susan Fox from *Poetic Form in Blake's Milton* by Susan Fox, copyright © 1976 by Princeton University Press. Reprinted by permission of Princeton University Press.

"*The Four Zoas:* First Things" by Leslie Brisman from *Romantic Origins* by Leslie Brisman, copyright © 1978 by Cornell University Press. Reprinted by permission.

"Los and Apocalypse" by Leopold Damrosch, Jr. from *Symbol and Truth in Blake's Myth* by Leopold Damrosch, Jr., copyright © 1980 by Princeton University Press. Reprinted by permission of Princeton University Press.

"Transformations" by David Wagenknecht from *Blake's Night: William Blake and the Idea of the Pastoral* by David Wagenknecht, copyright © 1973 by The President and Fellows of Harvard College. Reprinted by permission of Harvard University Press.

"The Feminine in Blake" by Diana Hume George from *Blake and Freud* by Diana Hume George, copyright © 1980 by Cornell University Press. Reprinted by permission.

Index